Extramural Shakespeare

Reproducing Shakespeare: New Studies in Adaptation and Appropriation

Reproducing Shakespeare marks the turn in adaptation studies toward recontextualization, reformatting, and media convergence. It builds on two decades of growing interest in the "afterlife" of Shakespeare, showcasing some of the best new work of this kind currently being produced. The series addresses the repurposing of Shakespeare in different technical, cultural, and performance formats, emphasizing the uses and effects of Shakespearean texts in both national and global networks of reference and communication. Studies in this series pursue a deeper understanding of how and why cultures recycle their classic works, and of the media involved in negotiating these transactions.

Series Editors

Thomas Cartelli, Muhlenberg College
Katherine Rowe, Bryn Mawr College

Titles

The English Renaissance in Popular Culture: An Age for All Time
Edited by Gregory Colón Semenza

Extramural Shakespeare
Denise Albanese

Extramural Shakespeare

Denise Albanese

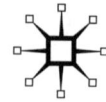

EXTRAMURAL SHAKESPEARE
Copyright © Denise Albanese 2010.

All rights reserved.

First published in 2010 by
PALGRAVE MACMILLAN®
in the United States—a division of St. Martin's Press LLC,
175 Fifth Avenue, New York, NY 10010.

Where this book is distributed in the UK, Europe and the rest of the world, this is by Palgrave Macmillan, a division of Macmillan Publishers Limited, registered in England, company number 785998, of Houndmills, Basingstoke, Hampshire RG21 6XS.

Palgrave Macmillan is the global academic imprint of the above companies and has companies and representatives throughout the world.

Palgrave® and Macmillan® are registered trademarks in the United States, the United Kingdom, Europe and other countries.

ISBN: 978–0–230–10513–3

Library of Congress Cataloging-in-Publication Data

Albanese, Denise.
    Extramural Shakespeare / Denise Albanese.
      p. cm.—(Reproducing Shakespeare)
      ISBN 978–0–230–10513–3 (alk. paper)
      1. Shakespeare, William, 1564–1616—Criticism and interpretation.
    I. Title.
PR2976.A55 2010
822.3'3—dc22   2010004229

A catalogue record of the book is available from the British Library.

Design by Newgen Imaging Systems (P) Ltd., Chennai, India.

First edition: September 2010

10 9 8 7 6 5 4 3 2 1

Printed in the United States of America.

For my sister Maureen, who is too smart and sensible to believe in myths, and in memory of my mother

Contents

List of Illustrations ix

Acknowledgments xi

Introduction: Shakespeare in Public 1

1 Reframing Shakespeare for the Millennium: American Culture, "Elites," the Academy—and Beyond 11

2 Pacino's Cliffs Notes: *Looking for Richard*'s "Public" Shakespeare 39

3 Shakespeare Goes to School 67

4 The Shakespeare Film, the Market, and the Americanization of Culture 95

5 Social Dreaming and Making Shakespeare Matter 119

Notes 145

Works Cited 165

Index 175

Illustrations

1 *Looking for Richard* 57
2 *Hamlet* 103
3 *Hamlet* 104
4 *Romeo + Juliet* 113
5 *Romeo + Juliet* 115

Acknowledgments

Since I think of myself principally as a scholar of seventeenth-century literature, it's a surprise to me to have produced a book on Shakespeare. But his centripetal pull on my class schedule in my home Department of English, combined with my joint appointment in Cultural Studies, has resulted in the happiest sort of project: one informed by my teaching the most potent, revered, and mystified figure in Anglophone literary history on the one hand, and by the forms of critique and analysis that make possible the broadest positioning of Shakespeare in the totality of cultural and social practices on the other. So my first thanks must go to all the students, both undergraduate and graduate, to whom I've taught Shakespeare, Horkheimer, Adorno, Bloch, Jameson, and a host of others, for their patience, skepticism, devotion, independence of mind, smarts, and enthusiasm.

Although the form of this analysis has little in common with the modes of criticism to which I was introduced both as an undergraduate and as a graduate student, it would be impossible for me to have a thought about Shakespeare or early modern culture that was not in some sense informed by those who have taught me: Richard Harrier, Eleanor Prosser, Terry Comito, John Bender, J. Martin Evans, Ron Rebholz, Wesley Trimpi, Louis Adrian Montrose, and especially Dustin Griffin, whose graduate course on the afterlife of Milton in the eighteenth century, to which I was admitted as a drastically underprepared undergraduate, first introduced me to a way of thinking about the cultural work that authors do, the afterlives they possess. But the end of graduate school was not the end of my formal education: when I first came to George Mason University, I took a seminar entitled "Big-Time Shakespeare" at the Folger Shakespeare Library with Michael Bristol. This book is the long-overdue culmination of a series of conversations he and I have had ever since, which began with an invitation to pinch-hit for Larry Levine at an MLA session. Though no trace remains in the following pages of that paper, this project would likely not exist were it not for the Folger seminar and my subsequent time as a Mellon postdoctoral fellow at the Center for Humanities at Wesleyan, which first taught me about cultural studies while I finished a more historicist project.

As is appropriate for a book whose stakes are in the present, many of my debts are owed in the here and now to the myriad colleagues and friends who have listened to all too many versions of this project and who have given bibliographical, argumentative, critical, and personal support to me in the years this project has been in gestation, mutating, it seemed, every time I sat down to write. I owe a particular debt to my former department chair, Deborah Kaplan, whose support of me has meant more than she can know; to Cindy Fuchs, my colleague in film studies, whose enthusiasm for and acuity about American popular culture first led me to think about Shakespeare in relation to his putative other; and to my wonderful colleagues in early modern studies, Devon Hodges (ever incisive and ever sane) and Robert Matz (whose own work on Shakespeare's sonnets is a model for anyone seeking to address the public appetite for Shakespeare). Thanks to my friend and colleagues, present and erstwhile, in Cultural Studies, Paul Smith, Tom Moylan, and Aine O'Brien, for good times and good arguments. Zofia Burr and Alok Yadav have been dear friends as well as keen interlocutors. For insights, conversations, and general jollying I am grateful to Caroline Bassett, Curt Barger, Lorraine Brown, Steve Brown, Peter Brunette, Dympna Callaghan, Dina Copelman, Julie Eisenberg, Rosemary Jann, Glenn Hennessey, Inderpal Grewal, Kim Hall, David Kaufmann, Winnie Keaney, Roger Lancaster, Roger Lathbury, Susan Lawrence, Madhavi Menon, Bobbi Ponce-Barger, Phyllis Rackin, Shelley Reid, Roy Rosenzweig, Amelia Rutledge, Jessica Scarlata, Laura Scott, Scott Shershow, Jyotsna Singh, Chris Thaiss, Susan Tichy, Valerie Traub, and Terry Zawacki. David Levy has given me a great deal, only some of it information about conservative discourse in the United States.

The work on this project has been furthered by many people and in many fora: Amy Scott-Douglas, Jonathan Gil Harris, and Jacques Lezra organized seminars at the SAA (Shakespeare Association of America) at which portions of chapter 5 were presented; thanks to them and to all who attended for their insights, which can only have strengthened the study. Thanks as well to Tom Moylan and the audience at the Ralahine Center for Utopian Studies at the University of Limerick, whose searching questions have made this chapter better. Thanks to the Folger Library's March 2007 conference, "Shakespeare in American Education," and to NEH funding in relation to that conference, I was able to undertake a significant portion of my archival research and to benefit from the work of my fellow participants. Another portion of this study was initially written at the behest of Jean Howard and

Scott Shershow; I owe thanks to them as well as to Crystal Bartolovich, whose invitation to give a paper at the Group for Early Modern Cultural Studies conference sparked the analysis in chapter 4. And I am grateful for the interest and support shown by the series editors, Thomas Cartelli and Katherine Rowe, who, like the anonymous reader secured by Palgrave Macmillan, also offered keen and useful responses to the manuscript.

Thanks to the University of Delaware Press for permission to print portions of my chapter "Canons Before Canons: College Entrance Requirements and the Making of a National-Educational Shakespeare," which will appear in *Shakespearean Educations: Power, Citizenship, and Performance,* ed. Mimi Godfrey, Coppèlia Kahn, and Heather Nathans (Newark, DE: University of Delaware Press, forthcoming). Thanks as well to Routledge UK for permission to print a revised and expanded version of the book chapter "The Shakespeare Film and the Americanization of Culture" from *Marxist Shakespeares*, ed. Jean Howard and Scott Shershow (New York: Routledge, 2000), 206–226.

My thanks to the special-collections librarians and university archivists at Stanford University, Columbia University, the City University of New York, Howard University, and the University of Virginia; and to Dr. David Ment of the Board of Education Archives in New York City. And I owe a real debt of gratitude to colleagues on the faculty of the College of Visual and Performing Arts at GMU, who were willing to help out a less-than-tech-savvy humanities professor with improving the quality of the images that appear in this volume: Edgar Endress and especially Sean Watkins and Lynne Constantine.

One final note: I wish Larry Levine, who after his retirement from Berkeley became a colleague of mine at Mason, and I had had more time to talk about this work, which owes so much to his groundbreaking research. I suspect he'd have liked the possibility that Shakespeare might be more a form of public property than he ever suspected.

INTRODUCTION

Shakespeare in Public

Why this, why now? A familiar pair of questions to anyone affiliated with a cultural studies program, as I am, but not quite so evidently necessary in the realm of Shakespeare studies, where I also do my work. While topical criticism of Shakespeare flourished in the 1980s and into the 1990s, more recently it has fallen into abeyance, perhaps because the suspicion with which ideology critique viewed Shakespeare, as agent of hegemony and property of the ruling class, offered little possibility for a more complicated, even dialectical development.

This is a book that aims to offer just that sense of complexity, that possibility for dialectical readings, in accounting for Shakespeare outside the walls of academia, that is, Shakespeare in public. Its aim is to argue that in the years around the turn of the millennium, Shakespeare is no longer located where prior critical accounts have placed him—at the top of a cultural hierarchy that maps out onto a social and economic one—but is both more elusive and more pervasive. That there is a great deal of complexity whenever Shakespeare's place in the social world is the subject of conversation is more or less a given: through the course of the twentieth century and into the twenty-first, Shakespeare has become a flash point for all types of cultural battles. He or his texts have been used variously to "civilize" non-Anglophone immigrants; to signify elevated taste (or tasting good, in the case of Charlie the Tuna); and to rouse cultural warriors fighting to preserve eternal verities from the contaminating effects of mass culture.[1] As the materialist work of the 1980s and 1990s has enduringly taught us, Shakespeare is a site (and sign) of political struggle as well as the name of an author.

On that front there will be more to say, since this study aligns itself with the materialist work to which I've alluded, while aiming to update its dependence on a now-superseded hypostasizing of Shakespeare principally as an agent of high culture in the United States. But by way of preamble to the larger task, it is necessary to acknowledge that it is sometimes hard to figure out what the future of such political work might be. The home questions critics such as Jonathan Dollimore, Jean Howard, Alan Sinfield, John Drakakis, Marion O'Connor, Ivo Kamps, and many others once raised about Shakespeare, dominant culture, and ideology have apparently been settled, or else they have receded both in urgency and in currency: in effect, the professional conversation (which was in any case always more vigorous in Britain than in the United States) has moved on.[2] If I may be permitted an overly schematic description of the field, the many species of politically inflected analyses characteristic of early modern studies in the 1980s and 1990s have largely been put aside, even as more strictly archival or literary work has begun once more to rise in professional importance. Meanwhile, any challenges posed by Shakespeare as a cultural object of continued topicality have been transmuted: some political energy has been taken up with the question of Shakespeare in relation to the performative or the postcolonial (including postcolonial formations in America), while questions of status, in particular, have been deferred onto the study of Shakespeare and film, new media, or other manifestations of popular culture.[3]

On some level, of course, increased specialization is the natural turn for any emerging area of study. But insofar as that specialization often leaves behind broader questions and the sense of a social totality within which cultural formations operate—and thus within which the political analysis of Shakespeare finds its greatest urgency—many of these studies have also left behind a critical sense of what John Joughin has analyzed as a "national culture."[4] For instance, while it is likely that residual colonial anxiety accounts for some aspects of Shakespearean relations in the United States, the economic and geopolitical priority this nation has held during much of the last fifty years suggests a fundamental disjuncture: between the colonial understood as a recent and defining fact central to the imagined life of the nation-state, and the colonial as a residual ideological trace that can be reactivated by elites for the purposes of establishing hegemony—as when Shakespeare's Englishness became central to the educational system within which increasing numbers of non-Anglophone immigrants were to be inserted at the turn of the last century. And since much work in the category of film and popular culture in particular, undertaken within the disciplinary confines of literary study, reflects little familiarity with a rigorous, energetic, and highly elaborated discourse on politics and mass culture as put forth by cultural studies scholars, the former work seems curiously compartmentalized, even at times deprived of the tools needed to continue to reflect on Shakespeare as an iconic element in a complex cultural field.

I'll have more to say on these matters in the pages that follow. But whatever the myriad virtues of a return to the archive, a reassertion of specifically literary discourse, or the development of a postcolonial or mass-mediated subfield taken in and of themselves, it remains the case that Shakespeare as public object—extramural Shakespeare, in the terms of this study—is in need of further articulation. Hence the pertinence of the two questions with which I began. It is only by understanding Shakespeare via models and critiques that move beyond textual practice and into an ensemble of interpretive strategies that cross disciplinary lines, as cultural studies does, that Shakespeare's place in perimillennial American culture may be understood. In fact, given the cultural shifts I will be describing in the pages that follow, such a rearticulation is urgent, if the valuable political lessons put forth by materialist scholars are not to be turned into mere historical artifacts, moments in the discipline's trajectory whose present utility and further development are no longer at issue and may even have become the object of embarrassment.

Yet it need not be true that the time for "political Shakespeare" has come and gone, since it has been the development best oriented toward acknowledging Shakespeare's manifestations in, and meaning to, the nonacademic realm—which is precisely apposite to the present moment. Of late, the profession has become institutionally inclined to recognize the existence, even the pull, of a "wider public"—an inclination that is sometimes inchoate or inherent, visible as trace in the recent abeyance of the "high theory" that once dominated English studies as a whole. Such an inclination is, however, sometimes made quite vivid by more concrete occasions, as betokened by the exceptional success of Stephen Greenblatt's *Will in the World* or the more typical and market-based pressure to produce classroom-friendly studies rather than highly annotated and densely theorized scholarly monographs.[5] At many points, then, it seems as though academics are being encouraged (and driven) to seek a world elsewhere. But it is a world whose interest in Shakespeare is operantly defined as the simple "outside" of scholarship, the real world beyond the putative ivory tower.[6]

As that suggests, it remains the case that understanding that public in complicated, even well-theorized ways has not been part of the institutional conversation. Indeed, the very need to think through what is meant by "the public" has by and large not been recognized as a problem, despite the fact that the term denotes a complex, inevitably discursive object. Naturally, it represents a demand for practical address, even as it constitutes an artifact of modern techniques concerning the statistical management of populations as epistemological aggregates (as with, say, opinion polls); more tellingly still is the fact that the public is the site of fantasy for academics—our "other," as it were. The prominence of concerns about the accessibility of scholarly work to a larger audience relates to an inarticulate desire, one born of perimillennial fears of irrelevance, supersession, or even suppression by, among other things, a state whose recent manifestation was squarely on the side of an uncritical and anti-intellectual orthodoxy all the more effective for its efforts to cloak itself as a depoliticization of knowledge and to legitimate itself as the will of citizens and taxpayers. Attacks on academics that have continued since the emergence of cultural materialism usually seek to represent themselves as serving the "public interest" in higher education and usually, although not always, take state-funded universities as their battleground. When, therefore, the study of early modern literature spontaneously moves away from addressing public formations around Shakespeare as a species of politics *and* a new generation of scholars emerges to take up strictly literary-historical and archival research agendas, it is useful to think about how relatively autonomous moves within a discipline might nevertheless be conditioned by changing circumstances outside it—and about how varying invocations of the public that lurks outside the academy's walls cannot but be central to the pursuit at this historical juncture.

At the end of this study I shall have more to say about Shakespeare's public, and with troubling what count as extramural formations. Even so, my principal goal is less to try to pin down the myriad and often contradictory dispensations within which an idea of a larger forum for Shakespeare is summoned forth—to define that public operationally—as it is with offering a complex rearticulation, sometimes argumentative and sometimes principally descriptive, of Shakespeare's place in American culture in these perimillennial years. As I've already begun to suggest, to the extent that extramural formations demand a wall—depend, that is, on an embedded notion of the academy as ivory tower or as a space that's unreal or otherwise exempted— every concern with extramural Shakespeare must also constitute an indirect argument about Shakespeare in the academy.[7]

One aim of this study is, therefore, to return to the position with which I initially took issue and which has constituted the central problem for much materialist work: that of Shakespeare in relation to power and dominance, in particular social class and the way it is presumed to be expressed by taste—which is to say, by cultural capital. After arguing that it is no longer useful to identify the possession of that capital with the work of dominance, in *Extramural Shakespeare* I suggest that an even more nuanced case must now be drawn in the case of Shakespeare: regardless of the status of elite culture *in general*, Shakespeare's status as a synonym for an ensemble of elite cultural goods needs to be challenged, a challenge that in turn necessitates a historically nuanced recalibration of the sociopolitical field. It thus becomes important to recognize that this current moment is very different from the one in which Shakespeare came to signify highbrow culture at the turn of the twentieth century, which Lawrence Levine has influentially described. But even more is required, since, as I shall suggest, this perimillennial conjuncture is also not identical with the Reaganite-Thatcherite one in which the culture wars first arose and which gave rise to "political Shakespeare" in the 1980s in the first place.

As I hope the preceding sketch of the social totality suggests, the aim of this study is to reposition debate on Shakespeare by challenging the failure to rethink how certain cultural properties relegated by analysis to high culture, Shakespeare preeminent among them, might nevertheless have migrated from the position of privilege to which they have been all-but-permanently consigned. Given the economic crisis that began in 2008, it would be especially foolhardy to argue that class is irrelevant to understanding national culture: doing so would in any case speak to the long-standing resistance in American analyses to accept class as a constitutive reality. Even more pointedly, it would echo the way in which the realities of growing economic inequity have become part of a rhetorical (and highly ideological) shell game, where matters of taste and consumption magically take the place of that inequity as the subject of criticism.

Nevertheless, what might be called the Shakespeare-function—the sum of the myriad roles Shakespeare plays and is made to play institutionally and publicly—is far harder to read as the leading edge of economic and social relations in the perimillennial United States than it perhaps once was. That does not mean that Shakespeare has no privileged locations: in fact, one through-line of my analysis concerns the persistence of pedagogical agendas—of the social fact that Shakespeare is, above all, schoolroom matter—in media and forms that are ostensibly anything but pedagogical. Nor do I intend any sentimentality, either about cultural commonalities or, for that matter, about the fact of social resistance to Shakespeare from those who have been construed (by discourse, by self-positioning, by objective social relations) as somehow located "below" such presumably rarefied cultural property. My claim is simpler and yet, I hope, with greater productive possibilities. First, I argue that Shakespeare is part of a public culture in the United States precisely because the mass-educational project of the twentieth century made him so. Second, as a consequence, Shakespeare needs to be read dialectically: while bearing in mind the myriad ways Shakespeare still functions as a sign of rarefied status in the American imaginary, it is also important to remember that the uses of Shakespeare are not exhausted by his semiotic role, and that under some circumstances Shakespeare—his plays and what he represents—might still hold out the possibility for what Ernst Bloch has deemed "the dream of a better world," the momentary glimpse of a utopian horizon that can propel longing for a more just future that has yet to arrive.[8]

Chapter 1, "Reframing Shakespeare for the Millennium: American Culture, 'Elites,' the Academy—and Beyond," therefore begins by addressing the continuing National Endowment for the Arts (NEA) initiative on "Shakespeare in American Communities," a program meant to take Shakespeare performances to cities and towns presumed otherwise to stand outside the dispensation of his plays. Rather than offer a skeptical and symptomatic reading of this state-sponsored program, I call attention to its contradictions instead: the NEA produces Shakespeare both as an inalienable part of the U.S. imaginary and, somehow, as external to popular American experience. But, as I argue, political discourse about Shakespeare in academia has in effect chosen to reproduce the latter half of the contradiction as the whole story. That is to say, the claim that Shakespeare is elite, a rarefied cultural property rather than a public object, has hardened into a kind of fact beyond which there is no going. Whatever its historical truth (cf. Levine), it certainly has not been held to the test by a searching engagement with the concrete mechanisms by means of which Shakespeare is made pervasive in U.S. culture. Inspired by Raymond Williams's crucial volume, I offer a *Keywords*-type treatment of the concept of elites: I thus consider the way the term "elite" has increasingly lost its shoring in status distinctions and has become a way to punish regimes of dissent from conservative hegemony. Yet elitism persists as a term of art in academia, a fact the more mystifying in that there has been increased awareness that academic privilege is itself ephemeral, increasingly subject to the rationalizations of the market.

From there, Chapter 2, " Pacino's Cliffs Notes: *Looking for Richard*'s 'Public' Shakespeare," considers *Looking for Richard,* the 1996 documentary focused on *Richard III* that Al Pacino produced and starred in, as an index to the Shakespeare-function in America: that is, what values, resistances, and fantasies attach to him, what role the Bard is seen to play in the American imaginary. After all, it is not until mystifications are subject to analysis that I can begin to demonstrate the truth of my claim. Performance, as has been recognized, looms large in the documentary, and I allude to the way in which Pacino's interest in bringing Shakespeare "to the people" might be correlated with (or perhaps haunted by?) Joseph Papp's Public Theater, whose superficially similar aims were characteristic of an earlier, more clearly progressive social and political conjuncture. Pacino's film seems both more personal and more apolitical—more in line, that is, with the general invocation that Shakespeare constitutes a "universally lovable object." Even so, that Pacino starred in a Broadway production of the play in which his nonclassically trained intonations were subject to criticism opens his documentary up to the larger question of how naturalized Shakespeare is—and is recognized to be—in Britain's former colony, more than 200 years after independence and more than 100 years after Shakespeare first became an educational inevitability. The documentary evinces an anxiety on this subject, an anxiety linked to what I deem its hidden pedagogical imperative, even though the film ostensibly values performance over scholarship as a way to know Shakespeare truly. Both because of Shakespeare's fantasmatic ties to England and Englishness and because Shakespeare is always produced as somehow anterior or "other" with respect to U.S. culture, Pacino's film winds up recapitulating overfamiliar pedagogical topoi in cinematic form, much like the Cliffs Notes the actor tellingly brandishes as a prop. Meanwhile, the complex ensemble of everyday responses to Shakespeare found in the documentary goes by and large unexamined, with resistance to Shakespeare introduced only so that the film can offer itself as the preeminent vehicle by which distaste and indifference may be overcome. The implicit claim seems to be that film will succeed where school has failed, a claim rendered the more contradictory for the documentary's having been offered precisely as an adjunct to formal education.

But how did the association between education and Shakespeare come to dominate the American imaginary in the first place? Given that this persistent conceptual link has been underexplored in political scholarship, I devote chapter 3, "Shakespeare Goes to School," to addressing the educational substrate that interpellates American citizens in the regime of Shakespeare. Beyond the need to sketch a historical description, my aim in the chapter is dual. First, it is to suggest that the mass culture with which Shakespeare ought most tellingly to be linked is a culture of *mass education*, which began to be consolidated at the turn of the twentieth century. In this I differ from a critical practice that, like Pacino, somehow needs to locate Shakespeare "elsewhere" in order to mystify the appearance of his texts in extramural venues other than academia or some other forum of elite culture—for instance, in a hypostasized "popular culture" whose relationship to its object is figured as appropriation rather than ownership. My second aim is to focus on the College Board's role in rendering Shakespeare an inescapable part of that mass-educational culture. The necessarily selective analysis of Shakespeare in American education I provide touches on the history leading up to the College Board, where extracts from selected plays that appeared in primers such as McGuffey's served as rhetorical training in a nascent citizen- and subject-formation. When the mass-educational project emerges in a United

States pressured by non-Anglophone immigration and responding to the exigencies of industrialized capital, this earlier practice comes to compete with, and be supplanted by, a newly productive—and eugenicist-inflected—understanding of Shakespeare as part of the "race knowledge" of America, even as the concept of "elites" is being refashioned to allow for newcomers. Hence, I argue, the consolidation of a pretertiary canon of plays: although reading practices were themselves increasingly drawn from an autonomous literary aesthetics, the very selection of plays to be prepared for college admission reveals a political intention at work. That intention, like the reason Shakespeare became compulsory in high school in the first place, has gone all but dead in the critical understanding. Yet without such historical insight, it is impossible to realize how Shakespeare has been mispredicated in current political criticism. This inattention also makes possible such missionary agendas as the NEA's "Shakespeare in American Communities," within which, as I have noted, Shakespeare is produced both as an inalienable part of the U.S. imaginary and, contradictorily, as somehow external to popular experience.

In chapter 4, "The Shakespeare Film, the Market, and the Americanization of Culture," I turn to the plethora of Shakespeare films in the 1990s to indicate that Shakespeare, while still understood as pedagogical property with strong affiliations to Britain, is increasingly becoming a market phenomenon, not unlike American education itself. As has been argued, from the beginning of the film industry, Shakespeare has been seen as a vehicle of mass uplift, a way to redeem a medium from contempt, and evidence of a sustained fantasy about popular forms rendering elite objects "accessible." By contrasting Branagh's monumental (marmoreal?) *Hamlet* with Baz Luhrmann's *William Shakespeare's Romeo + Juliet*, I argue that filmed Shakespeare has become a prime forum for renegotiating the Shakespeare-function. While Branagh's film echoes a reverential, pedagogical, and Anglophilic dispensation toward the Bard that is increasingly belated in American culture, Luhrmann's insertion of capitalist tropes is of a piece with his stylistic refashioning of Shakespeare along familiarly domestic popcultural lines. Luhrmann's film stands in for a Shakespeare understood as a direct apparatus of the market, rather as much of U.S. public culture is now itself understood.

But the story does not end with the interpenetration of Shakespeare and the market in the new millennium. For all that questions of production are and should be at issue, there remains the possibility of a utopian surplus, of Shakespeare as a repository for "social dreaming"—a recognition, that is, that Shakespearean formations, even when imbricated in questions of political economy and acts of hegemony, can still be *useful*, can still signify beyond those confines. In a final chapter entitled "Social Dreaming and Making Shakespeare Matter" that addresses the contradictions posed by a public radio show featuring a production of *Hamlet* by prison inmates, I consider how the distance established by public radio from its objects unexpectedly redoubles a a discourse within which "identification" with Shakespeare has become an object of suspicion: the resistance to the Shakespearean manifested by political criticism has, it seems, become the toothless new dominant. I argue nevertheless for the necessity of acknowledging what these prisoners say of their own relationship to the play and for accepting the challenge of understanding how Shakespeare, despite the constraining features of prison education programs and despite the fact that the texts cannot but be fetishized and ideologically fraught, might nevertheless represent the possibility of enlargement in all the complex and variable senses of that word. If, as I conclude, Shakespeare is a public object, then there is a progressive politics in allowing anyone who deems himself or herself addressed by the texts—who is constituted as part of Shakespeare's public—to escape the hermeneutics of suspicion and the charge of class treachery with which the desire to be Shakespeareanized has for too long been embroiled.

In closing, I offer a few meditations on the utility of a model of public culture, perhaps most recently popularized in the field of anthropology and via the journal to which it has given a name. It seems increasingly evident from its practice, if not from its accounts of itself, that academic scholarship no longer fears to embrace questions of value as they accrue around Shakespeare. If I am right, then this study is timely: in arguing for a salutary displacement of Shakespeare from the realm of the elite and his consequent and complex embeddedness in a public culture broadly construed, I hope to keep critical reflection on Shakespeare as a cultural object alive to new possibilities and new conjunctures.

CHAPTER 1

Reframing Shakespeare for the Millennium: American Culture, "Elites," the Academy—and Beyond

> This was not a fight we looked for... All those East Coast elites had to take it to the courts...
> > Rick Santorum, July 2004, in favor of the constitutional amendment against gay marriage

> The Pennsylvania Republican [Santorum] directed his colleagues to link... Democrats to the "Hollywood/entertainment elite," and asserted that "Hollywood's values are not America's values."
> > Mark Preston, *Roll Call*, July 19, 2004

> Governmental, nonprofit, and communications elites in particular are overwhelmingly liberal in their outlooks. So are academics. The radical students of the 1960s have become tenured professors, particularly in elite institutions. As Stanley Rothman observes, "Social science faculties at elite universities are overwhelmingly liberal and cosmopolitan or on the Left. Almost any form of civic loyalty or patriotism is considered reactionary." Liberalism tends to go with irreligiosity as well.
> > Samuel Huntington, "Dead Souls: The Denationalization of the American Elite" (2004)

> In an elite composed of individuals who find their way into it solely for their individual pre-eminence, the differences of background will be so great, that they will be united only by their common

interests, and separated by everything else. An elite must therefore be attached to *some* class, whether higher or lower: but so long as there are classes at all it is likely to be the dominant class that attracts this elite to itself. What would happen in a classless society—which is more difficult to envisage than people think—brings us into the area of conjecture.

T. S. Eliot, *Notes Towards the Definition of Culture* (1948)

* * *

In keeping with the extramural agenda of this study, I begin by stepping outside the confines of a particular text or formation to get our bearings on Shakespeare in American culture in the years around the millennium. If, as is my premise for this study, a new conjuncture has emerged whose contours challenge received descriptions of Shakespeare's writing as metonymous for elite culture, what, precisely, has changed? How has the concept of elitism shifted in register and function from the period some one hundred years ago, when, as Lawrence Levine has argued, Shakespeare first became "highbrow"? Is elitism still a discourse reliably linked with the myriad forms of social, political, and economic power beyond those circumscribed by the academy, where Shakespeare is undeniably ensconced? Do changes within academia in any way affect the questions I've raised? And most significantly, if Shakespeare is not strictly elite, then how can we link the answers to the questions I've already posed to offer a more complex, more accurate account of the place his plays occupy in the American imaginary?

My epigraphs have already indicated that recent political discourse has registered a shift in what might be called our national conversation around the place and value of elitism: certainly, the more recent statements emerging from the right side of the political spectrum suggest that at the very least, to be a member of an elite is no longer a good thing.[1] But however suggestive such remarks are that elitism has changed in affective sign and register, I need to demonstrate that the change is more than adventitious rhetoric and that it subtends more than mere excoriation of dissent. Hence the significance of an ongoing initiative first announced on Shakespeare's birthday in 2003, "Shakespeare in American Communities," by the National Endowment for the Arts (NEA). The NEA's role in the funding of culture (or, rather, Culture) has made it a bellwether of national ambivalence about—indeed, queasiness at—the meaning of elitism in art for the nation-state ever since the so-called culture wars in the late 1980s and 1990s.[2] Even as such skirmishes have mutated into aggressive maneuvers around religion and state policy that usually leave the arts behind, the agency that occasioned them with its individual artist grants to controversial performance artist Karen Finley and others, and its support of an exhibition devoted to the queer-themed photography of Robert Mapplethorpe, has drastically shifted its emphasis: in the perimillennial period, the NEA has operated to ratify a tacit consensus about the official limits allowed to art with respect to formal experimentation and ideologically challenging content, limits enforced in the name of the nation-state and its standards of aesthetic and corporeal decency (at least as subtended by and equivalent to taxpayer dollars). It is worth noting that the year before Santorum spoke against elites on both East and West coasts, the NEA, former sponsor of outlier art, saw its place as bringing Shakespeare to America in order to counter what Dana Gioia (former chairman of the NEA) described as the institution's "inherent problem of elitism."[3]

As might be expected, the substitution of Shakespeare for more avant-garde artistic practitioners was duly celebrated among conservative commentators: witness the *National Review* opinion piece by Roger Kimball, which ran under the celebratory headline "Goodbye Mapplethorpe, Hello Shakespeare."[4] But it is equally worth noting that the project continues, even flourishes, to this day under the Obama administration. Given the fact of its continuation, the NEA's definitive shift in investment from Finley and Mapplethorpe to Shakespeare seems to reveal that any comcomitant shift in the discourse of elitism has proven more durable than the circumstances of its emergence. Even so, those immediate circumstances are pertinent to my argument. Performance art such as Finley's might arguably, as Shakespeare so frequently has, be called elite, at least in the sense common to most experimental and avant-garde practices of being intelligible as a complex intervention in the field of artistic production, and acceptable as such, only to a comparative few. The rarefaction of her art, however, was not precisely the problem. Instead, the art that generated controversy was understood only too well, on an inchoate, emotional level, as an affront to "community standards"—standards, that is, whose ad hoc manufacture, by politicians and media alike, nevertheless had some indeterminate purchase on a broader horizon of value. This implicit linkage between elite formations and a "general public" is historically distinct, and it tells us a lot about the horizon on which Shakespeare has since loomed large. In moving from Finley to Shakespeare, the NEA has effectively offered the Bard as a fantasmatic corrective to the coterie practices of an art elite inclined to give offense by an agency newly rededicated to serving the "public good" in its potentially most anodyne form (and thereby increased the agency's funding during a time when such financing has been increasingly hard to come by). For this substitution to have the political efficacy intended for it, and the endurance it has shown, it is important that Shakespeare be, precisely, *not* elite; instead, he must be represented as a birthright.

When "Shakespeare in American Communities" was first announced by Dana Gioia, it was designed to send noted regional theater companies across the country to perform a limited repertory of Shakespeare plays: *Romeo and Juliet, A Midsummer's Night's Dream, Richard III,* and *Othello.* Thus its twin aims: the reinvigoration of a touring theater-company tradition and the introduction of "a new generation of audiences to the greatest writer in the English language."[5] As the phrase "new generation" betokens, this initiative presents the future as a form of return, a recourse to a moment in history when other generations also got to know their Shakespeare through the efforts of acting troupes dedicated to his works; as part of its legitimation narrative, the NEA's associated pamphlet provides a capsule overview of Shakespeare's theatrical pervasiveness in America, especially in the nineteenth century.[6] Gioia makes clear what's at stake in this return when he avers that a genealogical relation exists between national formations and Shakespearean ones: "I think it's impossible to understand American culture or American theater without understanding Shakespeare," a sentiment that would be roughly familiar to anyone who attended the breaking of ground for the Folger Library, or, for that matter, who recalls the 2007 initiative in the U.S. capital, "Shakespeare in Washington."[7] At the same time, however, the state's interest in Shakespeare is not strictly as an already-democratic alternative to decadent and offensive coterie practices, but as one that is *potentially* so—or, rather, one whose relation to the nation-state is both national precondition and an occasion for messianism. Hence the need to fund renewed national exposure to this "once universally accessible dramatist" who is now (lamentably) "our most sacred dramatist—to whom most audiences [are] not able to relate."[8]

In keeping with the rhetoric of outreach, the Web site for this initiative, also funded by Sallie Mae and with honorary co-chairs Laura Bush and the late Jack Valenti, the former president and CEO of the Motion Picture Association of America, suggests that its efforts to promulgate Shakespeare are unprecedented, and unprecedentedly wide, in terms that might raise the suspicions of skeptically minded interlocutors. In the words of Valenti, "unless you know, read, and hear [Shakespeare's] magic stories, there is a vacancy in your life."[9] And presumably such vacancies are pervasive, given the necessity of bringing productions of the plays to all fifty states, and especially of sending NEA-funded Shakespeare to counties and regions that have seldom if ever seen federal arts money or, it has been claimed, professional Shakespeare. "Shakespeare in American Communities," therefore, presents us with an apparent contradiction. On the one hand, Shakespeare is foundational to American culture; on the other, he is beyond the experience of far too many Americans. Gioia's postulation of Shakespeare's centrality must be at odds with Valenti's belief that Shakespeare has not been seen outside major urban population centers: it appears as a difference between Shakespeare's dominant place in official ideologies—what critical consensus has generally deemed his "elite" status—and the fact of his removal from the everyday lives of many American citizens. Valenti's sentiment is of a piece with his words on the necessity of exposure to Shakespeare; or, rather, the second sentiment constitutes a corollary to the first. In this dispensation, completeness of life and, notably, education is coextensive with knowledge of Shakespeare. Because this is so, and because Shakespeare, like many cultural objects on which a high value has been placed, is presumably more readily found in major cities on the coasts rather than in the putative heartland, "Shakespeare in American Communities" exists to bring—or is it restore?—ever-greater numbers of U.S. citizens into the purview of sweet triumph, witty composition, and profound relevance.

It is worth noting that the initiative appears to be flourishing: during 2009–2010, for instance, thirty-seven theater companies in twenty-five states and the District of Columbia will have conducted performances under its aegis.[10] Notable, too, is the fact that the initial rhetorical emphasis on performance has been supplemented in practice by the dissemination of educational materials and by pedagogical agendas in middle and especially high schools: it thereby makes good on a historically durable linkage between Shakespeare and pedagogy, a linkage I will explore in chapters 2 and 3. But for now, I want to focus on the readiness with which a critique of the NEA's inevitably contradictory rhetoric could be sketched. Indeed, perhaps too readily. Its apparently familiar claims about Shakespeare's centrality might lead one to misdiagnose the shifts in underlying conditions that generate the symptoms and thus ignore what may be new in their articulation. What interests me about the publicity materials for "Shakespeare in American Communities" is not the way they seem to confirm a number of already-available narratives about the hegemony of the high literary, the fetishization of an apparently anodyne Shakespeare, and the insistent alignment of aesthetic and national values carried over from the old into the new millennium, even though all these points might still have their place. Nor am I interested at the moment in addressing the historical ignorance that gives rise to a missionary zeal to promulgate Shakespeare—a zeal all the more puzzling since it seems to contradict its own postulate that Shakespeare, as foundational, is constitutive of Americanness itself. Rather, what draws me to the project is the way it does *not* wholly respond to the obvious critiques, the way its meaning exceeds the provocation of immediate circumstances.

The critical analysis to which the NEA project might yield itself is not precisely exhausted by an indignant focus on ideology; to the extent that this is so, "Shakespeare in American Communities" betokens the necessity to find a new way to talk about the politics of Shakespeare in perimillennial America, the motive for this study.

Curiously enough, the NEA's rhetoric—and, for that matter, the aims of the initiative as a whole—rhymes with the way that progressive academics have characterized the Shakespeare-function during the last twenty years or so. As my emphasis might have already suggested, the central feature of this harmony is the claim that geographical rarefaction means something: it is the sign of the uneven dispersal of high culture and also of the preferred habitations of the privileged few whose access to Shakespeare is a matter of propinquity, not only of elective affinity.[11] Such cities are also home to many of the United States' best-known cultural institutions. Thus bringing Shakespearean plays to "cities and towns" that have not had the opportunity to witness them is tantamount to leveling the cultural playing field, presumably while prizing Shakespeare from rarefied clutches.

Topical fantasies of democratic access aside, however, the view of Shakespeare espoused by "Shakespeaee in American Communities" does not seem all that different from that propounded by leftist critics in the 1980s and 1990s, and taken as given ever since. While matters of location have not in themselves loomed large in academic discussion, that Shakespeare is elite is all but an article of faith in academic discourse seeking to address literature as a social formation. It is a governing premise of this study that such a characterization is that rarest of Barthesian myths: one that, for different reasons, solicits assent from both Right and Left, and one that it is more than time to question.

As Barthes familiarly argued, at the heart of such mythmaking lies a motivated tendency to substitute Nature for History and so to naturalize power-saturated assertions concerning social reality.[12] Myth is typically a bourgeois activity—which is to say, an apparatus of cultural dominance; for this reason, Barthes pronounced myth on the Left a rarity, deeming it "inessential" with respect to the commonplaces about family, marriage, nation, and value necessary to bourgeois life. But that is because his notion of leftist mythography is derived from obsolescent socialist-realist modes, with their emphasis on "man the producer" (Barthes, 146–147). Current progressive myths concerning elite formations take on a different form. Rather than celebrate the laboring masses directly, these myths (promulgated until recently by, among other elements, cultural studies scholars) honor their habits of consumption, particularly when it comes to mass culture. That mass culture is presumed to be coextensive with the tastes of subordinated or economically disempowered populations, and that, moreover, the study of mass-cultural representations constitutes a form of solidarity with those populations, have become near-articles of faith in academia among scholars interested in relating the study of literature and the possession of literacy with power.[13]

To say as much is not to deny that such study has had progressive agency, nor that the many subtle readings of mass-cultural artifacts generated under this dispensation have been merely celebratory and undialectical in their response to popular tastes. But it is not my aim to identify what political impulse might continue to be honored in the name of mass culture. Instead, I want to call attention to the two significant questions that have been laid by the wayside as a result: whether, in general, elite cultural forms in the per-imillennial United States continue to have the power historically ascribed to them; and above all, whether Shakespeare, in particular, is the inalienable *property* of elites—as opposed, strictly speaking, to their taste, avocation, or phantasm of privilege, but also as opposed to the possibility that at the beginning of the twentieth-first century, Shakespeare is so widely dispersed, and so institutionally plural, that it makes little sense to think of his texts as anything but public culture.

Unlike its conservative counterpart, leftist mythographic discourse has not been altogether guilty of dissociating the Shakespeare-function in the United States from the material determinants that undergird the production and promulgation of Shakespeare. But in choosing to work within the either/or hydraulics of a culture understood as permanently divided between high and low, materialist Shakespeare criticism, like much cultural criticism in general, has found itself retracing the movements of a debate that began half a century ago, with the ever-greater accommodation of cultural products to the forces of industrialization. The influence of the culture industry, whose mass-produced fantasies were held to traduce genuine art, was an urgent point of argument for Frankfurt School critics such as Walter Benjamin and Theodor Adorno, as well as for American intellectuals such as Clement Greenberg and Dwight Macdonald.[14] Such argument, however, now has the character of a received gesture, a truth beyond which there has been no going. The current stasis is all the more peculiar in that it was originally the purpose of cultural studies in general, and of cultural materialist analyses of Shakespeare in particular, to question whether such truths were as fixed, as "natural," as they appeared to be. Surprisingly, later proponents of this position seem to have chosen to ignore the fact that the historical conditions isolating Shakespeare from "the masses" continue to shift, and that progressive criticism interested in examining Shakespeare as a cultural object needs therefore to shift correspondingly. What was once a salutary observation—that Shakespeare, understood as cultural capital, is the antithesis of demotic culture—has come to seem an immutable state of affairs. This is despite the fact that an increasingly pluralistic and market-based model of cultural goods has effectively put paid to the long struggle between high and low, elite and popular, that consumed twentieth-century debates about culture, class, and the production of public consciousness. When, however, what sells is an increasingly privatized, and endlessly customizable, range of texts and pleasures, and when the NEA motto of "A great nation deserves great art" equates that art with the narcissistic reward structures of the market writ large enough to accommodate the self-aggrandizing state, it no longer makes sense to quibble about binary cultural hydraulics. And when the privileges (real and fantasmatic) of academia have increasingly come under ideological and economic siege, it seems misplaced to apologize for having once had faith in redemptive cultural objects and for the forms of high literacy that it takes to profess them.

Although the United States is my principal locus of engagement, the fact is that critical studies of Shakespearean relations, like much of cultural studies itself, first flourished in Britain, where the relationship between access to high literary capital and class privilege has been pursued with greater vigor than it has tended to be here. Notable in this regard is the critical formation cultural materialism. While not all of its practitioners engaged with present-day cultural registers, they nevertheless variously worked to demystify the presumptive value neutrality of literary studies and to position Shakespeare as a principal vehicle of hegemony and national heritage. Indeed, it was within this formation that the first linkage between Shakespeare and mythography was articulated. As Graham Holderness suggested in the preface to his edited collection *The Shakespeare Myth*, that myth functioned like a particularly valuable piece of British currency bearing the image of the Bard: "The fortunate holder of a Shakespearean banknote possesses both monetary wealth and aesthetic richness; and by virtue of that possession is integrated, both materially and culturally, into the hegemonic ideologies of bourgeois society."[15] At the time his collection was published, Holderness's elegantly compressed formulation and the work it introduced represented an exciting and urgent demystification of Shakespeare worship, and hence of myth as understood in the hegemonic terms that principally preoccupied Barthes. And attention to popular culture was of a piece with that demystification, since popular culture, whatever the problems with its relationship to democratic formations of taste and whatever blind eye it turned to industrially imposed practices of consumption, was deemed nevertheless to represent a realm of comfort and familiarity for nonbourgeois subjects. Hence to find Shakespeare contained in popular forms was to find evidence—or perhaps, to express a hope—that the authority of dominant culture was being burlesqued, and with it the hegemonic values that Shakespeare was presumed to perpetuate.[16]

The most frequently used critical term to describe this act of popular burlesque has been "appropriation"—but this is a term whose utility to formations around Shakespeare demands further scrutiny.[17] Appropriation is akin to theft, the taking of private property: in critical circles the concept was given initial currency by the conceptual artist Sherrie Levine's "appropriations" of Walker Evans's photographs through rephotographing them, making her copies all but indistinguishable from the originals and thereby erasing any boundary between authorized and unauthorized. That is, she treated those originals, attached to the name of an author and possessed of discrete market value, as a form of *public* property, to be taken and drawn upon as needed, and hence as part of a cultural repertory transcending mere propertarian relations. What started off as embedded in propriety and possession ends up dissolving the distinction between realms: the appropriated image enters public culture.[18]

To reposition arenas thought to be opposed and antithetical is, I aver, the real legacy of an act of "appropriation." And that repositioning is what renders Holderness's demystification—and the myriad other moments associated with cultural materialism as well as with cultural studies—in danger of calcification. Insofar as the discourse of appropriation has been understood to depend on an apparently unending dynamic of elite and popular, of possession on the one hand and theft for the purpose of reuse on the other, it turns, as Barthes observed apropos of myth, the historical into the natural. Such stasis reappears, comparatively dematerialized, in American studies of popular Shakespeare, as in Douglas Lanier's admirable *Shakespeare and Modern Popular Culture*, which usefully explores a wealth of texts in a number of different registers—film and music among them—and which principally defines its twin objects in familiarly binary terms.[19] Indeed, merely by supposing surprise at finding a reference to Shakespeare in popular culture, Lanier cannot but reify the cultural registers that are the site of his interrogation:

> One way to answer the question "What is Shakespeare doing in popular culture?" is to recognize that these allusions are *doing something*, that pop culture uses Shakespeare to create meaning and not merely as an inert decoration or simple-minded token of prestige. Shakespeare's appearances in pop culture typically involve interplay between two cultural systems—high and pop culture—that operate in parallel realms, two bodies of reference, sets of cultural institutions, canons of aesthetic

standards, modes of constructing cultural authority. That interplay takes many forms, some harmonious, some reciprocal, some recuperative, some competitive, some antagonistic, and even some unstable combinations of these. But at its heart is a contest for authority between the two cultural systems and the institutional interests they represent. (16)

The very fact of the initial question asserts that Shakespeare cannot be said to properly belong in any of the myriad locales the study details. As is inevitable with such governing premises, Lanier's study effectively polices a boundary that it purports merely to describe; even more, and more perversely, while submerging its object in the detritus of the everyday, it winds up confirming Shakespeare's privilege simply by suggesting that it *can* be polluted by submersion, if only in passing.

Although the passage I've cited acknowledges the conservative position still articulated in publications like *The New Criterion*, which defend high culture from the siege it is presumed to be under from the taste of the masses, in practice any sense of dialectical possibility collapses into a unitary vector. Indeed, Lanier's position, like that of other critics working in the field, represents a mere inversion of the earlier intellectual orthodoxy. In this latter view, a high culture whose authority has been contested for at least a century has, for all analytical intents and purposes, remained unaffected by any struggle for cultural dominance, not to mention any changes in the material conditions to which this struggle might be related. This exemption of a hypostatized elite culture from scrutiny renders popular culture always agitating and yet, pathetically, always without agency. Dominant Shakespearean formations apparently maintain their hegemony by inertia, since their propositional and ideological content remains unaffected by the emergence of other spheres of cultural production. Curiously, then, a popular culture that interests critics because it hints at resistance expressed via a politics of taste remains interesting despite, or perhaps because of, its very lack of success in accomplishing its goal. In effect, a contest between cultural registers becomes a licensed, indeed formalized and highly structured, carnival.[20]

Hence another of my aims, which is to suggest that that political work continue by other modes of intervention, that it not rest at rendering Shakespeare as merely an object of theft and suspicion. To reiterate that claim is to be involved in an unconsciously duplicitous motion, where academics' own ambivalently experienced yet unabated access to Shakespearean goods is straitened into a narrative of repudiation and disavowal, a sign, perhaps, of guilt at the possession of a cultural capital presumed (I would argue, wrongly) to be inalienable from the power to oppress.

That the conversation about political Shakespeare, when it still occurs, is often identified with the need for self-recrimination needs little effort to demonstrate. Take, for instance, Sharon O'Dair's passionate and provocative repudiation of her own formation, her movement from child of the working class to an academic with a Ph.D. who teaches Shakespeare.[21] Her study suggests that her gradual investment in academic discipline and performance marks the occasion of her tacit treason to her class, a treason betokened by her willingness to jettison the preferred markers of class taste, preeminent among them a *distaste* for Shakespeare. The melancholy fact must be acknowledged that such a claim, while laudably conscious of academia's imbrication in social relations, makes one's entire career an act of bad faith, or a sin of commission that an academic monograph can inevitably do little to expiate. Apart from what such acknowledgment reveals about widespread academic self-criticism, however, there remain two larger hypotheses undergirding O'Dair's argument pertinent to my analysis. The first concerns the apparent belief that the connection between social class and aesthetic taste is both immutable and uninflectable—that Shakespeare, having once been identified *with* elites and *as* elite, is understood to be of little interest to working-class subjects everywhere and at all times except insofar as they are "ideological dupes," captive of a collaborationist impulse.[22] (Rejecting this belief is not the same thing as a critic's believing all such subjects *ought* to be exposed to Shakespeare; there is a difference between understanding social complexity and missionary advocacy that I will strive to maintain.) The second, far more important, is that matters of taste still constitute the leading edge of politics, a position that has as its corollary the assumption that popular culture is genuinely a "culture of the people" and hence that the affirmative study of it carries more progressive political value than the study of the canon.[23]

Of the latter of these two questions I have already written at some length elsewhere: as John Frow has acutely suggested in his analysis of what counts as "value" in cultural studies work, academic interest in popular culture is not an escape from canon formation and the drawing of distinctions but an extension of such work, as one might expect when it comes to professionalized writing about representation and aesthetics.[24] Whatever political efficacy the analysis of popular forms might offer has been subject to contestation for some time: even avowedly utopian critics such as Fredric Jameson can offer only hypotheses about reading potentialities, confined as they are to the ambit of the text and to the historical as a form of allegorical figuration.[25] And because the high-cultural text has suffered from being cast, in terms made (in)famous by Matthew Arnold, as a vehicle of uplift, the myriad ways in which it might work other than as ideological mystification have eluded the institutional capture of cultural studies critics. That is, although one point of emergence for cultural studies was the study of canonical literary texts, the field has long since shifted its energies to popular forms, leaving the status of so-called high culture apparently unaffected by the social, political, and economic changes to which the popular forms are considered subject. Strangely, such inattentiveness to how high culture might function in a new historical conjuncture—if, indeed, it is to have an important role—winds up reinforcing the very ideological postulates of universality and timelessness with which that culture has been taxed. Exchange the earlier, anodyne propositions about "the human condition" with somewhat newer ones about hegemony and domination, exchange reflexive reading strategies with equally unenergetic propositions about high culture's power continually being subverted from below, and you wind up more or less in the same place: stuck. It is perhaps no wonder, then, that the kind of cultural criticism in which I am engaged has all but vanished from Shakespeare studies.

The impasse to which I've just alluded circles back to the first of my hypotheses, concerning the one-to-one correspondence between elite cultural goods and elite social status. As is well-known, Lawrence Levine, in his influential *Highbrow/Lowbrow*, argues that Shakespeare, like opera, went from popular entertainment in the nineteenth century to the preserve of the moneyed and educated in the twentieth, a place where to all analytical intents and purposes both remain to this day. In the place of a culture united in enthusiastic enjoyment of, and familiarity with, a wide range of Shakespearean plays, in Levine's version of American modernity there opens instead a yawning division between popular taste, which the entertainment market exists to serve, and the more rarefied palates for which bel canto singing and Shakespearean theater are habitual pleasures. And in place of an engagement with the specificities of historical subjects understood via the complex interplay of regional factors, race, educational levels, class, ethnicity, and gender, Levine instead definitively registers a linear shift in the ground of discussion to practices of consumption and hierarchies of taste.

While Levine's groundbreaking study can scarcely be held accountable for the way that these questions of taste have become linked to what is and is not "authentically" American, it is worth noting the extent to which his descriptive model seems to have conquered the field. Even critics of Shakespeare who with some justice point to Levine's work as a nostalgic evocation of a common culture disagree mainly about relative emphasis rather than with the continuing utility of placing Shakespeare in the superlunary realm.[26] However, the parallels he draws between opera and Shakespeare as comparably elite forms do not stand up to material scrutiny, and it is the collapse of those parallels that reveals the inadequacies of his model to the present moment. It is of course true that Shakespeare and opera benefit from the support of privileged institutions and classes such as Levine touches on: witness the NEA. It is also true that both can be united under the sign of Europhilic culture, a generally bourgeois aesthetic disposition toward the Old World and its cultural goods. But analysis need not stop there. The expenses associated with opera as it is put forward in the United States, from training singers and musicians to mounting large-scale productions to the cost of attendance, are not in any way reinforced or valorized by a national educational discourse in which Verdi, Wagner—indeed, even music training in the form of school bands—are considered central. That Shakespeare is an increasingly ineluctable part of education in America is not, in contrast, open to much contestation: the focus on pedagogy added by "Shakespeare in American Communities" to its originally performance-focused initiative makes that clear enough. Perhaps even more tellingly, though, opera has thus far appeared to be beyond the imaginative and ideological reach of a demand that its stage be in some sense a microcosm of the nation-state in its representation of the civic body, a demand that, when it is made, cannot but suggest there is something at stake for the national imaginary in who plays its parts.[27] While the many accomplished African American opera singers are of course duly noted and celebrated, casting practices that would now be considered offensive on the Shakespearean stage still seem to pass without very much remark in opera. It is no longer remotely thinkable for any white actor, let alone one of the stature of Laurence Olivier, to put on black face in order to portray Othello; however, there appears to be nothing at stake for American public culture when a tenor such as Placido Domingo has done the same to embody his Verdian counterpart Otello.

As I've been told, a good tenor is hard to find. When aesthetics trumps politics, indeed, when the separation between the two remains highly naturalized, we might imagine that that is simply because the forces of ideological enforcement have not yet stormed the battlements, that opera constitutes a zone of exemption from the culture wars to which I've earlier referred. Precisely: opera can have continued its embrace of a practice that has long been delegitimated and found offensive when it comes to the Shakespearean stage, because its comparatively rarefied, indeed, recondite, status protects it from wider scrutiny. One is of course not to imagine that all operagoers are secretly reactionary partisans of a high-class minstrel show.[28] Rather, it is because opera, unlike Shakespeare, does not *matter* to the imaginary of the United States that its racial impersonations do not incite controversy. Opera's very internationalism—manifested in everything from casts and conductors to the still-general practice of not translating the sung lyrics into English—represents an outmoded metonym for the dominant class, or, rather, represents a taste that, while once indeed the sign of social and economic preeminence, is now in danger of being associated with un-Americanness in the current political climate. Hence my initial epigraph from Samuel Huntington.

One hundred years after the Gilded Age brought into being a network of institutions dedicated to displaying and preserving an Arnoldian notion of culture as "the best that has been thought and said in 'the world'" (i.e., Europe and particularly Britain)—and one hundred years after Shakespeare first became an entrance requirement for admission to elite universities—governing elites no longer need a public dedication to European art forms as a leading sign for, and legitimation of, their power. At issue here is the continued utility of the idea of cultural capital, a term derived from the reflexive sociology of Pierre Bourdieu and widely adopted in American academia, thanks in part to John Guillory's book of the same name.[29] Michèle Lamont's comparative sociological study of the upper middle classes in the United States and France confirms what might well have been suspected of a nation sometimes adjudged "anti-intellectual": acquiring cultural sophistication and symbolic capital—what John Guillory described as the high literacy for which the canon is a simply a convenient vehicle and which is generally comprehended by "cultural capital"—does not matter very much to professionals and managers in Indianapolis and New York; it matters far less than it does, in fact, to their counterparts in Paris and Clermont-Ferrand.[30] Lamont's study serves as a salutary reminder of the need to emulate Pierre Bourdieu's nuanced attention to the specificities of a national formation even as we adapt his terms of analysis. For all the conceptual power of "cultural capital" in delineating some historical aspects of the interplay of class, taste, and power, in America there persists an alternative crystallization around the self-made, pragmatic subject as the avatar of success within American capitalism, a crystallization that governs most popular articulations of power and influence.

Such myths are perhaps on the ascendant, given the glee with which Bill Gates's lack of academic credentials has been circulated, and given as well the promotion of the relentlessly self-mythologizing Donald Trump as a point of mass aspiration. His television show, "The Apprentice," which until its turn to celebrity charity work featured applicants eager to prove their business moxie, merely makes overt the governing premise that most "reality" shows cover over with an arbitrary grid of exoticized difficulty: the model of success on offer, and defined in terms of a pot of money at the end, is an enactment of the imaginary of capitalism—and it depends on grit, luck, dirty tricks, and mass-cultural star appeal. If Golden Age plutocrats at the turn of the prior century sought the inoculation provided by philanthropy and the trappings of traditional Europeanized high culture, and educational reformers of the time increasingly positioned Shakespeare as a gateway to university admission, their latter-day counterparts generally feel no such pressure, no need to assume the protective coloration even of residual Anglophilia (Trump's excessively gilded and mirrored residence is a domestic, almost "vulgar," simulacrum of high bourgeois taste in European decor: Vegas-style luxury with precious materials). Increasingly, bourgeois tastes have become disarticulated from bourgeois power; instead, those tastes constitute a residual formation, regardless of whether they are espoused from Right or Left. Indeed, given the rush to affiliate Shakespeare with elitism and the failure, thus far, to make good on the belief that he can be disarticulated from hegemonic formulations, it appears sometimes that the only people left who articulate the affirmative value of bourgeois culture are politically reactionary, fighting a rear-guard action not only against "tenured radicals" but against the emergent market populism of an even newer Right than has been on the ascendant in the United States. Coincident with that ascension, the power of "elite culture" as a sign has increasingly shifted from positive to negative, as the epigraph from Huntington suggests. Even his title, "Dead Souls," tropes (via its reference to Gogol's text) the cultural capital ascribed to elites, while suggesting it is a form of baggage that murders the American spirit.

Although public figures such as Huntington do not reserve the scorn for opera that they do toward national avant-gardes and the production of new aesthetic forms, when governing elites in the United States effectively repudiate European cultural production and values—the aesthetic products of the political formation "old Europe," in Donald Rumsfeld's dismissive phrase—it is to position themselves securely within a fantasmatic national consensus that sees popular taste not just as a market but as the core point of reference for identity as an American. In fact, that taste has become an increasingly valuable locus of reduction and condensation for a host of economic and political agendas—a form of alibi, as it were, in which attending to popular entertainment or market demographics stands in for attending to the material conditions under which most American citizens live. Under current conditions, in which economic power, popular taste, and the state are united hegemonically, the persistence of initiatives such as "Shakespeare in American Communities" cannot signify that the same old ideological work critiqued by cultural materialism is being performed via Shakespeare, despite their superficial similarity to past formations.

All the more reason, then, for any study of Shakespeare in American public culture to be suspicious of the stories we already know how to tell—or, to put it more pungently, of the performances that actually inscribe what they purport merely to reflect. If increasingly state institutions and their agents reject the elitism signified by European high culture but strenuously protect Shakespeare, it is not simply because of the structural hypocrisy of power, which says one thing and means another—although, as I shall suggest later, the referential register of "elite" in American discourse is far from coherent or straightforward. Partly, it is because Shakespeare's nationalization goes beyond the control of the elites to whom Levine has the Bard surrendered at the turn of the last century. But partly it involves recognizing how the political study of Shakespeare has become disarticulated from the structural transformations of academic labor that have occurred in these perimillennial years. Academics' use of the term "elite" to designate Shakespeare (and, by extension, themselves) is not only a misapprehension of its textual object: it has become an unwitting concession to the hegemony of the market and its political agents.

* * *

One way to bring the unwitting concession into view is via a study of the semantic field within which elitism emerged and now operates. "Elite" and "elitism" are among the terms ripe for the *Keywords* treatment identified with Raymond Williams, since they are politically efficacious terms whose historically determinate semantic and ideological shifts stand in need of unconcealing.[31] Although in cultural criticism "elite" and "popular" seem, like high and low, a natural and mutually constitutive binary, in fact they are radically asymmetrical, since the career of the latter term is far longer and more substantial, and thus a significant index of changing social relations.[32] In what seems like a fortuitous coincidence for a study on Shakespeare and the public imaginary, "popular" emerges in the last quarter of the sixteenth century, in senses both political and cultural. It is unclear what purchase, if any, the word had on actually existing formations drawing on the will of large number of the underclass; nevertheless, it is plausible to suggest that the word operated not unlike a structure of feeling, a semantic-historical promise of a realm of broader-based practices.

And yet, unlike "popular" or, for that matter, such words as "literature" or "culture," "elite" is a term whose history startles most for its apparent brevity rather than for its mutating signification. A search of the *Oxford English Dictionary* (*OED*), for instance, reveals an unexpected discontinuity in the history of usage. "Elite" first comes into the English language in the fourteenth century as a synonym for "elect" and was used, like that word, to denote someone chosen (from L. *eligere*) in a specifically religious sense—hence the few citations, all to bishops and other episcopal persons.[33]

Then, if the historical dictionary is to be trusted, "elite" all but disappears from usage for some 500 years—even during a period in which distinctions based on rank were, by common agreement, being challenged by those based on wealth. This is not to say that the discourse of choice and distinction disappears altogether. Rather, it was signaled by the word "aristocracy," which, in addition to the familiar modern sense of a distinction of nobility based on blood and heritable title, was used more broadly, in a way concomitant with its Greek etymology, to refer to a mode of government by the "best" citizens of a state. Hence Elyot's 1531 *Booke Called the Governour*: "In the Greke tunge called Aristocratia...in englisshe, the rule of men of beste disposicion." Indeed, a supporting citation in the *OED* to *Volpone*, in a passage that also mentions the Senate, seems to suggests a deliberate, and potentially conservative, classicism—a usage that by extension brings education to the forefront and potentially furthered by Hobbes, who, in 1651, defined the aristocracy as the formation "wherein the highest magistrate is chosen out of those that have had the best education." Gibbon's 1781 usage appears to translate political referentiality further into the terms valorized by Enlightenment discourse: hence "a perfect Aristocracy of reason and virtue." Although in 1850 Thomas Carlyle wrote straightforwardly of "the attainment of a truer and truer Aristocracy, or Government again by the Best," the apparent (and unqualified) nostalgia of that "again" suggests not some lost and Periclean Golden Age, but rather, a semantic slippage that the *OED*, in a rare bit of overt editorialism, laconically locates with the French Revolution: whereas earlier usages launched themselves against pervasive monarchy, later ones, the dictionary avers, see democracy, the rule of the many, the "popular," as opposed to the chosen, as the competing form of political life. Over time the sense of the word mutates still more: as the *OED* definition suggests, "The term is popularly extended to include all those by birth or fortune occupy a position distinctly above the rest of the community" (*OED*, "aristocracy," 5).

If the *OED*'s genealogy is to be trusted, the more recent connotations of "aristocracy" all but set the stage for the reemergence of "elite," which returns to English through French, overtly stripped of its religious connotations, to denote the "choice part or flower (of society or of any body or class of persons)."[34] Byron's 1823 *Don Juan* is the first text cited—"With other Countesses of Blank—but rank; / At once the 'lie' and the 'elite' of crowds"—a phrase whose mocking employment of the term juxtaposes aristocratic title with namelessness and rank with the mob, effectively undermining any purchase on actually existing status distinctions, while it raises the question of what sort of discursive and social universe Byron was thus trying to put to the sword. Few usages are so dismissive, however: apart from technical extensions of the term into botany or typography, "elite" has seemed rather durably to take over the functions of a politically delegitimated "aristocracy," a word that since the late eighteenth century had assumed the taint of heritable privilege, of a nobility of the blood. Of particular interest is T. S. Eliot's *Notes Towards the Definition of Culture* of 1948: the truncated phrase from it cited by the *OED*, "An elite-governed society," barely hints at the connection the poet sought to forge between power and privilege, the better to defend a British culture he perceived to be under siege at the end of World War II.[35]

Eliot's text is both an oddly illuminating choice for the *OED* and a displacement of the word's more usual field of engagement in the earlier part of the twentieth century. That the illustrative quotation chosen should come from Eliot little reveals that its more habitual context was debates in the comparatively new field of sociology, which Eliot signals (but does not exhaust) through his references to Karl Mannheim's writings. Although the word itself returned to English through French, the comparatively new concept it subtended found its initial formulations in the writings of Gaetano Mosca and Vilifredo Pareto, two Italian thinkers whose theories of cultural segmentation, of the domination of the many by the few, helped set the terms for a long series of sociological debates that have been associated most often with Max Weber.[36] Yet for all the attention the discursive category has generated, elite theory is not, in most senses, conceptually elaborate; it focuses on modeling how social forms make and remake themselves through the actions of talented or otherwise distinctive individuals who do not have inherited access to power. The power of elite theory lies in its historical effects, the way it both displaced the revolutionary model of class struggle associated with Marx and responded to the threat that nascent democratic institutions posed to the very division between orders of society. Thus Tom Bottomore:

> The concept of the political elite was pursued by Mosca and Pareto as a key term in a new social science, but it had another aspect which is scarcely less apparent in their writings: namely, that it formed part of a political doctrine which was opposed to, or critical of, modern democracy, and still more opposed to modern socialism.[37]

That is to say, the concept of "elites" was located at the intersection of state politics and power-knowledge. It emerged not all that long after another event of interest to Foucault: the demographic management of population, through statistics and other techniques, which renders the various denizens of both the nation-state and the colony discursively knowable, discursively masterable.[38] As such, sociology, in particular its elaboration of elite theory, is subject to the same critical gaze that Foucault directed at its juridical, medical, and psychologistic counterparts. Unlike those other fields, however, sociology, as yet another of the sciences of man, was in the process of constructing an *overtly* self-legitimating model of cultural differentiation, one whose conservatism was in effect a reaction formation in favor of centralized state power and of the elites who did its work, directly or indirectly.

Matters of academic provenance aside, however, the word "elite" has come into increased prominence in the rebarbative and opportunistic discourse of American politics at the recent turn of the millennium. As several of my initial quotations indicate, "elite" has gained vigor as a term of reactionary political abuse, a way to dismiss and demonize a regime of values that represents an exhausted social liberalism. What seems most obvious, however, is not simply that the term constitutes an abnegated, indeed abject, subject position from which its putative designees recoil in fear (these days, people duck the term "elite" at least as much as young and affluent urban residents once dissociated themselves from the dismissive title "yuppie"). It is that the term itself has come to have no stable referent and so represents a mode of othering whose motility is as much to the point as the falsely universalized populism for which the attackers of elitism claim to speak.[39] Sociological theory suggests that elites can be replaced when they no longer serve the essentially conservative function to which their pursuit of distinction entitles them—when, as I've already suggested, they withdraw from, or rebel against, the tacit equipoise between power and the ostensibly disinterested promotion of knowledge to which academic and intellectual elites are enjoined. John Guillory notes that the word "liberal" has been in the process of becoming so contaminated that it is all but delegitimated as a political possibility in American public discourse, echoing the fate of Marxist radicalism extirpated by McCarthyism in the 1950s: hence, presumably, the newly ascendant "progressive." But both "Marxist" and "liberal" have some recent history of referentiality, which is to say, some anchor, however vexed and in need of complication, in material history. The rhetoric of "are you now or have you ever been?" tried to pin down a definitive affiliation, and the rubric of the "fellow traveler" at least denoted that there were, in fact, such things as actually existing Communists with whom one might consort. And to the extent that liberalism was a self-constituted discourse and, in certain regions of the country at least, an actual political party, it too has some purchase on institutional fixity.

Not so, precisely, with elite. Not only has the term changed in affective sign, from a positive to a negative value. Its recent career shows it to slide with a rapidity that would put reactionary fantasies of a deconstruction unanchored in the material world of fixed meanings to shame, the more peculiar given the conservatism of some of its most ambitious articulations. Even so, I hope it is clear that my interest is not in making obvious, and straightforwardly partisan, argumentative points. Rather, it is in thinking about how the present prominence of anti-elitist discourse signifies a tacit reversal of vector for the political conditions under which the term itself emerged, and the consequences of that reversal for how we think about Shakespeare right now.

Mosca's and Pareto's theorizing on elites as a positive force was, as Bottomore suggests, inflected by the beginnings of socialism and of democratic political cultures in Europe. At this conjuncture, however, elites defined in terms of culture and taste and evoked as a distorting deviation from popular will, serve as useful straw figures: their demonization gestures in the direction of mass political projects even as the feint guarantees that concentrated financial and corporate power, a growing and far more pernicious form of authority wielded by a select few, remains generally uninterrogated. As long as there are cultural elites to attack, this dispensation might suggest, then democracy remains strong—and, rhetorically at least, socialism a threat. It is perhaps no accident that the term "class struggle" has been revived to delegitimate even the mildest criticism of economic inequality or the most middling efforts at health reform, for it reveals that the conditions of democratic dissent subtended by the Keynesian state are readily substituted for the historical possibility of socialism they kept at bay. Indeed, the collapse of the one into the other might be read still more pessimistically. For all the ideological connections forged under neo-liberalism between the necessity of a free market and the maintenance of social and political liberties, to the extent that actually existing democracy tends to hinder the excesses of untrammeled capital, the democratic state form must be preserved as sign while its propositional content is reduced to that which it defines by a condition of exteriority.[40] "Liberty," they cry, when their real concern is license—arrangements by mean of which capital can be multiplied ever more effectively, even more freely, through transnational flows.

Under such elusive discursive and material conditions, what does it mean when progressive academic discourse has insisted on Shakespeare's elitism—and when, in a strangely handy (if unconscious) capitulation to right-wing rhetorical baiting and an equally strange resistance to dialectical thinking, it insists on seeing *itself* as shamefully elite? In an analysis of the "torsioned" class position of academics-as-intellectuals, Guillory has noted that in recent times, "an intellectual is interpellated now as a peculiar kind of *political subject*."[41] This politicization attaches itself in particular to those working in the humanities, even as their field becomes subject to increasing marginalization in a university dedicated more and more to technocratic rationality. While the truth of any connection between academics (understood as a privileged category in crisis) and the institutional nexus is undeniable, in setting up his analysis via a historical disjuncture between academics and journalists as competing models of the intellectual, Guillory cannot anticipate the extent to which anti-academic sentiment has migrated beyond the sphere of those who might reasonably share the title "intellectual" and entered a political discourse for which the distinction has little force. In the gap between his term and mine, "intellectual" versus "elite," we glimpse the difference between a class-centered formation with the academy as its focal point and one with an alarmingly protean capacity to infiltrate other realms of discourse while precisely obscuring any home questions about academics' mutating place in the relations of production.[42]

* * *

Perhaps one reason for the resistance to changing the discourse around Shakespeare has to do with the question of its unacknowledged self-servingness, the way in which polarities keep us fixed in the category of elites—at least discursively. Stanley Aronowitz has, after all, described academia as "the last good job in America," and his description of the working life of a moderately privileged academic, a life that affords autonomy both of work and of the intellect, mental challenge, camaraderie, a comfortable if not lush standard of living, and a pleasing interpenetration of labor and leisure, is indeed enviable, one reason many of us became academics in the first place.[43] This sense of autonomy and privilege might well correspond to academics' ability to exercise power in their chosen fields—or rather to equate the possession of expertise with the exercise of power. Leftist academics have acknowledged the consequences attendant upon the possession of cultural capital, understood here not merely as a matter of field-dependent competence but rather as the sign of a distinct privilege within a small substrate of capitalist society. Inspired variously by Foucault as well as by Weberian arguments about class and status, Althusser's work on education as an ideological state apparatus, the Ehrenreichs' discussion of the professional-managerial class, and, most recently, Pierre Bourdieu's *Distinction*, academic discourse has pursued a self-reflexive analysis concerning its role in reproducing the relations of production and more broadly in the benefits it receives from status distinctions that do not always correspond to the hard data of annual income.[44]

In 1976, Richard Ohmann, for example, subjected the practices and institutions of English as a discipline to materialist scrutiny in the wake of the 1960s, the better to diagnose its collusion with technocratic regimes in terms that all but speak of an implicit allegiance with the bourgeoisie.[45] More pointed for my purposes, in that same year Stephen J. Brown used the occasion of the American bicentennial to suggest that the emergence of a curriculum with Shakespeare at its center represented "the imposition of white Anglo-Saxon Protestant 'civility' from above." As the title of his brief essay indicated, to trace the place of Shakespeare in America was to recognize how education's chosen fetish object was ancillary to class domination, rawly conceived.[46]

There is much historical truth to Brown's particular argument, as I shall indicate in chapter 3, when I analyze the role of the nascent College Board in demanding knowledge of Shakespeare for entrance to colleges and universities. But that truth needs to be sufficiently recognized *as* historical, with respect both to academics and to Shakespeare. Failure to do so produces a strange consequence: to the rarefied object that is Shakespeare is compounded the equally rarefied subject who is his *essentially* privileged institutional counterpart. If all academic intellectuals are forever guardians and gatekeepers of privilege, then those who teach Shakespeare must, by the logic of agglomeration, be the most restrictively elite of them all. Positing that formations that emerged a century ago persist (as thought they constituted steady-state systems) yields not only the familiar assertion that reading, understanding, or enjoying the plays requires an extraordinary and rarefied level of education—an assertion that is certainly not entirely wrong as far as it goes—but also the presumption that through the magic of the hypostasized discourse of cultural capital, acquaintance with the plays conveys the elite status that is its own precondition. Elitism is both cause and effect, object of suspicion and blameworthy end in itself.

What good does it do to keep status and Shakespeare in the United States coextensive at the present conjuncture? And for whom? As I shall argue in chapter 3, the inextricability of his plays from education at the secondary level and, indeed, even at educational levels below high school means that durable fantasies about the texts and their author coexist with an ever-widening Shakespearean net into which more and more of the population is increasingly drawn, and which the rhetoric of innovation characteristic of the "Shakespeare in American Communities" endeavor partly obscures. Certainly the simple directness of Brown's and Ohmann's insights is specific to the time in which they were produced: a time when English professors were indeed part of a small and (more or less) demographically uniform cadre trained, and often teaching, at the most ostentatiously restrictive universities, and possessed of a largely unexamined and therefore mandarin power to reproduce the canon, define high literacy, police the linguistic practices of their students, and in general serve as social as well as intellectual gatekeepers. But literary academia is now far from demographically uniform, as O'Dair's more recent account of her working-class origins avers. Indeed, her description of how she became a hyperliterate subject—a docile, ready pupil whose taking knowledge on board was reinforced and validated—forms the counterpart of Stephen Brown's: if Shakespeare is part of a mechanism of "Anglo-Saxon civility imposed from above," then O'Dair is retrospectively eager to reveal what those operations look like from below, by evoking the costs of assimilation, and by valorizing popular resistance—indeed, indifference—to the Shakespearean lessons she has apparently learned far too well.

Such an analysis raises the specter of inauthenticity, even apostasy. Hence the frequent recourse to something akin to anxiety in O'Dair's study, a regret at possessing, and being possessed by, a cultural capital that inevitably separates her from a culture where such things are not valued. Whatever its considerable biographical pathos, as a structural analysis this argument can only be called sentimental; indeed, it forms the personalist counterpart of the fetish popular culture has become, not simply in the academy, but in the political formations I have already begun to discuss. As with much cultural studies work, it locates all value with "the people"—and a strangely monolithic and uncomplex version of a working class at that: as though resistance to Shakespeare were truly the sign of organic intellectualism, and as though American populism were not, these days, a phenomenon needing far more subtle tools of dissection. I am struck by how misplaced, indeed politically inefficacious, this shame is.[47]

In general, all the positions I have discussed seem belated with respect to the power of "literature" in general, and Shakespeare in particular, as ideologically laden signs of a distinction that primarily serves dominative ends. Thanks to Marjorie Garber, many of us are familiar with remarks made by Lynne Cheney in 1988 concerning Shakespeare's universality, in which criticism of politicized readings of Shakespeare was propped up by an opportunistic citation of Maya Angelou,'s claim that the sonnets must have been written by a black woman; those remarks infamously manifested how merely invoking Shakespeare's name represents a form of policing in the right mouths.[48] Yet Garber's critique of how Cheney's rhetoric simply reproduces the national fetish that is Shakespeare seems as inadequate to the present moment as a paralyzing abeyance in the face of the privilege intellectual training has been held to convey.

Certainly, the "universal" Shakespeare Garber attacks can still operate as a nostalgic fantasy: "That Shakespeare is the dream space of nostalgia for an aging undergraduate (that is to say, for just about everyone) seems self-evidently true, and, to tell the truth, not all bad. He is—whoever he is, or was—the fantasy of originary cultural wholeness...to believe in something, in someone, all-knowing, and immutable. If not God, then Shakespeare, who amounts to a version of the same thing" (243). Still, it is worth noting that Garber sidesteps the real focus of Cheney's attack: the universities' supposed politicization of knowledge. Indeed, Garber's ready parenthetical equation of the fantasies of a fictional "aging undergraduate" with "just about everyone" reveals, albeit unintentionally, the gap between her own naturalized framework and the rhetoric of populism that has only gotten more insistent, more strident, in the years since Cheney opined and Garber rejoined. Hence the latter's closing statement: "What is less clear is how we can get beyond this particular ideology. For Shakespeare as fetish, in this time of perceived crisis in the humanities, has become the ideology of our time" (250). For Garber, what needs "getting beyond" is partly the way a fixed and universalized Shakespeare, a Shakespeare whose meaning cannot be subject to contestation or deconstruction without great peril, refers back to the "maternal phallus" that is England. Yet Anglophilia is not particularly a telling form of power at this moment in the American imaginary, even if Blair's adding Britain to the American-dominated "coalition of the willing" in the Iraq war brought forth nostalgic evocations of World War II–era allegiances in a public discourse all too willing to use the legitimation of historical precedent. Evidence of that is not far to seek: even if Shakespeare made it into the curriculum at the turn of the twentieth century precisely as the sign of an Anglo-Saxon "race knowledge," my analysis of Branagh's *Hamlet* in chapter 4 suggests that Anglophilia is but a residual formation at this moment in the United States.

And just as important, in effect, is the once-durable connection between academia and elite social status. As many readers will already know perhaps too well, segments of academia are themselves undergoing a form of proletarianization—a structural deprivileging in which punitive economic agendas, especially those imposed at and by a number of state universities, become a significant register of what *can* and indeed *may* be subject to the conditions of underfunding, of what is ideologically vulnerable to the rhetoric of scarcity and belt-tightening. To put it more bluntly: academic status is not an objectively existing index of comparative privilege; nor is the place of academia in guaranteeing the continued reproduction of capitalist social relations an essential characteristic of academia as a profession, however significant the historical relationship between industrial protocols on the one hand and the rationalized structures within which universities produce knowledge on the other. Rather, status dependent on the possession of cultural capital operates as part of a fantasmatic public pact. When one or more of the parties to this pact withdraw their consent to its terms, the persistence of the status claim is far from guaranteed, except as a lingering trick of rhetoric, or (to speak more materially) the trace of a residual formation. Indeed, the withdrawal of resources from certain state-sponsored higher-educational institutions is a surer indication that many humanities academics are not, in fact, as privileged as some persist in claiming that all academics are.[49]

I am far from the first to suggest that higher education has also become something of a market. That Ivy League and other historically privileged universities and colleges vie against one another to recruit economically and (presumably) intellectually desirable students via restrictive early admissions policies is but one index of how competition between postsecondary institutions has greatly increased in recent years. And, indeed, the emergence of for-profit universities alongside their historically nonprofit counterparts attests to an important shift in the way capitalism, power, and education have become interrelated. Where once higher education, to which access was comparatively restricted, was designed to (re)produce a distinct class of privileged subjects whose role with respect to the maintenance and expansion of wealth was by and large as secure as their admission to a historically prominent university, the broadening of access to colleges and universities was but one step in an ongoing transformation of the relationship between education and labor markets. Bill Readings's *The University in Ruins*, whose melancholy title hints at looming devastation, suggests that "the wider social role of the University as an institution is now up for grabs."[50]

To argue as much is not to deny the straitened circumstance within which many state budgets now operate, nor the relationship between economic trends and the post-Keynesian withdrawal of the federal government from social agendas whose funding has now been pushed back to state and local governmental levels. But the obvious needs stating: at state institutions that have historically small private endowments, funding is largely dependent on state revenues; these, in turn, are determined by taxes. The need that some academics have encountered to make a case that we actually do work hard and long, albeit not in ways commensurable with the rationalized time structures of most jobs available in capitalism, is not so easily dismissed as a problem of information. Rather, it seems prima facie evidence that increasingly academics may be considered an elite only insofar as they can be made to pay for it—made, that is, to surrender the material supports of that discursive privilege. Claiming that university professors don't work hard enough becomes a prolegomenon to underfunding, to a withdrawal of revenues that has more than a little of the anti-intellectual about it.

But it is not anti-intellectualism per se, however much such a thing has been claimed as a persistent feature of popular democracy.[51] Rather, it is a historically specific suspicion of the professoriat that has been engendered in the wake of the culture wars with which I began the chapter and that has been the subject of extensive commentary within academia. A battle that has been engaged as a matter of representation—of Shakespeare versus pop culture, say—might also be understood as related to the modestly changed demographics within the profession. Nothing reveals the gap between conceptions of the professoriat based on status and those based on class quite so much as recognizing that status elites are subject to displacement if and when their constitution changes, or when they no longer affiliate themselves and their interests with the dominant class whose aims they are said to share, as my epigraph from T. S. Eliot evinces. To the extent that the academy has confronted issues of the relation between representation and democracy, within the demographics of the profession and within the aesthetic forum that is the canon, it has, in effect, broken its tacit contract. And since it is colleges and universities with the least amount of inertial density—the least accumulation of a history of quasi-autonomous practices, independent sources of funding, and historical prominence—that are most vulnerable to institutional remodeling in the age of what the cultural geographer David Harvey has called "flexible accumulation," it is most often they who symptomatize (a better word might be "endure") the changing place with respect to academics and the wielding of economic and political power in the United States.[52] Even within such motile institutions, of course, there are gradations of privilege: the college reliant on increasing numbers of adjuncts might well also continue to tenure its professors, although the rate of such hiring is inflected.

This brings me back to "the last good job in America." As might be expected, Aronowitz is not engaging in self-congratulation in essay form. Just as importantly, unlike Ohmann, Brown, or O'Dair, he is not castigating himself, or, indeed, college professors as a class, for all that like O'Dair, he too is self-identified as having come from a working-class background.[53] Indeed, his essay mimics those who would disparage academics in terms that make clear his impatience with how such discussions coincide with the leveling effect of the market:

> In this period of galloping reaction, some of which is coded as populism, these privileges may appear to some to be luxuries and our writing and our teaching merely the ruminations of a narrow academic elite. Some are even moved to attack my working conditions as evidence that the last good job should be ended. It's subversive for a labor regime that is working overtime to close the doors to work democracy and to freedom and poses endless paid work as the ideal to which we should all strive.

For this tendency, I am one of a (thankfully) diminishing fragment of the professoriate whose privileges must be rescinded, the sooner the better. After all, if hardly anyone else enjoys these conditions why should I? (Aronowitz, "Last Good Job," 212)

In place of capitulation to the governing logic he parodies, Aronowitz insists that the myriad satisfactions rendering his job "good" were once available in kind in many forms of labor and argues for the restoration of those satisfactions as worth the struggle: "Rather than proposing an equality of alienated labor we should fight to universalize throughout society the autonomy and shorter working hours of the senior professoriate at research institutions, not just for those in higher education" (212).

It is worth noting that the "good job" Aronowitz describes is not really the same as an elite one. Some tenured and tenure-track academics are indeed privileged because they possess jobs that cannot all that readily be outsourced or otherwise be made to disappear. But job security is no cause for apology; to offer one is to engage in something perilously close to survivor's guilt. And it is all the more telling that such guilt about having a stable and rewarding job is the material counterpart to an intellectual regime in which pleasure in Shakespeare—which persists, I am sure, despite the hermeneutics of suspicion—goes underground even while it publicly becomes tantamount to a breaking of faith with "the people."

* * *

In spending as much time discussing academia as I have, it may seem that I've left the world "beyond," in which Shakespeare exists in myriad forms, little place for reentry. As I've already suggested, however—and even apart from an appropriate concern, derived from cultural studies, with understanding historical conjuncture across a range of domains and discourses—there is no pure outside to academic formations. If the place of Shakespeare in the American imaginary must be affected by broader political and economic shifts, shifts that also affect the academy, then it is also true that instantiations of Shakespeare that present themselves as "apart" from academia, indeed from school culture at large, might nevertheless be haunted by what they seek to bracket or deny.

Witness Al Pacino's *Looking for Richard*, a film that presents itself as the remedy to elite conceptions of the Bard. Seeking to escape the pressure of authority, of a Shakespeare deemed unappealing to the mass public precisely because of the dead weight of elite rarefaction, scholarship, and tradition, it offers its medium—film—as central to its redemptive, indeed messianic, message. Mass form, it seems to aver, will succeed where the schoolroom has failed, will render Shakespeare appealing to a "wider public," a term to be used with caution. In that, Pacino travels along a highly familiar path—and offers a highly familiar account of popular resistance to, and love of, Shakespeare. In fact, it is precisely because the assumptions that undergird Pacino's documentary are so familiar, so fixed, and yet, given the terms I've set up, so belated, that it serves as an important index of how to identify fantasies of Shakespeare in perimillennial America.

CHAPTER 2

Pacino's Cliffs Notes: *Looking for Richard*'s "Public" Shakespeare

When it comes to Shakespeare outside the walls of academia, film will inevitably be an object of discussion. Even as new forms of media generate new modalities of interaction and splinter the heretofore dominant notion of a collective audience, it is fair to say that the twentieth century has been dominated by mass-cultural forms such as film, and thus by the mass public, whether material or fantasmatic, to whom they are addressed. When Shakespeare takes mass-cultural form, therefore, it cannot but be significant; hence the proliferation of Shakespearean films in the late 1990s, which might constitute an imaginary resolution to the long-standing dilemma caused by opposing high and low cultural forms and occurring even as that bifurcated model of culture falls into abeyance.

In a later chapter, I consider this cinematic glut as, among other things, a referendum on the function of Shakespeare in America in these perimillennial years, a referendum in which ever-ascendant market forces vie with a residual aura of British-inflected literary prestige. However, one particular film, Al Pacino's 1996 documentary *Looking for Richard,* demands to be considered on its own.[1] Pacino's film interests me not so much as part of a broader Shakespearean formation in and as cinema but as a representation of pervasive anxieties about Shakespeare in America conducted in documentary mass-cultural form. Indeed, the troubled relationship Pacino's film asserts between Shakespeare and its version of "the public" makes it necessary to consider as a concrete point of departure for this study. Rather than read the text in its particularity as both an ideological and material force in culture, then, I want instead to think about how the very fact of the documentary—that is, the perception that such an intervention, and from such a quarter, is *needed*—can be used to diagnose persistent national fantasies about Shakespeare. As I will argue, *Looking for Richard* is informed ("haunted" is perhaps a better term) by perhaps *the* preeminent discourse about Shakespeare in public: that which attaches to Joseph Papp's Public Theater, famous for its long-term ambition to desacralize Shakespeare and make the plays accessible to nonelite audiences. To the extent that Pacino, like Papp before him, takes Shakespeare as his text, performance as his preferred vehicle of appeal, New York as his stage, and New Yorkers—particularly streetwise types—as his (diegetic) audience, Pacino's project echoes Papp's as a form of populist address on behalf of Shakespearean pleasures, even as it updates the medium from stage to screen in an all-but-natural progression.

But Papp's passionate seizure of Shakespearean performance on behalf of a capacious and multitudinous urban public was historically timely, of a piece with social movements opening myriad institutions to diverse participation. In Pacino's earnest film, the impulse seems more depoliticized and personal, even idiopathic, however much it is aimed outward. But, as I will argue, the power of performance, so important to the Public Theater's instantiation of Shakespeare, is displaced by the ghost of its other, by the institutionalized, intimidating Shakespeare of the schoolroom. As this displacement from performance to occasional lesson might suggest, *Looking for Richard* is somewhat divided against itself, from a formal standpoint as well as a propositional one. Filmed over a number of years as a side project for Pacino, assembled from over eighty hours of footage by no fewer than six editors, it cannot seem to decide what it is: the latest avatar of the apparently never-ending quest to disseminate Shakespeare more broadly, or a performance diary, complete with glimpses of read-throughs and snippets suggesting a larger project, a filmed version of *Richard III* that appears to live "elsewhere."

Given the gap it measures between Papp's "public Shakespeare" and what I am calling perimillennial Shakespeare, such confounded aims and ontology signal the way *Looking for Richard* operates as a useful register of the confused (not to say contradictory) place Shakespeare holds in the national imaginary at the current moment. The film figures forth an American relation to Shakespeare at once universalizing and exclusionary, anxious about whether the English playwright has ever been naturalized in the United States; believing, like the NEA, in the priority of performance (which, as several scholars have noted, depends on a Method-inflected focus on character pragmatics) but fearful of being found wanting; exuberant about popular appeal, but gnawingly suspicious that true meaning might be found elsewhere, among experts whose knowledge is both honored and ridiculed.[2] In all these things, the documentary's strategy is of a piece with the assumptions it makes about its audience, particularly concerning that audience's relationship to Shakespeare. *Looking for Richard* strives to acknowledge that in a city rich with high-cultural resources, hostility and indifference to Shakespeare are widespread. But it cannot take those attitudes seriously enough to explore them. Nor does it unambivalently assert a faith that performance in itself is the key to pleasure, the royal road to knowledge. Even given its moments of engaging self-mockery, or, rather, precisely because of them, it treats anything but reverence toward Shakespeare as a problem to be solved: a problem whose solution is known in advance. Because his film's self-mockery resembles nothing more consequential than the trope of comic relief made famous by orthodox interpretation of subplots in the tragedies, Pacino effectively redeems all forms of resistance to Shakespeare by putting them in the service of a higher message. Like the wit of the Porter of Hell Gate or the Gravedigger in *Hamlet,* the laughter of his public audience constitutes a subordinate recapitulation of more serious themes. This unknowing is represented as a form of ignorance—of, in the end, never having been exposed to the right approach—to which Pacino's documentary offers itself as the salutary corrective.

Hence my claim that *Looking for Richard* enacts the fantasy that pervades much national discourse on the Bard, in which the dissemination of Shakespeare is always undertaken on behalf of unnamed others, of resistant segments of a fantasmatic and unitary public who are understood to reject the playwright only because the proper appeal has not yet been proffered. And like much national discourse (witness the NEA's "Shakespeare in American Communities"), the documentary cannot quite acknowledge the history that brought it, and us, to this pass: a history, that is, of prior moments of engagement with Shakespeare, when Shakespeare has been imposed, offered, rejected, partially taken up, used opportunistically from below and from above, a history that spans the life of the republic. That in perimillennial American culture, Shakespeare seems always marked by displacements—by the sense that he is elsewhere, hovering above or beyond, neither fully naturalized nor fully rejected as alien—and that those displacements must be endlessly conjured only to be endlessly corrected for: these are dispensations that permeate *Looking for Richard.* It is for this reason that I read the film as in some sense an index to the Shakespeare-function in the United States in the perimillennial era. In the case of Pacino's film, it is performance that becomes the vehicle of restoration. In this particular case, of course, the filmic appeal to "the masses" (a term I use advisedly) cannot be disarticulated from the power of the star and of the mass-cultural realm that Pacino subtends, a realm that has long taken polemical advantage of its opposition to high culture—and one from which Papp's public Shakespeare sometimes profited itself.³

As I've already suggested, however, in this film the appeal to the masses also cannot be disarticulated from the ostensible other of the performer's Shakespeare: the Shakespeare of study and scholarship, the hearth god of the secondary school classroom for approximately one hundred years. As though despite itself, *Looking for Richard* evinces a particularly durable formation around Shakespeare in twentieth- and twenty-first century America, which I call the pedagogical imperative: the sense that, where Shakespeare is concerned and no matter the status of performance, there are always lessons to be learned.

* * *

Although I have suggested that Pacino's film may be read as a continuation of Joseph Papp's earlier efforts to promote Shakespeare as a civic good in New York beginning in the 1960s, *Looking for Richard* contains few overt references to Papp's institution. Papp's name, for instance, is never mentioned, nor is any interview conducted with any current director or representative of the Public Theater. However, a scene early in the film reveals how the imaginative landscape of the film is necessarily inscribed by Papp's celebrated efforts to disseminate Shakespeare to wider audiences. As Pacino strolls through Central Park, wearing dark glasses and greeting fans, the camera affords a glimpse of a banner for the Delacorte Theater, Papp's enduring contribution to public Shakespeare, announcing the summer's productions of *Measure for Measure* and *All's Well That Ends Well*. That the young men whom Pacino tries to persuade to see the Central Park production worry about price, and that they seem only perfunctorily committed to attending despite Pacino's reassurances that admission is free and the play worth their attention, are but two indices of how the film might justify its existence. By inference, Papp's worthy efforts are, if not unavailing, then insufficient, his legacy in need of quickening—by a star come down to earth, a native son of the city gone on to cinematic glory.

Indeed, the opening sequence, which has been a focus of critical attention, reveals how important a New York understood both as densely urban and nonrarefied is to the film's representation of its mission.⁴ *Looking for Richard* begins with a British-accented voice intoning Prospero's lines from *The Tempest*, lines that, while not identified in the film, have long been taken out of context to stand as a metatheatrical self-reflection on the part of the dramatist: "Our revels now are ended..." What is shown, however, is not precisely a version of the stage, of performance; instead, there is a shot across bare tree branches which then slowly overlaps to the image of a church whose bells are presumably the ones heard under the voice-over. This church is seen again in another view, gabled, with rounded windows punctuated by Gothic points; the entire edifice is crowned with spires. According to the visual logic of the image, the theater is replaced by the cathedral, the stage by the altar. By extension, the art of drama is sanctified, the worship of Shakespeare a form of necessary devotion.

But that is not all that the opening shots of ecclesiastical architecture establish: they signify, retroactively, by that to which they give way and seem to set up a familiar argument about the relationship between New World and Old. As the voice reaches the lines "The cloud capped towers, the gorgeous palaces, the solemn temples, yea, the great globe itself," the spires are replaced by a stark high-rise apartment building; the camera pans down, over a wall inscribed with graffiti, to a basketball court, where Pacino is playing one-on-one with a light-skinned young man. That scene, in turn, gives way to a hand (Pacino's?) holding what appears to be a Folger edition of one of Shakespeare's plays: a page is turned back in slow motion as the voice completes the phrase "...shall dissolve." Although the proleptically elegiac moments of the opening are undeniable, there appears to be a visual argument (punning on the very idea of "dissolve") in juxtaposing those distant, Gothic (and English-seeming?) spires with their successor images.[5] Images that imply reverence, devotion, authority, even England—the space of those "gorgeous palaces," the source of that disembodied, even authorial, voice—give way to the demotic spaces of the New World, more specifically to the inner-city streets of New York and to the visual spectacle of an iconic American star at play. When the play is done, when the rarefied heights of high culture are left behind, there is the space of urban, extramural play. Is one the successor of the other, its equivalent, or its debasement?

While an initial reading of the series of shots linking the two edifices could be read to suggest either cultural succession or cultural disjunction, the ambiguity soon resolves itself. The visual argument of the opening arc, from *there* to *here*, chimes with the fact that much of the staging of *Richard III* that Pacino so labors over takes place in the Cloisters, a museum affiliated with the Metropolitan Museum on Fifth Avenue (whose front steps are an impromptu theater for Pacino's physical impersonation of the hunchback at another point in the film) and consisting of portions of medieval ecclesiastical buildings brought to the United States and assembled together into a whole. Apart from representing the closest thing Pacino might find to a period setting in the New World, the Cloisters nicely echoes the status of Shakespeare indicated by the opening dissolve from spire to tenement: like the history play itself, the museum is a presence from another time and place brought to dwell in urban America, a translation of cultural patrimony that (although such a translation does not interest Pacino) indexes the power of American capital and its erstwhile affiliation with, and investment in, European cultural forms.

And perhaps like the Bard's presence in American life, the Cloisters evoke the problem of authenticity. The museum in Washington Heights did not, after all, grow there organically, but was rather transplanted by bits and shards from Europe. If, as a potential initial setting for the play, it is somehow too real, that is, too literal, it is also not real enough to guarantee Pacino's efforts the authenticity he apparently seeks. What the Cloisters offer is not historical presence, but a simulacrum of history. This does not mean, of course, that American Shakespeare is likewise a simulation, since the cultural processes that resulted in such an edifice's being erected in New York are materially quite different from (and later than) those that brought Shakespeare to America and that at the turn of the twentieth century began to reassociate him with England. But insofar as American Shakespeare often seems conditioned by a reflexive Anglocentrism at least a century old, a habit of glancing over the shoulder and across the Atlantic, staging *Richard III* in the Cloisters calls attention to the gap between there and here even as it attempts to duplicate an originary presence. As I'll consider later, *Looking for Richard* seems beset with the gnawing anxiety that Shakespeare has never really taken root in America, a fear of national inadequacy that it renders as equivalent to the popular indifference toward the plays Pacino encounters in the street. To put it bluntly, as far as this documentary is concerned, Americans as a *people* don't own Shakespeare and have never quite owned him, any more than they own the history subtended by those transplanted medieval buildings.

Hence the frequent reversion to British actors as privileged sources of insight, a reversion that reads as a tribute to the power of origins. (Hence, as well, the trip Pacino takes with Frederic Kimball to Stratford, where his search for Authorial Presence in the bedchamber where Shakespeare is alleged to have been born is amusingly deflated——one of several moments of self-mockery that hint at the foreshortened possibility of a more complex and less earnest response to the weight of history that comes along with Shakespeare.) Derek Jacobi, for instance, suggests that it's not strictly necessary to understand Shakespearean language in all its subtlety; instead, he offers advice that seems perilously close to jollying condescension: "It's not important, just get the gist of it. Just trust it, you'll get it." (These sentiments are repeated by Pacino at another point in the documentary.) The snippet with John Gielgud that follows is perhaps more overt about the differing national stakes in gaining access to the Shakespearean: as he muses,

Americans are not surrounded by the art and artifacts, the all-but-innate knowledge of period and its possibilities, that make Shakespearean drama somehow natural for and to a British actor. In Gielgud's world, it would seem, class does not exist as a constitutive reality: you either get Shakespeare as a matter of birthright or you don't, and suffer thereby from the deleterious effects of postcolonial anxiety some 200 years after the fact of dissociation, as Pacino's film implies. The Cloisters can do little to erase so massive a deficit of cultural patrimony.

Even so, not all British actors interviewed in the documentary reify the gap between Britain and Shakespeare on the one hand, and the putatively tremulous American actor on the other. Vanessa Redgrave, for one, suggests that it is not the alienness of Shakespearean language to modern-day Americans that causes stumbling so much as the shift in historical relations between the signifier and the signified: "The music, literally I mean the music, and the thoughts, and the concepts, and the feelings have not been divorced from the words. And in England you've had centuries in which word has been totally divorced from truth, and that's a problem for us actors." Redgrave's words seem informed by T. S Eliot's famous characterization of the seventeenth century as a moment for the "dissociation of sensibility," when thought and feeling first became divorced: in the prelapsarian Eden of Shakespeare's time, words and things, musicality and meaning, went hand in hand. Insofar as Redgrave's words speak principally of and to the English actors who represent the authority of Shakespeare's home country, the distance from "truth" Redgrave articulates potentially undoes any hierarchical relation between Old World and New.

However, the provocative expansiveness about language and comparative history such considerations open up is forestalled by the construction of the documentary, which even if divided against itself remains in dogged pursuit of statements more readily assimilable to its agenda. To explore the regulatory characters of reviewing, actor training, the text itself, and a historically remote linguistic practice is to acknowledge the power the ensemble has to police what is acceptable in the realm of the Shakespearean in perimillennial America. Home questioning of what it means to perform Shakespeare when, for instance, one does not have the classical training that has been deemed by some cultural arbiters an inalienable aspect of the task would have consequences far beyond whatever accidental connection to Pacino's own history as a performer with which it intersects. Indeed, self-consciously considering how American-accented speech is too often established at some remove from "proper" Shakespearean diction would strike at the heart of at least one of the documentary's avowed aims, since diagnosing the lack of interest many Americans manifest in Shakespeare also means acknowledging the extent to which Shakespeare is always produced as anterior, other, elsewhere, "higher," with posh accents the auditory sign of his removal from the here and now.

Of course, Pacino also interviews American actors as well. Their mere presence signals a possible alternative to the foundational priority accorded England by glancing at a history of Shakespeare performed in America, a history that has frequently contested Anglophilic modes of performance and audience, the "proper" forms, tones, and bodies needed for Shakespeare.[6] But that is not how they function in the film. The American actors whom Pacino interviews or with whom he works on the play outside the performance fall, by and large, into two camps. Either they are actors, like Dominic Chianese, Penelope Allen, and Frederic Kimball (who serves in the movie as Pacino's principal sounding board), who participated in Pacino's unevenly reviewed production of *Richard III* at the Cort Theater on Broadway in 1979, in which Pacino's New York accent was subject to particular criticism. Or else they are actors who have worked both on stage and in films and whose Shakespearean affiliations include significant work with Papp at the Public Theater. Kevin Kline, for instance, not only appeared in a film version of *A Midsummer's Night's Dream* released more or less at the same time as Pacino's documentary; he also made his first appearance in a Papp production in 1970 and in fact starred in a 1982 production of *Richard III* at the Delacorte.[7] And James Earl Jones was among the actors whom Papp cast in his celebrated efforts at color-blind casting.[8] Jones's career with Papp seems to have begun in 1960, when he played Williams in a production of *Henry V*; in 1966 he shared the role of Macbeth with Michael McGuire in an all-black production, then went on to play Oberon in a 1969 *Midsummer's Night's Dream*, Claudius in a 1972 *Hamlet*, and the title role in *King Lear* in 1973. (As it happens, not all of his roles reflect quite such an indifference to race in casting: in 1962 he played the Prince of Morocco in *The Merchant of Venice*, the same year he also played Caliban. And he starred as Othello in 1964.) In fact, Pacino himself worked with Papp on Shakespeare at least twice: as Hamlet in a 1979 production, and as Marc Antony in *Julius Caesar* in 1986–1987.[9]

Oddly, however, neither Kline's nor Jones's credentials as actors in Papp productions are ever brought to light in their interviews. Nor for that matter are the Cort Theater actors identified: the only overts hint of that prior production are to be found in a glimpse of a background poster and a brief interchange about Pacino's prior familiarity with the play. In effect, the recent performance history of *Richard III* and, more broadly, of American efforts to democratize Shakespeare aren't overtly claimed. Indeed, they are put at some distance, particularly when it comes to the actors who worked with Papp: neither Kline nor Jones is shown addressing how to *act* Shakespeare.

Although Kline also comments on Richard's conniving character, he is given more space to mock the orotund pronouncements associated with a bygone high-Shakespearean style. However, rather than offer, or be asked to offer, an alternative mode of performance that recognizes the oppressiveness of the proper, Anglophonic Shakespearean voice, that critiques the weight of history deemed so ineluctable by the famously sonorous Gielgud and that acknowledges his own experience with Richard, Kline tenders an amusing anecdote—the everyman story of the teen who'd rather make out with his girlfriend than listen to a boring and pompously declaimed Shakespeare play. And although James Earl Jones's reminiscence of his uncle's recitations from *Julius Caesar* evokes an all-but-forgotten American schooling in oratory, in which Shakespearean set pieces once played an important part, this recollection stands in puzzling isolation. Lacking either support for this information from the documentary or even a connection to Jones's modern-day performance practice, the recollection, emerging as it does from a markedly raced body, primarily ratifies the ideology of big-tent Shakespeare while constituting a token interruption of the Shakespeare world Pacino has presented, which is almost, with one other significant exception, entirely white.

Doubtless it is primarily Jones's familiarity as a movie actor that accounts for his presence in *Looking for Richard*. And insofar as his career is, in its turn, defined by his well-known and commercially pervasive, and, yes, sonorous voice, his is a weighty star turn rather than strictly an actor's one. Kline's joking appearance, in contrast, is more in keeping with the occasional irreverence manifested in the documentary, a joking that might be enlisted on the side of raffish domestication. From the moment early on, when Pacino proclaims "Fuck!" after he peers out from behind a stage curtain and steps onto the stage as a modern-dress Richard, only to see the costumed figure of Shakespeare as his sole audience, the film invites the audience to laugh, relax, even identify with Pacino's dilemma, the better to participate in a collective sigh of relief: even trained professionals find Shakespeare daunting and obscure and, via the mass-cultural equivalent of the modesty topos, don't mind being seen revealing their inadequacy. The film star confronts the rigors of the stage and the most rigorous practitioner of dramatic art—and panics. The (presumably) un-Shakespearean expletive to which Pacino gives voice is the iruption of the American demotic into the space of worship, a tension-breaking moment that also tropes class and nationality, as well as mass versus high culture. To that extent, it echoes the response of the everyday "regular" American at the end of the twentieth century to the overweening demands of the English-derived high-cultural icon who is an ineluctable presence in American life—a response that is effectively resistance in one form or another, here embodied by the cinematic equivalents of the teenage couple of Kline's recollection, who would rather make out (and who are seen doing so during one of Pacino's other glimpses from behind the curtain). But as will be clear, such native responses are not—cannot—be taken seriously enough to be fashioned into a counternarrative. Instead, they must be tamed and contextualized.

Hence the "regular" Americans who can also be found in *Looking for Richard*, the pedestrians whom Pacino stops and questions in passing: many are native white ethnic New Yorkers, marked (as Pacino is himself) by unmistakable accents and stereotypical bluntness. These interlocutors operate as the diegetic stand-ins for the more fantasmatic American public whom Pacino presumes to address: that is, their statements of resistance—and, in one exceptional case, of pious appreciation—represent the sort of things Americans believe to be true when it comes to Shakespeare and the problem of pleasure, in correction or celebration of which Pacino's film is launched. In general, the men and women whom Pacino asks about Shakespeare don't have much to say on the subject—they shrug, they murmur, they cannot recall. More pointedly, however, some remember a strong distaste: one young man states that Shakespeare is "boring"; a young woman pithily assesses a recent staging of *Hamlet* she attended: "It sucked." Responses from the few English interviewees encountered during a trip to Stratford-upon-Avon stand in general contrast: although one young man allows he "can't get on" with *Richard III* despite working on it for six months, more typical is the loudmouth who asks the filmmakers, "What the fuck do you know about Shakespeare?" And the Englishman who flashes the holographic Shakespeare on his credit card seems quite canny about the currency of the Bard, in all possible senses of the word: as he says, Shakespeare is "a great export."[10]

It is precisely Shakespeare's status as imported cultural good that hovers about *Looking for Richard* as the great problem, acknowledged in passing but scarcely explored beyond Derek Jacobi's claim that scholars, critics, and commentators all collude in telling Americans they can't do Shakespeare. Between the rhyming monosyllables of "suck" and "fuck," of resistance, contempt, and dismay at cultural weight, lies a complex terrain; it is no surprise the film does not, probably cannot, given the personalist weight of Pacino's investment as it is represented, venture very far into. Why, for instance, is Shakespeare boring to that young man? Surely it's possible that a production of the highly familiar play *Hamlet* could be less than thrilling? What if there is not a universally convincing answer to the question of why, precisely, the "average American" ought to care about this long-dead British playwright? But the point of the American interviews is not really to learn what ordinary people think about Shakespeare, with all the potential complexity and refractoriness—and perhaps disappointment—attendant upon such a project. Rather, the interviews I've cited merely *illustrate* a familiar popular resistance deemed to be transparent and self-explanatory, a joking preamble to the important action, like Pacino's expletive from behind the curtain. However bracing their irreverence might be, its sole purpose is to be supplanted by what Pacino wants them, and others like them in the film's audience, to know as a substitute.

Or, perhaps, to feel. Thus Pacino's brandishing a Cliffs Notes early in the film, even as he offers something close to an explanation of his motive for the documentary: "It has always been a dream of mine to communicate how I feel about Shakespeare to other people." What gets communicated to "other people" in this film, however, is something other than the direct expression of personal aesthetic sentiment, since Pacino never offers a further explanation or exploration of the (presumably) affirmative content of his dream. Lacking the specificity of autobiographical revelation, "feeling" becomes merely a conventionalized sign, an autotelic placeholder for the psychic goods Shakespeare is presumed capable of bequeathing to each and therefore, perhaps, to all. "How I feel about Shakespeare" is not, in the end, a promissory note for personal revelation, despite the film's occasional jocular representation of Pacino's sense of inadequacy as well as his high seriousness when it comes to approaching the project. If the former seems overtly performative, the latter is not precisely innocent of scripting: indeed, if it were not the case that Pacino wants to be seen as deeply invested in looking for *Richard III*, it would not be possible to read the film as representative. And precisely to the extent it is, the necessary conjunction of "feeling" and Shakespeare is inevitably conventionalized.

Even so, the film affords tantalizing hints of why it is that Pacino is so drawn to *Richard III* in particular. I've mentioned the 1979 Cort Theater production, whose continuing relevance is felt not only in the working group he's assembled (almost none of whom actually takes part in the staging eventually put on) but also in one street exchange, when a young French-speaking woman expresses some skepticism about Pacino's doing Shakespeare with "[his] American accent." Such perceived vocal inadequacy was a focus for the notoriously waspish critic John Simon, who in his review pilloried what he saw as the poor fit between American accents, particularly Pacino's markedly New York articulations, and the matter of the play: "In this *Richard III* there are accents aplenty—every kind of accent you have ever heard in your life, except one that has anything to do with Shakespeare."[11] Indeed, knowing in particular of Simon's contempt for the way Shakespearean verse was enunciated by a cast at least partly composed of American actors from the white working class goes a long way to explaining the recurrent concern, in

Looking for Richard, with the difficulty of Shakespeare's language and with American actors' fear of it. That fear is never overtly owned: that is, at no point does Pacino ever suggest that speaking, laying claim to those distantly generated words, haunts him personally in any way. Nevertheless, the interviews on the subject Pacino conducts with British actors serve as a sign of the repressed.

Imagining that the documentary has as its motivation the demonstration of Pacino's—and, indeed, American actors'—fitness for acting Shakespeare despite normative evaluations to the contrary is not far-fetched: complicated "feeling" about Shakespeare could indeed be generated under such conditions. But that sort of complexity is not what the film puts on offer, nor what it appears to deem its mission. Instead, whatever individual response Pacino might have had with respect to the reviews of the Cort Theater production, whatever broader questions about naturalizing Shakespeare in America those reviews, critics, scholars, and commentators might raise, are blunted, deferred onto this latter-day project of mass edification. A more pointed way of putting it is to note that Pacino's devotion to Shakespeare cannot be separated from a durable national injunction that Shakespeare must be loved, regardless of any sense of professional inadequacy and how that sense is constructed, regardless of questions of relevance, regardless of popular indifference as evinced on the street.

A documentary project with the apparent agenda of Pacino's in these perimillennial years cannot but partake of cultural conservatism, regardless of its intent. Hence the very orthodoxy of the costumes, the setting, the ideas of fidelity to a historical past and place unrelated to the present: all suggest that there is a preexisting standard that must be addressed, even met, that any ambitions on the part of those involved be subordinated to a narrow and received sense of what is historically, phonologically, and, indeed, ideologically appropriate. While there is much in the documentary that could be adduced to underscore my claim, it is particularly useful to consider who among the ordinary speakers in New York is given space, whose words are privileged, when most passersby are seen to offer only a dismissive phrase or two. Preeminent among such interviewees is an African American panhandler (his last words later in the film are to ask a passerby for spare change) who speaks passionately for Shakespeare and who, for all the world, sounds like the most conventional, even conservative, policy advocate for teaching the canon:

> *Speaker*: "Intelligence is hooked with language. And when we speak with no feeling we get nothing out of our society. We should speak like Shakespeare, we should introduce Shakespeare into the academic. You know why? Because then the kids would have feelings."

Offscreen Pacino: "That's right."
Speaker: "We have no feelings, That's why it's easy for us to get a gun and shoot each other. We don't feel for each other."
Pacino: "That's right."
Speaker: "But if we were taught to feel we wouldn't be so violent."
Pacino: "And you think that Shakespeare helps us with that?"
Speaker: "He did more than help us, he instructed us."

It is clear this particular man in the street is a privileged interlocutor: of all the passersby Pacino films, only he is cut so as to air his views at such length. (Indeed, he returns later in the film discussing the relationship of language and truth, in something of an echo of Redgrave's concern.) But why? Perhaps in part because, like Pacino himself, he gives priority to emotion, which is represented not so much as an end in itself, let alone a complex psychic state, as a state of unspecified but optimistic possibility, of "feeling for each other" made possible by Shakespeare. In his purview, such feeling stands as the opposite of violence, just as for Pacino, feeling, as the opposite of resistance, is a sufficient motivation for the expanse of the film. Yet it is precisely their solidarity around redemptive faith in Shakespeare's capacity to generate positive emotion that bespeaks conservatism.

That solidarity between Pacino and the homeless man, signified by those off-camera murmurs of assent, ratifies the view of Shakespeare as a universal solvent, a way out of the complexity of social relations determined by forces far more material than a love of Shakespeare. The segment offers its audience an enervated ideology, a parody of utopianism, of a dream of a better world, rather than the real thing. That it is parodic—although, let me be clear, never intentionally so—is evinced not only by the cruel way the man's own words are inevitably qualified by his objective situation, but also by the fact that, strictly speaking, his wish for a more widely disseminated Shakespeare flies in the face of evidence when it is not simply a conventional thing to say. As I shall demonstrate at greater length in the following chapter, Shakespeare has long been taught in high schools and increasingly to younger and younger students, even if not in the experience of this man or those whom he might be said to represent in this documentary. Perhaps, that is: for if not in his experience, then where do his statements come from, since they seem precisely like the sort of things always said about Shakespeare, particularly in institutional settings like the classroom?

Sentiments like those of the homeless man have a long shelf life, particularly among those licensed to make public pronouncements—they emerged, for instance, in mainstream media outlets in New York and Washington, D.C., in the 1996 furor over Georgetown University's English department and its decision to cease making Shakespeare mandatory for majors. To the extent that such sentiments are subject to empirical demonstration, however, they are readily falsifiable. It hardly needs to be pointed out that the study of Shakespeare is far from sufficient to render those engaged in the study somehow more ethical and moral, a claim revealing a class-and race-based valence that goes back at least as far as the turn of the twentieth century. Studying Shakespeare is never a necessity for moral insight, for all that I might seem to contradict myself in discussing the reading of Shakespeare in a prison project offered in the final chapter. Yet when it comes to culturally privileged speakers and their obstinate belief in Shakespeare's capacity to generate moral improvement, empirical truth is less to the point than the mystification of social agency and of the complex origins of social problems to which Shakespeare has been lent for at least the last century. Members of the corporate media opine as though high culture really still had motive power in the ensemble of social relations that define the possibilities of a good life in the perimillennial United States. What does it mean, then, when an evidently deprivileged speaker is made their mouthpiece?

In a documentary that is (James Earl Jones notwithstanding) more or less unreflexively monoracial and one that in typical mainstream American fashion never attends to the politics of class, the fetishization of this black man with missing teeth is at best problematic. For reasons that my final chapter will intimate, it is analytically unsatisfying to discount the sincerity of the man's articulation, to reduce his utterance to false consciousness—as, for instance, Marjorie Garber has done in arguing against Lynne Cheney's opportunistically citing Maya Angelou on Shakespeare's universality in the 1980s.[12] There is, nevertheless, a critical difference between this man's beliefs about Shakespeare as such and the uses to which the documentary puts them. After all, when nearly every other interview shows comparatively prosperous white Americans on the street ignorant, sheepish, or dismissive, greater weight cannot but be placed on this one segment, if only by way of difference. And difference abounds in, and with, this one speaker. That being the case, there is something enervated, unreflexively pious about putting on display a man so clearly marked as deprivileged by the coalescence of race, class, and visible signs of personal neglect, only to privilege his insights about Shakespeare. This informant may be the sign of a real social problem, of an unequal dispersal of access to good education, of lowered intellectual expectations for a subset of the U.S. population too likely to suffer other signs of social and economic dismissal—or he may not. Without the work it would take to place the man properly, he becomes rather like the African soldier proudly saluting the French flag in an era of decolonization, whom Barthes so famously discussed in *Mythologies*: an alibi, here, not of imperialism but of a residual fantasy of dominant culture: that love of Shakespeare crosses class and racial divides and that his texts are a vehicle for social harmony and the American version of the civilizing project.

And it is significant that the informant's faith in Shakespeare is belated—overtaken, that is—by the shift from a redemptive model of high culture that derives from Matthew Arnold and a successor regime that valorizes mass audiences and their movement toward a market-driven multiplicity of cultural goods, none of which can be securely linked, these days, even to the ghost of a desire for an ethical disposition in dominant discourse: that is, for a dream of a better world through consuming and apprehending those cultural goods.[13] If Shakespeare still matters to U.S. culture, as I am arguing in this study, then he cannot but matter differently in a regime where questions of value are foreshortened by the market's prehensile readiness to interpellate consumers along the lines of individual taste. Pacino's privileged interlocutor is thus, despite his vastly different material circumstances, in the same position as all those pundits who fretted over what happens when those who aim to become policymakers, elected officials, and legislators are no longer compelled to learn their Shakespearean lessons at Georgetown: the ground has shifted underfoot, but has oddly left far too many people standing in the same place.

This failure to sense a shift may be further evidence of the latent conservatism that pervades *Looking for Richard* as a whole, of the quest that knows in advance what forms its answers concerning Shakespeare's importance must take, despite the intrinsic unruliness of the documentary form. Even so, that the documentary uses a black man to make a stale point lends his presence a certain poignancy. Whatever the source of his lessons on Shakespeare, he has learned them well—and yet, to the cultural critic at least, he does not seem aware that he speaks contradiction.

* * *

The commonplace that lessons of ethical goodness can and must be learned via formal instruction in Shakespeare naturally leads to considering the pedagogical imperative that pervades the documentary. To say that *Looking for Richard* is invested in a covertly instructional approach to Shakespeare is not to deny the film's own sense of itself as a form of populist evangelism on the part of an actor-director. One of its expressed conceits, after all, is that performance is the preferred point of access for *Richard III*, and by extension the Shakespearean canon. Although that conceit is initially a matter of inference, it becomes overt when Pacino and the other participants are discussing what could drive the recently widowed Lady Anne into the arms of Richard.

When Kimball proffers a reactionary interpretation—that she is in effect flirting by putting herself in Richard's path—that is rejected by Winona Ryder, the actor playing Anne, Kimball becomes upset at Pacino:

> You said that you were gonna find a scholar from somewhere who was going to speak directly into the camera and explain what really went down with Richard and Anne, and I am telling you that that is absolutely ridiculous, that you know more about *Richard III* than any fucking scholar at Columbia or Harvard…because you are making this entire documentary in order to show that actors truly are…the possessors of a tradition, the proud inheritors of the understanding of Shakespeare, for Chrissakes. And then you turn around and say, I'm gonna, I'm gonna go get a scholar to explain it to you.

Kimball's outburst is greeted with some good-natured hooting from the participants, and Pacino avers that the opinions of academics count as much or as little as anyone else's. Nevertheless, that outburst retains a core of propositional truth, at least as far as *Looking for Richard's* ambivalence toward privileged Shakespearean epistemology is concerned. What supposedly started out as a "a documentary about making Shakespeare a little bit more accessible to people, those people out there" (as the exasperated coproducer Michael Hadge puts it) has "turn[ed] into a movie about a play." This avowed shift in tenor, which occurs in a section of the film tellingly entitled "Getting in Deeper," reveals that dual-mindedness to which I earlier referred and from which the film never quite clears itself. At the same time, however, it also gestures toward an imaginary resolution of the contradictory duality. Kimball's words suggest that performance eclipses scholarship as a way to understand Shakespeare, that there is a direct line of descent from Shakespeare's time to the present through a continuing succession of actors. If, then, actors are the "proud inheritors of understanding," it stands to reason that performance is the royal road along which popular investment in the Bard must proceed. When, later in the film, Hadge continues to argue against the increasing dominance of staging efforts in the project because "[t]hose people can't get *Richard III*. I can't get *Richard III*, it's too complicated," Kimball's response—that *Richard III* is Shakespeare's most popular play, because it is staged more often than *Hamlet*—effectively ends the debate in terms that favor performance. And yet it never goes beyond mere facticity to explore why the play might be so popular to audiences who do not inhabit the history as birthright. Instead, performance and popularity go hand in hand as sufficient explanations in themselves.

To posit that the vitality of performance constitutes a corrective to a Shakespeare who is more embalmed because more literary is a familiar enough claim, albeit one whose belated polarities have been subjected to critical scrutiny.[14] The presumable opposition is actually more a relationship of supplementarity, with all the potential for erasure, struggle, desire, and lack the Derridean term implies. Despite the propositional attractiveness of Kimball's overschematic terms for the film's zealous sense of itself, however, it is the argument of this chapter that the specter of the pedagogue is never far offscreen in *Looking for Richard*, even if the movie never succeeds in producing a scholar "from Columbia or Harvard" to address the camera for the purposes of general illumination. Indeed, it cannot present any scholar (let alone an American one), not so much because to do so would expose the tendentiousness of Kimball's fervent claim as because the film could not bear the weight of scholarship as such. It goes without saying that scholarship is nonpopular; more to the point, though, is the fact that scholarship (one hopes) aims not to come to all the foregone conclusions, that is, precisely, a specialized system of knowledge production in which originality, whether actual or nominal, is the sign of high value.

Pacino's Shakespeare film, on the other hand, cannot escape the tried-and-true; it all but revels in perpetuating highly familiar claims and ways into the play, strategies that it equates with popular appeal. A more pointed way of putting it would be to say that *Looking for Richard* wants to teach the same old lessons heard in secondary schoolrooms, the presumable origin of disaffection and resistance in the first place. The documentary's very existence is predicated on that crucial misrecognition: it can't help imagining that the problem with such lessons is not their content but rather the vehicle of presentation. The movie is erected on the belief that what fails in the classroom must work in the theater—or, rather, in the cinematic representation of a theatrical process, one aided and abetted by Hollywood star power.

And yet there is seemingly little that is dramatic (let alone cinematic) about much of the interpretive process the film documents. What appears most perverse about this film is that it enervates a potentially seductive medium, and for that matter a potentially seductive way into the text. Indeed, the very fact that *Looking for Richard* is a documentary means that the immediacy and ravishment possible with performance, especially in the cinema, are occasionally put on display, only to be put at a distance, time and again. For instance, consider the earnest yet elementary way Pacino (who has just mentioned having performed Richard's opening soliloquy to an audience of uncomprehending students) sets out to explain the War of the Roses and the events that bring us to the play, which all but reeks of an introductory lesson in a Shakespeare survey class:

> *Pacino*: Before the play Richard III starts we gotta know a little bit about what happened before.... What happened is, we've just been through a civil war called the War of the Roses, in which the Lancasters and the Yorks clashed. Two rival families, and the Yorks won. They beat the Lancasters, and they're now in power. And Richard is a York. My brother Edward is the king now. And my brother Clarence is not the king, and me, I'm not the king. I wanna be the king. It's that simple....
> *Peter Brook*: The key word, clearly... right from the start, is "discontent."
> *Pacino*: So Richard, in the very opening scene of the play, tells us just how badly he feels about the peacetime world he finds himself in and what he intends to do about it.

The edited-in comment from Brook concerning "discontent" aside, however, it's worth noting that unlike professional pedagogues, when it comes to the play itself, Pacino and those he's working with do not so much explain the text as explain around it, even paraphrase it. There is little that seems to be a recognizable dramatic insight, one attuned to the subtleties of character, little of the way staging can clarify a relation as well as any footnote. Although a bit later Kimball elaborately explains the pun in "Now is the winter of our discontent, Made glorious summer by this son of York," that moment is one of the few where Shakespearean language as such is acknowledged a part of a process, rather than the puzzling obstacle that Jacobi diagnoses as a particular source of fretfulness to American actors.

This is not to say there is no concern whatsoever with language. But the nature of that concern is often characterized, as I have already suggested, by anxiety, not by wonderment, pleasure in difficulty, or even absorption of a complicated kind. A brief snippet of Kenneth Branagh stressing the mouth feel of words like "curd" and "posset" stands out: it is one of the few moments where a particularly verbal pleasure, that of articulating, tasting, unusual words, is given place in the documentary. In general, Shakespeare's text—which is to say, the script, the exploration of which is supposed to dispel the assistant's foreboding on behalf of "those people out there"—is presented as an obstacle to understanding. And it is an obstacle, it seems, one might be able to do without, or at least sidestep as much as possible, as students forcibly brought to the trough of Shakespearean goodness have inevitably tried to do. Although almost all the scenes depict some measure of collaboration, *Looking for Richard* contains little in the way of productive interaction over the language, where actors puzzle over how to say the lines, how to respond to the stimulus provided by another character. Even allowing for a general American preference for Method acting and Pacino's particular association with it, for starting with a character study rather than what he says, it is nevertheless clear that Pacino does not see the key to the play to lie with the page. In fact, a scene early in the film suggests a commonality between Pacino's film and that clandestine inhabitant of schoolrooms past whose role was precisely to bypass Shakespeare's words: witness the Cliffs Notes for *Richard III* that Pacino uses as a prop to introduce his motive for the film, his "feeling" for Shakespeare.

Brandishing the notes is, potentially, a bold gesture. Aligning his project with the emblematic study guide could lend to the film a gleefully nose-thumbing attitude directed at the academic class, in keeping with other irreverent gestures in the film, Kimball's outburst among them.[15] After all, Cliffs Notes might be taken to represent Shakespeare "from below," an illicit substitute for the sacred text that offers a minor resistance to the hegemony of the authorized version and the compulsory nature of bardolatry.[16] A film that offered itself as the equivalent of a study guide could, in confidently and sustainedly irreverent hands, carnivalize the cult of Shakespeare and mock the pretensions of its priests. However much Cliffs Notes themselves play it straight, bringing them into public view, celebrating them, and indeed deploying the resources of cinematic practice to do so might well turn the

Figure 1 *Looking for Richard.*

hierarchies of the Shakespeare world on their head. It might constitute a point in favor of those who think Shakespeare "sucks" but who are nevertheless again and again compelled to engage with him and account for themselves.

Militating against this possibility is surely Pacino's own reverence, which, given the film's very occasional gestures toward the politics of class, reveals something like the zeal of the convert. More important, however, is the nature of those notes themselves. That Pacino uses Cliffs Notes rather than, say, the more up-to-date SparkNotes is in the first instance probably a function of his age and of the age of the cliché such notes represent: the dominance of the newer product (which trumpets that they are generated by Harvard students) is comparatively recent. SparkNotes's *Hamlet*, for instance, is copyrighted in 2002 and is tied to the newly dominant Norton edition of Shakespeare, which features the most recent criticism and scholarship, whereas the Cliffs Notes *Hamlet* was copyrighted in 1971, with its most recent printing in 1994. In fact, until SparkNotes emerged, there was a curious lag between the concerns of study guides and the matter of the academic classroom, at least insofar as tertiary-level analytics of Shakespeare have been concerned: resembling flies caught in amber, Cliffs Notes were the province of outmoded interpretations and the dogged pursuit of themes like so many messages in a bottle. Innocent of more recent critical concerns with feminism, race, or sexuality, let alone the strategies of reading influenced by semiotics or deconstruction, they began to resemble quaint relics in university bookstores, evidence of a strange abeyance on the part of the market, of a bizarrely commemorative timelessness when it came to the bastard child of Shakespeare studies that seemed to exempt "interpretation" from the novelty-fetishizing agendas of commerce as well as of academia.

As the very fact of SparkNotes evinces, however, the market has awakened to the profitability of updated interpretive materials: the legend featured on their front covers, "Smarter Better Faster," unites the exigencies of competitive schooling betokened by the association with Harvard with the speeded-up exigencies of capitalism. The theme is continued with a front-matter sonnet entitled "Introduction: A Prologue from the Bard" in proper Shakespearean form, in which the grandly inflated exertions of the Harvardians who generate the guides are equaled by a mockery of its consumers and all the possibilities that "missing" implies (incomprehension; indifference; absence of effort; absence from class): "If patient or 'whatever,' please attend, / What you have missed, our toil shall strive to mend." The front matter also includes a plug for SparkNotes's Web materials, with which the paper form is equated as a secondary product. The individual volumes themselves meld old-style Aristotelian categories (e.g., "Rising action") with topical matter (the volume on *The Tempest*, for example, offers a section on "The Allure of Ruling a Colony" and identifies Caliban as a colonized subject).[17] The bibliography, in contrast, is less wholly forward looking: it lists many of the same venerable studies (e.g., A. C. Bradley, J. Dover Wilson) also to be found in Cliffs Notes, while supplementing them with newer studies. This effort at comprehensiveness makes clear that the newer study guides aim less to complement Cliffs Notes than to replace them entirely, as indeed they mostly have.

Given their mastery of postmodern self-consciousness, their opportunistic blending of old and new modes of textual approach, and their digital ontology, SparkNotes constitute on-demand student-oriented products for what the cultural critic David Harvey has characterized as the era of flexible accumulation. Indeed, their merging of academic smarts with market agendas is betokened by the corporate name form: SparkNotes, like ExxonMobil, a running together of words in which time can scarcely be spared for taking a breath. And the fact that they are assembled by a team of producers named only on the copyright page, and as "contributors," displaces the academic markers of Cliffs Notes—singly authored by possessors of degrees, and under the general editorship of a scholar as well—with the student-driven labor form of the group project. If SparkNotes are self-advertised as "Today's Most Popular Study Guides," it may well be because the social relations they subtend mirror the increasingly student-centered realm of academia as much as their subject matter does.

What, then, of Pacino's Cliffs Notes? Everything I have said thus far about SparkNotes would suggest that Pacino's symbolic guide be read as the sign of an outmoded interpretive agenda. This is a claim that in no way would violate the spirit of *Looking for Richard*. The need for a trot is doubtless increased by the fact that it is *Richard III*, not *Hamlet*, *Romeo and Juliet*, or even *Julius Caesar*, that fascinates Pacino. That is to say, *Richard III*'s history is not a part of native educational discourse, the relations among Lancasters and Yorks not made second nature through institutional practices that rehearse and thereby keep present the history and bloodlines of an ancient nation-state. For all its popularity in performance, few other plays would make quite so clear the ineffable Britishness of Pacino's view of Shakespeare or reveal the anxious inadequacies of the American. Indeed, at several points Pacino despairs of tracking the relationships among the various courtly factions: even the line where Clarence is imprisoned—"This day should Clarence closely be mew'd up About a prophecy which says that G Of Edward's heirs the murderer shall be"—confuses him. He contemplates changing the G to C in a gesture of nonce expediency; the film does not show anyone worrying about the loss of productive ambiguity—that is, the foreshadowing about Richard of Gloucester's own murderousness that "G" makes possible—that is lost if the initial were to be changed. The impulse to simplify is of a piece with what I have taken to be Pacino's decision to film in the Cloisters Museum in New York City: both constitute similarly literal-minded efforts at imaginative engagement with Shakespeare, and especially with a play highly marked by signs of historical remoteness and needing simplification by whatever means possible.

Hence, too, the section of the film devoted to iambic pentameter. While, strictly speaking, the discussion of metrics (which edits together the utterances of a number of speakers) is not right out of the outmoded study guide, why should the technicalities of iambic pentameter concern Pacino's audience at all, except insofar as all lessons about Shakespearean verse form begin (and many end) with a potted definition of feet and meter?

> Experienced classical actors have a few things that they can use at a moment's notice. The understanding of iambic pentameter, for one thing. Everybody says, "iambic pentameter." What is that supposed to mean? Some say there are no rules. I say there are rules, like the iambic pentameter, that must be learned and can be rejected once learned. "Pentameter" means "meter," and "pen," meaning "five." So there's five beats. Which, at its worst, sounds only like: "Why, so. Now have I done a good day's work." De-da de-da de-da de-da de-da. And iambic is where the accent goes. That's de-tum de-tum de-tum de-tum. And five of them—da-da da-da da-da da-da da-da—make a pentameter line, five iambs. An iamb is like an anteater. Very high in the back and very short, little front legs. Da-da! Shakespeare's poetry and his iambics floated and descended through the pentameter of the soul. And it's the soul, the spirit of real, concrete people going through hell, and sometimes moments of great achievement and joy. That is the pentameter you must focus on and should you find that reality, all the iambics will fall into place.

If this is a claim about acting rather than a classroom lesson, it is one curiously devoid of dramatic or performative consequence. There is scant insight into the act of speaking against the metrical pattern, to the tension between iambic form as regulation and the accentual promiscuity of ordinary speech patterns. Instead, we have the image of the anteater: perhaps a good mnemonic, but somewhat hard to work with as a productive insight for the demands of performance. As might be clear by now, iambic pentameter stands as a more-or-less unassimilated sign of "Shakespeare's language," a pedagogical topos that leads as if by magic directly to the "spirit of real, concrete people." When it comes to the reality and concreteness of the characters, their status as "people," though, there is Pacino's reference to discontent and Kimball's potentially retrograde suggestion that Anne is flirting with Richard when she asks that those bearing her slain husband's body stop in Richard's proximity—a position that, as I've noted, meets with Winona Ryder's skeptical resistance for its *implausibility*.

It little matters if Kimball's is a reading of Anne's character that might actually be put forth in a study guide to *Richard III*: what counts is that it looks backward, to an understanding of gender and desire of a piece with the general, pretheoretical and preconstructivist moment in which Cliffs Notes were produced. It is tempting to speculate on whether Cliffs Notes now seem more appropriate to the state-sponsored secondary school than to the college classroom; after all, in the former, canon and interpretation are subject to a particular inertia owing in part to the massive capital investment textbooks constitute for underfunded school districts, while local control of school boards means that many instructors are forced to shy away from controversy in favor of blandly generalizing interpretations.[18] Regardless of whether this is so in factual sense, however, the fact remains that the interpretations themselves seldom stray from the ambit of what is possible in such a setting—and what has been possible over the course of many years.

Offering anodyne lessons is where *Looking* finds itself in most matters. It is perhaps not surprising, then, that publicity materials for the film were mailed to Shakespeare instructors, advertising the availability of film-related aids to study and offering to help plan lessons using the film, presumably with students who perhaps think that Shakespeare "sucks"—and who need the blandishments of a Hollywood star (if one less than current in the adolescent frame of reference) to be led to regard him otherwise. Given my claims about the overfamiliar (not to say shopworn) character of Pacino's interpretive understanding, it might seem surprising that these materials were sent to college professors, as much as or even more than to secondary school instructors. Of course, the irony of Pacino's didactic film is that *Richard III* is seldom, if ever, part of the compulsory exposure to Shakespeare taking place in pretertiary education; it's not even guaranteed to be in any given college-level Shakespeare course. While in the first instance, this gap in object constitutes a simple misrecognition of the filmmakers' market, it also reveals the extent to which, as I shall later argue, the market as a larger entity itself has come to Shakespeare—come, that is, to see itself as a purveyor of cultural goods equal in power to, and greater in effectivity than, the formal educational institutions whose aims to inculcate culture it mimics. If nowhere else, this might be where *Looking for Richard* approaches the innovative relationship to the market more characteristic of SparkNotes.

* * *

If Pacino is the new form of the pedagogue, the students are "those people out there," the ones who, as I've noted, cannot be counted upon to ever understand *Richard III*. And those misapprehending subjects are inevitably the film's imaginative projection of its audience, its public, which may or may not coincide with the actual viewers of the film.[19] Despite the way in which academic talk has tended to insist on an opposition between mass and elite culture, when it comes to Shakespeare on film, and for that matter on television, there has been a notable series of convergences in aim. In the approximately one hundred years since cinema emerged as a commercial representational medium, for instance, it has from time to time presented itself as a vehicle for the transmission of cultural values to which it has been presumed to be inimical. Hence the work that William Uricchio and Roberta Pearson have done on Vitagraph Quality Films, which produced a series of Shakespeare films between 1908 and 1912.[20] The moment when these abbreviated, non-text-bound versions of the plays were produced represented a moment of high immigration from non-Anglophone countries, whose citizens, it was claimed, needed to be introduced to Shakespeare so that national Anglophilic values could be inculcated in them. At a later moment, there come the pedagogically inflected moments of Laurence Olivier's 1948 *Hamlet* and (switching to television) the complete Shakespeare canon produced for television from 1978 to 1985 that was a joint venture of the BBC and Time-Life Corporation.[21] More or less since the emergence of film technology as such, then, film takes on Shakespeare as an ideologically pleasing usurpation of the medium of mass pleasure by a bourgeois devotion to moral improvement and class acculturation by literature. And in all these cases, the imagined public for these cultural products is deemed in need of education, one way or another.

This mass-cultural formation succeeded a less reverential because more theatrically familiar dispensation in the nineteenth century, in which Shakespeare was part of entertainment culture, as Lawrence Levine has argued. Although Levine's nostalgic account is blind to the work of racial, regional, and gender differentiation the fact of performance makes clear, it is nevertheless broadly true that at the beginning of the twentieth century Shakespeare became associated, more and more, with a certain messianism, a sense that the plays were best understood as important elements in a civilizing discourse. At that period, however, the "masses" who were the subject of concern were clearly positioned as an underclass, by virtue of their relationship either to labor or to the Anglo-Saxon tongue, or, of course, both.

Today, however, overt condescension and overt preaching will not do: European-derived cultural capital does not have the same relationship to American political or economic power as it did one hundred years earlier, an elusive fact on which this study is premised. Nor is it the case that *Looking for Richard* contains no moments when matters of class and taste pressure the narrative; hence the cocky, pithy rejections, the graffiti and the basketball court, the occasional moments of demotic profanity. Nevertheless, when Pacino sets out to address nonenthusiasts, he does so not in the service of class-based models of taste but rather in a seductively double voice, at once personalist, even idiosyncratic, and implicitly democratizing. Pacino's swerving away from addressing class head-on is particularly American, an inherited mystification. But the cockiness of his urban interlocutors in response to his queries about Shakespeare also confirms the point of departure for this study: due to the increasingly and effectively mandatory role that achieving a high school diploma has taken on in the United States, and due as well to the pervasiveness of Shakespeare in secondary and even primary school classrooms, it is hard indeed to maintain the received wisdom that knowledge of Shakespeare is *in fact* solely the province of elites. Most of Pacino's interlocutors are not, after all, *ignorant* of Shakespeare, in the sense of never having heard of him. Nor is it likely they have escaped educational exposure: on what other basis would they offer their pithy assessments?[22] More scandalously for the evangelical purposes of this documentary, they merely prefer other pleasures—prefer, that is, to dissent from what I earlier termed the national injunction to love Shakespeare, in the devoted service of which *Looking for Richard* offers itself.

Even so, I would aver, theirs is less resistance from below, a politics of taste to be uncritically valorized, than a historically revelatory refusal to be shamed into obeisance, a refusal conditioned by the long ascendancy of mass culture and by the reverence given to popular taste by market forces, opinion polls, and shifting currents in intellectual work determined to approach the products and consumers of the culture industry with some seriousness. To speak more structurally, the casual repudiation of Shakespeare that Pacino encounters reveals the concomitant dissevering of political and economic power from the power of the authorized and literate word that Shakespeare above all represents. The bourgeois idiolect described by John Guillory and secured by a vesting in the canon no longer is automatically synecdochic for other forms of power. That was almost certainly the case when Shakespeare's plays were first introduced as college entrance requirements some one hundred years ago, as the following chapter will suggest. But, as I have been aiming to demonstrate, that moment—as well as the ideological formations attendant upon it—has all but waned.

When Pacino decides to film *Richard III*, then, he is occupying a ground already inscribed by contradictory, even competing, demands about both what film can do to render Shakespeare an object of desire and what performance has done as a historical practice. More to the point, his understanding of Shakespeare's place in public culture seems belated, marked by nostalgia for a time when unmediated performance held an almost mystical potency. This nostalgia is the more telling given Pacino's own career in Hollywood and the way that his capital as screen star is never far from the scene. Throughout, Pacino's Hollywood obligations are hinted at: a cap from *Scent of a Woman* here, shorter hair plus a beard for *Carlito's Way* there. Even the way in which Pacino stages the death of Richard—in Kimball's arms, on a New York street, calling out the latter's first name as though he were a character in *The Godfather*—reminds us of a context importantly different from the one before us.

And importantly different, as well, from the one out of which Joseph Papp's Public Theater emerged half a century ago. The so-called culture wars notwithstanding and quite apart from the question of Pacino's own investments, discourse concerning who owns Shakespeare has little effect on the way power, economic and otherwise, is apportioned in the perimillennial United States; as I've already indicated with respect to the NEA's agenda for "Shakespeare in American Communities," any arguments that claim as much are fighting a rearguard action. Color-blind casting having become the largely unmarked norm, it is hard indeed to remember that minority representation on the Shakespearean stage was, at the moment of its emergence, connected to the matter of political representation and voting rights being fought in public form, in public spaces, and at great risk. Papp's efforts to proselytize on behalf of Shakespeare in the 1950s and the 1960s were inseparable from a larger conjuncture, from broader social movements around civil rights, labor, and education that could not but involve a structural understanding of privilege and Shakespeare's relationship to it at the time. This understanding must in turn be linked to Papp's own history as a Left populist: his testimony in front of the House Un-American Activities Committee, during which he was accused of claiming Shakespeare for Communism, attests to the ease with which a shift in the deployment of symbolic capital was perceived to be coextensive with a threat to nationhood and the relations of production.[23] It is out of such a political history that Papp's taking Shakespeare to the streets on flatbed trucks and to inner-city schools in the 1950s emerged. Papp's Shakespearean innovations occurred on a number of fronts: among them were not just the color-blind casting practices to which I have already referred but also productions of Shakespeare and Jonson in Spanish that took place in the 1960s and collaborations with black and Latino theater troupes in the late 1970s.

These days, however, free Shakespeare in Central Park has become a New York institution almost as august as the Cloisters. If, technically, the performances are still open to all attendees, corporate donations and the privilege of priority seating attendant upon them bring the Public Theater in line with most cultural gatekeepers accustomed to maximizing sources of funding.[24] The allegiance between capital and cultural institutions is an accomplished fact whose supposed separation of content from donor interests has been subjected to scrutiny by installation artists such as Hans Haacke: a contrast may be drawn between the normative arts practice in which the current Public Theater participates and the fact that Papp once turned down a grant from the NEA.[25] And perhaps more insidious a mode of exclusion than the comparatively few seats given over to corporate donors are the "free" seats that require prospective attendees to devote several hours, often during a working day, to wait in the distribution line: it is not surprising if the commitment to sit, wait, and picnic in anticipation of a nighttime performance exerts a cost that a comparative (and comparatively privileged) few can afford to pay. Paradoxically, the fact of the tickets' being free but distributed in order of patrons' arrival greatly increases the perceived, and perhaps actual, burden on potential audiences, and potentially lends this once-democratizing institution a restrictive air that Pacino's initial "peddling" can do little to dispel. It is inevitable that with time and shifts in management, the inertial tendencies accompanying institutionalization would overtake once-mobile practices such as Papp's inaugural Shakespeare productions and obscure, even domesticate, the innovative, contrarian, and radical impulses out of which those productions arose. Even so, it is worth noting that what is lost is a clear sense of unreservedly public access that was perhaps the most striking feature of Papp's intended presentation of Shakespeare.

Movie Shakespeare looks like a way out of the perplexity of latter-day theatrical performance: if not free, then affordable; if lacking a sense of occasion, then all the better for being an "ordinary" and (given the plurality of viewing practices) tractable experience. But as the preceding analysis has tried to demonstrate, the medium alone cannot serve redemptive purposes. Nor can it readily escape the drive to pedagogy, so deeply entrenched is that mode of apprehending Shakespeare in the American imaginary. If the connection between Shakespeare and the classroom, between lessons and mass experience, is deeply enough naturalized that what looks like an alternative becomes a redoubling, then understanding how Shakespeare went to school in the first place is, paradoxically enough, the only way that extramural formations can be understood for what they now are.

CHAPTER 3

Shakespeare Goes to School

In the previous chapter, I used *Looking for Richard* to demonstrate that these days it's hard indeed to escape the pedagogical imperative, a contradictory formation in which the demand that the public find pleasure in Shakespeare is countermanded by a quasi-evangelical practice, emerging from a range of sites, in which Shakespeare is inalienable from pedagogical agendas. The classroom thus occupies a contradictory position: it is the presumable source of disaffection in the first place, yet at the same time it often affords the tacit structuration within which that disaffection is meant to be overcome. So it is only fitting that I dedicate a chapter to Shakespeare in the schools. My purpose, however, is not to show how disaffection arises, nor to advocate for other or better approaches to teaching the plays. Disaffection, where it exists, is overdetermined and is ineluctably, even dialectically, related to the widespread demand in American culture that Shakespeare constitute a universally lovable object. As such, it far exceeds the capacity of noncollegiate instruction for countering (although I do not concede that it needs to be countered): the school is its scapegoat as vehicle of transmission, not its source.

Rather, I want to show how things came to be as they are, how Shakespeare is above all the locus of pedagogical experience for Americans. Thus the aim of this chapter is to show how Shakespeare went to the schools—that is, how a select handful of his plays became a nearly inescapable aspect of secondary education during the twentieth century, a state of affairs that persists into the present. The history of Shakespeare in American education is only beginning to be written, and it is far beyond the scope of this project to contribute to it in anything but a fragmentary manner.[1] It follows that many mechanisms doubtless contributed to Shakespeare's pedagogical centrality;

that being so, however, understanding how Shakespeare, elite culture, and education first came into a productive relation will go a long way toward explaining the source of the continuing misrecognition I am arguing against in this study. Hence my focus on the reading lists prescribed or otherwise influenced by the College Entrance Examination Board (CEEB) around the turn of the twentieth century and that, in a more diffuse way, rendered the ability to demonstrate knowledge of Shakespeare inseparable from collegiate-level literacy—that is, from a level of education then an inalienable privilege of a demographically pressured Anglo-Saxon elite.[2] As the fact of that pressure might suggest, literacy was not the sole issue leading to Shakespeare's being enshrined in the schools: given that mass immigration from non-Anglophone countries was held to imperil the social reproduction of the nation-state, Shakespeare and what he represented were enlisted, sometimes overtly, to serve the cause of a eugenicist "race knowledge" then widespread in educational discourse.

The recognition that Shakespeare was in some sense overtly politicized long before the advent of cultural materialism, or for that matter of interpretive strategies attentive to ideologies of race, gender, and sexuality, reminds us that historical research is the ally of more topical work. At the same time, however, it also nudges us to remember how readily decisions made for one reason harden into self-evident facts requiring institutional support but no further explanation. Witness Shakespeare's career in formal education. Once the plays found their way into the secondary school curriculum for the purposes of college preparation for a few, it seems to have been determined they would stay, despite the fact that admission to college has (in public discourse at least) long since hinged on the scientistic testing of aptitude rather than on the acquisition of specifically textualized cultural capital. This unhinging, which is perhaps better called a disarticulation, represents all the more reason to consider Shakespeare a public cultural entity rather than an elite one. Having outlasted his real utility to the work of a once-restrictive higher education in the service of industrial capital and of the racial imaginary of the nation for which his texts were enlisted approximately a century ago, Shakespeare lives on in the schools, a compulsory good and residual formation from that earlier moment.

Demonstrating this two-pronged claim concerning emergence and residuum, even in the necessarily partial ways to follow, is fundamental to the argument of this book. It is not possible to argue against the claim that Shakespeare is elite until and unless one can demonstrate the systematic manner in which his texts are widely (if not deeply) impressed into the U.S. imaginary, the better to serve as a reservoir for fantasy, resistance, investment, and counterinvestment. The secondary school, the completion of which has taken on the character of a national educational minimum in effect if not in practice, is thus the preferred conduit for such impressment.[3] The twentieth century has been the epoch of mass education, during which ever-greater numbers of students were brought farther and farther into its institutional embrace. And Shakespeare has been an ineluctable part of that embrace, often beginning in grammar school but especially in high school: indeed, secondary education in particular, regardless of changing college entrance requirements and, for that matter, changing demographics, cannot seem to do without the Bard. A handful of plays, most frequently *Julius Caesar* and *Macbeth* but also often *Hamlet, A Midsummer's Night's Dream,* and, more recently, *Romeo and Juliet,* have become pervasive in the experience of Americans who have completed a high school degree.[4] This state of affairs, I argue, renders it impossible to maintain a simple equation between Shakespeare and elite cultural property. The issue is not whether everyone can or is willing to read the plays; rather, it is a matter of all-but-compulsory exposure.

Examining the mechanisms by means of which Shakespeare first emerged in the curriculum, when competence in a select few Shakespeare plays "as we know them"—in full text, from versions edited for classroom use—began to be demanded as a requirement for those few seeking entrance into college is only part of my aim. Equally important is to recognize the way in which even my fragmentary data argue that the imaginative and ideological life of the nation-state—from a discourse of citizenship to matters of race as well as of class—was negotiated, reproduced, and even contested under the quasi-official sign of Shakespeare. In this regard, silences speak as tellingly as acts of commission: where the pressure occasioned by the growth in European, but non-English-speaking, immigrant populations seems to have forced some Shakespeare plays into prominence as resources for projecting a spectral notion of Anglo-Saxon privilege, other plays, once more popular, fell by the wayside. While some, like *Othello*, were prey to a durable and conjunctural embarrassment about the mingling of black and white in the wake of Reconstruction and the Civil War, others, like *King John*, disappeared for reasons it is harder to guess at but that may have to do with the growing autonomy of literary criticism as a mode for apprehending the plays. Nevertheless, that extra-literary concerns could and did attach themselves to Shakespeare indicates that even when his texts were part of a movement to distinction, they could not but prove central to American life.

* * *

The requirement that high school students know some Shakespeare bears a complex and yet all-but-invisible relationship to the mass-educational project being systematized in the United States at the turn of the twentieth century. To put it with some bluntness, without the emergence of a national educational project, it is not at all clear whether Shakespeare would have remained as available to the national imaginary as Lawrence Levine and scholars influenced by him argued he had been in the nineteenth century.[5] In a sense as important as it is underacknowledged, it is the educational apparatus, which during the twentieth century more and more inevitably takes the entire country as its horizon, that has afforded Shakespeare his most durable mass-cultural presence at the present time, rather than more critically canonized loci such as film or television.

In fact, until the relatively recent (and still highly contested) flowering of the homeschooling movement, there has been scant escape from the ambit of a national educational project, a fact with important consequences for the often-tendentious conjuncture of Shakespeare and mass culture. The critical arguments that have tried to place Shakespeare in relation to that culture have understandably mistaken both their object and its historical predication. Shakespeare is not the marmoreal and oppressive other of the carnivalizing lower stratum wrought by the culture industry; for that matter, neither are his plays the always-already popular forms on behalf of which the historical gap separating the present conjuncture from Shakespeare's epoch ought to be gainsaid by an evangelizing popular medium in search of the material and ideological benefits of providing uplift. The mass culture most immediately pertinent to a discussion of Shakespeare, in perimillennial America is the *culture of mass education,* an institution whose production began, as I have already suggested, with the rising to prominence of industrialized capitalism at the turn of the twentieth century, and hence with the concomitant links forged between universities (especially research universities) on the one hand, and the agenda of Gilded Age capital on the other.

Rather like the economy of mass production to which it is conjuncturally related, the national educational project of the early twentieth century represented a demand for standardization: it strove to eliminate local idiosyncrasies while aiming to construct an educational continuum (for whites, at least) that stretched from early childhood to the threshold of the university. For approximately the first quarter of the twentieth century, it identified and reproduced a body of knowledge that students seeking admission to college would increasingly be expected to know and write about. Hence the importance of the College Board as a guarantor of national standards: according to Mary Trachsel, "In large measure, the unification of American education was accomplished through the articulatory function of entrance exams that effected a consolidation of the originally unrelated systems of public and private schooling as well as secondary and higher education."[6]

Of course, the influence of the College Board, especially in the first years of its existence, was not empirically equal to its aims: I invoke it rather as fantasmatic projection of a certain dispensation, a dispensation to which Shakespeare was necessary.

But, as I've already indicated, equally necessary to the mass-educational project was the shifting population of the United States at the turn of the twentieth century. As is well-known, Lawrence Levine has generally associated the alignment of Shakespeare and education with the emergence of the category "highbrow," which originally signified a racialized presumption that cranial capacity, betokened by the cant of the forehead, was an index of intelligence and cultural value. Certainly, scholars active in the early twentieth-century promotion of the Bard have provided ample evidence of a connection between the plays as a sort of Anglo-Saxon patrimony on the one hand, and the inculcatory effects of didactic practice on immigrant populations on the other: hence the analytical parallels between education as such and the Vitagraph project. So explicit a linkage among education, Shakespeare, and standardized education for immigrants persisted at least as late as the dedication of the Folger Shakespeare Library in 1932, as the strangely ambiguous words of Joseph Quincy Adams, supervisor of research for the library and formerly professor of English at Cornell, attest:

> Fortunately, about the time the forces of immigration became a menace to the preservation of our long-established civilization, there was initiated throughout the country a system of free and compulsory education for youth. In a spirit of efficiency, that education was made stereotyped in form; and in a spirit of democracy, every child was forced by law to submit to its discipline. The discipline devised was not, perhaps, ideal; but it was virtually the same in every state and territory, and had the merit of giving one training to the heterogeneous population which now filled our land. As a result, whatever the racial antecedents, out of the portals of the schools emerged, in the second or third generation, a homogeneous people, speaking the same language, inspired by the same ideals, exemplifying the same culture. Indeed, to the European mind, Americans possess a likeness that borders on fatal monotony; they dress alike, behave alike, think alike, throughout the length and breadth of our vast territory...
>
> On the side of the humanities, that schooling concerned itself mainly with the English language and literature—a choice, of course, dictated by practical considerations...
>
> And here Shakespeare, the object of general idolatry, was again called upon to play a part in American cultural life, this time on the stage of

education. In our fixed plan of elementary schooling, he was made the corner-stone of cultural discipline. A study of his works was required in successive grades extending over a period of years...

This study and veneration did not stop with the grammar and high schools; it was carried into the colleges and universities, and there pursued with still more vigor...[7]

Written after entrance examinations moved in the direction of aptitude testing, Adams's words afford a glimpse of the immigrant citizen as stamped out by enforced discipline in the somewhat dubious service of a democratic ideal and gathered under the sign of Shakespeare. New Americans emerge from educational apparatuses like so many new commodities, mass produced into a standardization that seems, to Adams, at least, the necessary price to pay for keeping the immigrant "menace" at bay. Oddly, however, he apparently reverses the vectors of causation: in his account of the national educational system, the study of Shakespeare begins from the ground up, rather than being driven by decisions at the highest level of instruction that percolate downwards. Perhaps this is because he is focused on the looming threat from below rather than on the comparatively loftier gatekeeping practices such as entrance examinations that seem to have resulted in Shakespeare's becoming enshrined in the curriculum in the first place. But his very misrecognition is important, since it nevertheless reveals the extent to which Shakespeare's early centrality to mass education must be triangulated with "race knowledge" as well as with industrialization.

It would in any case be difficult to deny that the College Board was both a force for standardization and an agent of exclusionary practices implicated in preserving the racialized boundaries of the nation-state: hence its foundational status to this account. But its deployment of Shakespeare as a pedagogical touchstone could not have come out of nowhere, as Adams's remarks about "the object of general idolatry" suggest. Although popular performance has loomed large in historical accounts of the time before Shakespeare went to school full-time, this deployment could not have been secured only on the basis of performance-based acquaintance. For Shakespeare to have been available to serve as a meaningful sign for college-appropriate literacy, there must have been a history of prior textual, educational apparitions.

* * *

As that last remark suggests, the prominence to be given here to the College Board and the entrance examinations that universities administered around the turn of the century should not create the impression that there was no pedagogical Shakespeare beforehand. Rather, Shakespeare could be found in school texts dating from at least the end of the first quarter of the nineteenth century, and hence, presumably, in various pedagogical venues. However, precisely because standardization of grade level and the type of institutions appropriate to certain ages and grades—the state-supervised educational system best suited to producing a mass public—was an unevenly emerging issue, the nineteenth-century pedagogical forms and practices that preceded the time of my greatest concern defy easy summary. Not only were there significant variations in educational standards and teacher training, by region and by state, regardless of the discourses that took national practice as their frame of reference. Some forms of education, such as mechanics' associations or the "forest schools" of the antebellum South, where freemen and slaves who had temporarily slipped away from their masters often learned to read, defy the very nature of archival research by virtue of their informal or even fugitive character.[8] Some education was undertaken autonomously or else flourished with the quasi-institutionalized support of itinerant lecturers or such local formations as the chautauquas.[9] As a corollary, the various uses to which Shakespeare might have been put in those myriad locales are just as hard to characterize. Even when local records do survive, they can be uninformative for the purposes of tracking how Shakespeare was used in precollegiate education: for example, a search of the Board of Education archives in New York for the years before the borough school districts were combined in 1898 offered little information about what students were asked to study.

Or, more properly, to declaim, since one fact about which it is comparatively easy to be sure is that speeches from the plays were above all understood as an occasion for oratory: nineteenth-century primers and oratorical manuals evince as much. These volumes made free use of passages from the plays, not to exemplify "literary" or aesthetic value, but to serve as performative supports for the fashioning of the nascent American subject via the exercise of declamation. Regardless of encounters with the plays onstage, many nineteenth-century subjects would also have learned to value Shakespeare as an adjunct to early training in literacy—a literacy in which oratorical exercise was connected both to the mimesis of histrionic passions and to the inculcation of moral, as well as civic and patriotic, values, if the selection of passages is any indication. That is to say, early pedagogical uses of Shakespeare were intrinsically public, directed outward either in a literal sense—via the fact of speeches marked and practiced for performance—or in the sense of the imaginative projection, as in Benedict Anderson's "imagined community," required to be a member of a nation-state.[10]

Many readers meant for primary and even secondary schools seem to have been published in the Northeast, particularly in Boston, as well as in Ohio and Kentucky. Given that there is some evidence of regional taste when it came to Shakespeare in performance before the twentieth century, the fact that primer publication was comparatively centralized suggests the possibility of a protocanon formed by institutionally and geographically privileged means.[11] The numerous readers associated with William Holmes McGuffey serve as an important case in point.[12] According to Dorothy Sullivan, over 22 million copies of McGuffey's various textbooks were sold between 1836 and 1920: although extracts from Shakespeare appeared only in the Fourth and Sixth Eclectic Readers, the popularity of the series is strong evidence of its capacity to determine what counted as Shakespeare for many Americans.[13] And what counted was itself selective. In the Sixth Reader, generally aimed at the equivalent of high school or college students, the selections from Shakespeare were more extensive and generally comprised speeches from a range of plays chosen to illustrate various moral positions or virtues, as the titles given to the selections at times attest: witness a selection entitled "The Folly of Intoxication," from *Othello*. Among the other Shakespearean extracts singled out for declamatory exercises, some requiring more than one participant, were Henry V's address to the troops at Harfleur; Hamlet's most famous soliloquy, "To be or not to be"; "Clarence's Dream," from *Richard III*; the aftermath of the Gad's Hill prank featuring Hal and Falstaff from *Henry IV Part I*; and, most unlikely perhaps to modern eyes, two passages from *King John* as well as one from *Henry VIII*.[14]

But McGuffey's readers were far from the only schoolbook available. Henry William Simon notes that John Pickett's *The Juvenile Mentor*, originally published in 1820, had no fewer than twenty-three passages from Shakespeare intended to teach students how to perform "the passions"; the twenty-first edition of Olney's *Natural Reader*, published in 1845, had a list of passages almost identical to McGuffey's, with the significant substitution of Othello's "Apology for his Marriage" for the play's treatment of Cassio's drunken rowdiness.[15] In any case, these Shakespearean extracts (which were sometimes silently edited in revealing ways) gesture toward a wealth of questions for the scholar more used to whole-text pedagogy. What, for instance, was the principle of selection in any given text? How might Shakespearean extracts be read alongside or against other selections? Were the selections themselves, as well as the cues for oratory that accompanied them, tacitly pressured by recollections of performances, and if so, to what end? Is there any significance to the different selections to be found among primers, or enough duplication across their range that one can already speak of a redacted canon whose apparently miscellaneous character belies a principle of consensus beyond market logic not now easily visible? When, if at all, do literary aesthetics make themselves felt?[16]

Unfortunately, I cannot begin to hazard answers to most of these questions. When it comes to the matter of consensus, however, my content summary suggests that some Shakespearean extracts were reprinted more frequently than others. For instance, from the first it seems as though *Julius Caesar*, still a presence in secondary school curricula, was a privileged locus for oratorical training. According to Ruth Miller Elson's extensive study of nineteenth-century textbooks, selections from *Julius Caesar*, notably Brutus's speech preferring his love for Rome to his love for Caesar, appear in numerous other readers besides those I have mentioned: Brutus's speech in particular initially functioned to naturalize by rhetorical inscription the self-sacrificing patriotic values of the emergent nation-state.[17] Elson's claim follows along a history of performance that suggests the play has borne the freight of politics more or less from Revolutionary times, if the hint in 1906 account offered by George B. Churchill is to be trusted:

> How full of promise appears that record of the years before the Revolution! Before 1769 all Shakespeare's great tragedies save "Julius Caesar" are already on the stage. Before the Revolution that play has been added, and with it "Cymbeline," "The Tempest," and "King John." They took their work seriously, these early actors, and boldly essayed the highest.[18]

Churchill's sense of what counts as a "great" tragedy is more expansive than many more recent lists: besides *Julius Caesar*, it includes *Othello*, *King Lear*, *Hamlet*, *Macbeth*, *Coriolanus*, *Antony and Cleopatra*, even *Timon of Athens*: everything, that is, but *Titus Andronicus* (whose inclusion in the canon, despite doubts about its authorship, Churchill does not dispute). Since in 1906 Churchill claimed to find evidence that all these plays, and others besides, were being actively performed in America before 1769, the fact that *Julius Caesar* was **not**, despite its being considered estimable, of "the highest," seems remarkable.

But perhaps not, given that, laconically, Churchill notes its appearance "before the Revolution." In the period preceding the start of the Revolution, the comparative paucity (suppression?) of performances of *Julius Caesar* attests to the potential volatility of the plot; its entrance onto the stage "before the Revolution," then, invites us to read it (along, perhaps, with the otherwise unlikely *King John*) as a successful and indeed rhetorically compelling allegory of the struggle of the colonial nation-state against tyranny.[19] And about a century later, in the years following the Civil War and the assassination of Abraham Lincoln by the actor John Wilkes Booth, *Julius Caesar* offered virtually a topical reference. Not only had Booth joined his brothers, Edwin and Junius Brutus, in a notable performance of the play the fall before the assassination, a performance in which he played Marc Antony, but also his diaries reveal an identification between himself and Brutus, and his public cry, "*Sic semper tyrannis*. The South is avenged," links the death of the president imaginatively with the historical events that subtend the play itself.[20] Indeed, when one considers the evidence that productions such as Edwin Booth's *Richard II* were received with marked difference in North and South, it is even possible that John of Gaunt, Bolingbroke, and the deposed king himself spoke in terms appropriate to Southern Anglophilia while presenting a referendum of sorts on tyranny and political legitimacy, the melancholy disappearance of "traditional" bonds, and a brutally exploitative agrarian, if not precisely "emerald," way of life.[21]

The language Ruth Warren employed as recently as 1955 in discussing Shakespearean reception in America bespeaks the readiness with which *Julius Caesar* constitutes a site of political projection even after purely literary analysis has become the new national dominant with respect to Shakespeare: "*Julius Caesar* presents a complicated moral problem, involving loyalty, moral right and wrong, true patriotism versus self-interest disguised as love of country, the rights of the people shabbily used by rabble-rousers, and the whole perplexing matter of when a politician ceases to be an honest man..."[22] Here the resonances with McCarthyism represent a more recent manifestation of an impulse to assimilate the play to the polis, an assimilation that, it seems, persists into the present, albeit not with the same object.[23] And in a revealing back-formation, a recent guidebook for teaching *Julius Caesar* gives students a series of readings that ask them to connect the play to the Booths and the Lincoln assassination, thereby recovering a political logic that has been obscured by more recent pedagogical dominants.[24] Such histories need to be recovered, if only to remind us that "political Shakespeare" is far from a new invention. However, as the discipline of English became institutionalized and as plays were increasingly read in and for themselves, *Julius Caesar* seems to have become less immediately instrumental for the imagined community of the United States. And as the trajectory of that play suggests, significant shifts took place within education itself, from a Shakespeare understood theatrically, declamatorily, and by bits and shards, to a Shakespeare who became a vehicle for aesthetic analysis and of a literary value to be found in "completeness."

The lessons to which Shakespearean extracts might have been put in the nineteenth century were not always so civic. Witness *The Merchant of Venice*, a play that informal surveys suggest has largely dropped out of secondary education, but that once had a great deal of currency. Nineteenth-century primers were not innocent of discourse about race: they had, for instance, often been divided on the subject of slavery. Given that several of these texts were produced in abolitionist Boston, it would be no surprise to find that in general they condemned the institution. This condemnation was, according to Elson, offset by the contempt and horror with which Africa and Africans were sometimes described, in schoolbooks widely used in both North and South (Elson, 85–86). Many textbooks apparently concerned themselves more widely with the construction of an Anglo-Saxon national identity that sought to put even European others in their place and to provide a rationalizing discourse on ethnic and racial difference. Hence Antonio's speech bitterly declaiming the hardness of Shylock's Jewish heart was frequently reprinted (Elson, 84). In contrast, at least one earlier primer prefaced the lines thus: "It would convey a false moral, if it should be made to cast any reproach on a Jew, as such; for a Jew may be a good member of society; and, like every other man, ought to be judged according to his acts, and not according to any prejudice which current error or bigotry has established."[25] Shakespearean extracts, it seemed, could be used to disseminate racial typology, or to argue against its "false moral"—a dialectical possibility the more complicated when one remembers that the speeches were destined to be performed.

Even when the movement to whole-text Shakespeare and hence to an autonomous literary object had begun, such instrumental ends did not disappear altogether: witness the emphasis given both to selections from a very few plays, such as *The Merchant of Venice,* and to Shakespeare himself, as the source of Anglo-Saxon "race knowledge." To understand both shift and persistence, it is necessary to turn to the emergence of the College Board.

* * *

In his essay parodically entitled "Give an Account of Shakespeare and Education, Showing Why You Think They Are Effective and What You Have Appreciated about Them. Support Your Comments with Precise References," Alan Sinfield has described how examination questions for admission to elite universities in England demand that students provide a representation of Shakespeare that is at once celebratory and anodyne, deprived of any complicating subtexts, ambiguities, or counterplots that might interfere with understanding Shakespeare as a poet of national values.[26] Even more fundamentally, for Sinfield such examinations revealed that Shakespeare functions as cultural capital in the British educational apparatus, a metonym for the privileges of class. To "have" Shakespeare in the sense elicited by the entrance examinations is, it would seem, to be marked out as a once or future member of a comparatively rarefied and privileged category of student. At base, then, Shakespeare's presence on a college entrance examination in Great Britain brings together plays, privilege, and precollegiate pedagogy in a union as much naturalized as it is revealing.

While, as I've indicated, it has been commonplace to consider Shakespeare symbolic of class privilege in the United States no less than in the United Kingdom, one cannot use Shakespeare's name to track how access to higher education in America is currently connected to highly restrictive admissions practices. Granted, Shakespeare is included among the authors recommended for study in an AP course in English literature, and the ability to present evidence of high competence in literary analysis and interpretation is presumed to be quite helpful in the admission process.[27] Correspondingly, there is evidence that elite college-preparatory institutions offer more variety and sophistication than public secondary schools when it comes to which Shakespeare plays are studied and which editions used.[28] I am not, therefore, suggesting that there is no correlation between how, where, and by whom Shakespeare is studied, and the chances of gaining admission to a selective college. Although this study depends on acknowledging that Shakespeare no longer seems to possess efficacy as a form of cultural capital, in very delimited educational contexts his is still a name to contend with. Even so, it would be hard to argue that doing well on the standardized tests that serve as national sorting mechanisms for college admission depends on knowing what to say, and how to write, about a select list of rarefied texts. In keeping with national ideology, an apparent free market with respect to subject matter obtains for those seeking to enter college, and Shakespeare is not, it would seem, an escapable purchase.[29]

Undeniably, the development and transformation of secondary school curricula follow a complicated trajectory, within which issues peculiar to the institution and the locality cannot but play a large role. If, however, there no longer is a test for college admission as such in the United States that demands even a selective knowledge of Shakespeare, there once was, thanks to the efforts of the College Board, which was founded around the turn of the twentieth century and which sponsored examinations based on selected reading lists from 1901 until 1931. The board united a select group of college professors with masters and instructors in a few academies and secondary schools, the better to work from both ends toward the point of contact. Its emergence was symptomatic of a disappearing consensus about the value of a classical education—an education, that is, largely steeped in the study of Latin and Greek. Spurred on by the reforms first proposed by Charles William Eliot, the president of Harvard, but implemented particularly in the Midwest and the West, higher education was slowly being refocused to reflect competence in technical and scientific subjects, designed to educate a new type of man (or, less frequently, woman) to play a significant part in the creation and reproduction of wealth. As David Starr Jordan, chosen by the Stanfords to serve as the first president of their new university, suggested, the times did not seem to call for "Greek-minded men," where "Greek-minded" represents an obsolescent notion of quasi-aristocratic distinction and the pedagogical preparations that subtend it.[30]

Apparently, however, the times did call for Shakespeare, whose plays seem to have been brought into curricular prominence by the same shifts, as well as by a related discourse whose aim was to articulate the British, indeed Anglo-Saxon, racial and cultural foundations of the United States against shifts in immigration bringing more and more non-Anglophone speakers to the country.[31] (Hence publicly funded lectures in Italian and Yiddish on Shakespeare in New York City shortly after the turn of the century, which were offered alongside lectures on the history of U.S. democracy, the evils of socialism, and on proper sanitation techniques in the household as a matter of public health: taken together, these lectures indicate a wholesale municipal effort to administer to the immigrant medically, politically, and ideologically.) More and more, that is, Shakespeare was Janus-faced: a sign both of college-level literacy and of the more demotic, less rarefied knowledge associated with the burgeoning interest in a uniform national educational system and allied to the economic transformations (themselves based on iterability and mass production) of approximately one hundred years ago.

Even so, it is striking that Shakespeare, while made newly important by the board as a whole-text author, is nevertheless not initially *more* important than such writers as Sir Walter Scott. Given how many of the non-Shakespearean texts deemed significant by turn-of-the century educational reformers have dropped out of circulation, there is even more reason to claim Shakespeare's persistence as a reservoir for public use. Of course, I wish to avoid making the tendentious and lazy claim that Shakespeare survived where Scott did not because of the sheer quality of the former's texts, although it seems likely that literary aesthetics and standards of taste are themselves formed in relation to the Shakespearean, rather than having an independent and abstract life as arbiters of Shakespeare's quality. Nevertheless, I want to stress that the very fact of survival is itself significant: just as a selective knowledge of Shakespeare was positioned as a condition of admission to higher education, it was shortly thereafter abandoned as a marker of accomplishment, as colleges moved to standardized testing. And yet Shakespeare, an artifact of complex historical forces, remained inalienable from the high school curriculum, where the texts persist to this day.

It must immediately be acknowledged that, rather than a single test for college admission demanding knowledge of Shakespeare be demonstrated, there were, in actuality, several, based on a more-or-less common reading list that, once consolidated, seemed to vary little from year to year at a given institution. And even though the College Board reading lists were influential, they were not uniformly and immediately adopted in the Northeast, among the institutions that generally supported the board's aims or, as in the case of Harvard, helped spur the innovation. Moreover, even the decision to adopt its lists did not result in a uniform national exam: complete standardization awaited the arrival of the multiple-choice test. But the earliest board-inspired college- and university-specific materials I have been able to examine shared the fact of Shakespeare: as I have suggested, the ability to write well-crafted paragraphs on selected plays seems to have been considered all but identical with college-level literacy in English at the turn of the twentieth century.[32]

And if there was unanimity about the importance of Shakespeare, there was also significant convergence around certain plays in particular, a convergence that puts the occasional point of difference in high relief. A great deal of emphasis was devoted to *Macbeth,* particularly in and around New York City, where College Board member and president of Columbia University, Nicholas Murray Butler, worked to have board texts set the examinations not just at Columbia and Barnard but at New York University as well. (He seems also to have had influence over teacher training for the newly constituted New York City Board of Education: its teacher-licensing examinations, too, reveal a single-minded emphasis on the same play.)[33] *The Merchant of Venice* and *Julius Caesar* were also frequently to be found on entrance examination reading lists, and it is these texts that appear to have had a durable career in the high school curriculum of the twentieth century. At the same time, however, in the late 1890s and for at least ten to twenty years thereafter, variation elsewhere among the plays chosen reveals at times some lingering affinity with the collection of Shakespearean set-pieces for oratorical and rhetorical analysis that appeared in handbooks of oratory and rhetoric and in readers such as McGuffey's, which were drawn from a wider range of plays than the College Board embraced. This variation also reveals that at times institutions that were either geographically or culturally distant from universities such as Columbia, Harvard, Yale, Penn, and the other founding members of the College Board seemed to have had differing ideas about which Shakespeare texts ought to be known.

University bulletins and registers, the chief sources of my data, began to publish annual lists of texts and textbooks in a variety of disciplines, from history to mathematics and usually including German and French as well as

Latin or Greek, that had to be mastered in order to sit for qualifying examinations. In some universities, a category of English vernacular texts was simply added on to an already-extant body of readings; in others, the new appearance of such lists signaled participation in the burgeoning project of mass education on a national scale. It is worth noting what other readings were considered mandatory in addition to Scott's *Ivanhoe*. The books suggested for either "Reading" (to be discussed generally) or "For Study and Practice" (for more nuanced understanding) were Milton's *Comus, L'Allegro,* and *Il Penseroso*, with books 1 and 2 of *Paradise Lost,* choices that may seem more or less natural to us: less so, surely, are such texts as Webster's First Bunker Hill Oration; Longfellow's *Evangeline*; or William Macaulay's writings, whether his life of Johnson, or his essays on Addison, Milton, or Dryden.[34] Shakespeare persists, while these texts have declined in importance: hence discussing Shakespeare's place in a changing educational system is a way to mark how a pervasive cultural good is refunctioned to suit new exigencies and how a precollegiate canon—a canon, that is, of Shakespeare plays known via reading and analysis to an ever-growing public formed by state education—begins to emerge.

To appreciate the influence of the College Board in enshrining Shakespeare's plays in the secondary school curriculum, it is necessary to review the period leading up to the first examination of 1901. Preliminary research indicates that Shakespeare was not particularly central in many college courses themselves. In New York, during the period just prior to the turn of the century, for instance, mentions of Shakespeare in the curriculum are scarce: in the 1880s, Columbia's entrance requirements were heavily influenced by classical curricula, which led into a related college curriculum. The first appearance of a Shakespeare text in Columbia College's handbook seems to have been in the degree requirements for the "classical course of study" during that period, which stipulated *Macbeth* as the central reading in a sophomore requirement. When women were first admitted to Columbia as special certificate students in 1887–1888, however, they were given *Love's Labor's Lost* to study "with analysis of plot, language, figures and allusions." The following year, while the men persisted with *Macbeth,* the women were assigned *The Tempest.* (The year after that, Barnard was officially established.) It is hard not to see in this brief divergence a certain horror at the prospect of educated women being asked to contemplate the ambitious virago that is Lady Macbeth—and, indeed, the play may well have functioned broadly in myriad educational venues in the service of gendered self-regulation. If horror, there was, however, it was comparatively short-lived: by 1898 Barnard women were reading *Macbeth,* even as the men had moved on to *Othello.* This shift might have been influenced by the fact that a Columbia faculty member, Thomas Price, published a study on prosody in *Othello* in 1888. As befits an increasing concern with linking the study of English with a discourse of Anglo-Saxon origins via Germanic philology, Price's study resembles nothing so such as an approach to prosody reminiscent of that dedicated to Anglo-Saxon verse forms.[35]

But Shakespeare does not yet appear as part of the entrance requirements. It is not until the handbook for 1892–1893 that students are asked to present knowledge of Shakespeare for admission—specifically, of *Julius Caesar* and *Merchant*—and continue to be until the formal adoption of college entrance examinations in 1901.[36] At that point, entrance examinations in English get divided into two parts, reflecting the divisions between "Study" and "Reading" to which I have referred: students are tested on *Merchant* for Part I, "Reading" and *Macbeth* for Part 2, "Study." In 1903–1905, *Merchant* and *Julius Caesar* are assigned for Part I, while *Macbeth* persists through at least 1905 for Part II. Indeed, the New York City Board of Education archives suggest a remarkable municipal convergence around *Macbeth* in particular, since the qualifying examinations for those aspiring to become school principals that were published in the superintendent's annual report also demand a knowledge of this play above all.

In contrast, *Macbeth* loomed far less authoritatively in the City College of New York, which served a population that was far more ethnically diverse (unlike Columbia, it had no restrictive quota on Jews) and far less exclusionary in terms of preparation. Having originally begun as the "Free Academy," it combined the functions of the high schools New York City was a historical laggard in setting up with the functions of a college. When Shakespeare makes an appearance in this less elite environment, it is, strictly speaking, neither at the collegiate level nor at the level of entrance requirement; rather, it is as part of a five-year degree designed to meld preparatory study with college, and so represents an institutional form that diverges from the College Board's belief that there should be a clear separation between secondary school and university. In 1895–1896 we find the first mention of a Shakespeare text, *Julius Caesar*, designated for the third year of study, a state of affairs that appears to persist at least until 1897–1888. By 1901–1902, the third-year students were asked to read an extensive number of Shakespeare plays: *A Midsummer Night's Dream, As You Like It, Hamlet, King Lear,* and *The Tempest.* If *Julius Caesar* is likely introduced to the curriculum as a vernacular substitute for the classical texts demanded at more elite institutions, the 1901–1902 course of study looks far more like comparable university-level courses. Notable, however, is the apparent idiosyncrasy of most of the selections, taken from plays that did not figure in the early years of College Board entrance requirements. And offering a tantalizing possibility for speculation is the fact that in the years I've considered, while *The Merchant of Venice* is being read widely elsewhere in the city, it is not being studied at City College of New York, whose registers of students and alumni attest to the large number of Jews it admitted and graduated.

A similarly wider range of plays also characterized the examination practices at Howard University and the University of Virginia, two telling instances of institutions more remote from New York and New England as centers of educational influence. For all that these universities now may be considered comparatively elite, during the period with which I am concerned their institutional forms looked a great deal more like those of City College than of the colleges and universities participating in the College Board—and for comparable although historically distinct reasons. And as one might therefore expect, the place of Shakespeare in both curriculum and entrance requirements does not precisely mirror what is going on in elite Northern universities. For instance, Howard, founded in 1867, insisted on the rigorousness of its course of study even as it included a preparatory department (later renamed "Academy") in acknowledgment of the practical difficulties involved in preparing emancipated slaves as well as freemen and freewomen for college-level work. In its 1894–1895 catalog, Shakespeare first appears outside of a "Rhetoricals" requirement in the preparatory department, under the heading of "Collateral Exercises," which appear to be a list of ancillary readings: texts specified include *Julius Caesar* and *Henry VIII*. The collateral exercises of 1896–1897 ask for *Merchant* and *As You Like It*. Thereafter, Shakespeare disappears from mention, although collateral exercises are specified, and in 1900–1901 the catalog proclaims that Howard's "requirements for admission are higher than in most Southern Institutions."

Several larger-scale institutional transformations signal this movement to intellectual distinction as defined by white Northern standards, transformations that, it seems, culminate with the publication of examination readings lists for admissions. Around the turn of the twentieth century, a formal English department apart from the certificate-based general training began to emerge at Howard; by 1903–1904, it had developed a College of Arts and Sciences, and entrance requirements began to be specified more fully. At the same time, its Teachers College asks students to take a course in Shakespeare, with half a year on *Romeo and Juliet* and selected comedies and half a year on *Macbeth, Hamlet, King Lear, The Tempest,* and *Richard II*. In 1904–1905, "Shakespearean drama" is indicated as the object of English composition; in 1905–1906, *Macbeth* is assigned to the middle year of the preparatory school. In 1908–1909, the College of Arts and Sciences merged with the Teachers College to become the School of Liberal Arts. It is at this comparatively later moment that Howard's entrance requirements come to resemble those of universities officially affiliated with the College Board, an affiliation signaled rhetorically by its division of preparation into "study and practice" on the one hand and "reading" on the other. Notably, however, the selection of Shakespeare plays published for admission at Howard is broader than those generally found on College Board lists. Just as in College Board examinations, *Macbeth* is designed "for study and practice," while for reading, a longer list of Shakespeare plays, including *As You Like It, Henry V, Julius Caesar, The Merchant of Venice,* and *Twelfth Night,* appears. Howard's emulatory stance with respect to standards and its extensive commitment to the plays constitute a tacit rejoinder to the frequent allegiance between Shakespeare and an implicitly racially exclusionary patrimony found in the Northeast. If in elite Northern universities Shakespeare carries the sign of "race knowledge," then Howard's insistence on making so many of the plays available to the freeborn black and emancipated slaves whom it matriculated offers the possibility of a counterinscription, of a reserve for the fashioning of an educated citizen of color apart from the ideological ballast with which the plays were customarily fraught.

As Howard's telling reference to "most Southern institutions" might suggest, white Southern schooling historically lagged behind the Northeast and the Midwest and, like the education of emancipated slaves, was the object of reform by Northern philanthropists in the postbellum period. Rather like Howard, the University of Virginia had by charter long combined the functions of a college and a preparatory school; moreover, the state charge to admit any white male student who presented the appropriate credentials meant that, in this precarious, postbellum period at least, the university necessarily had less restrictive entrance requirements, which is partly signaled by the fact that little mention of Shakespeare occurs in them. But when Shakespeare does appear, the intensity with which study of the texts is advocated suggests, if anything, a redoubling of the racialized investment of the North, a sense, that is, that the association between Shakespeare and "race knowledge" may be being asserted all the more forcefully in the postbellum South.

The matter of curricular reform, therefore, necessarily assumes different contours in this institutional nexus. While in the historically prominent colleges and universities of the Northeast Shakespeare is being introduced as a way to reform the curriculum and make it *less* overtly elitist than the study of the classics, during approximately the same time period, at the University of Virginia, the increasing presence of Shakespeare seems to have been the sign of *greater* curricular, and hence greater preparatory, rigor. In a 1905 entrance examination, students were asked to write about only "An English author of the 19th century," "Any period of American Lit," and "An English dramatist of the Elizabethan period"; a little earlier, in 1901, they were being asked to write "a good paragraph on Lady Macbeth" and to discuss the role of the witches in the play. But by 1908, under the influence of the Association of Colleges and Preparatory Schools of the Southern States, a regional institution set up to parallel the aims of the College Board, the University of Virginia was announcing standard exams with reading lists at least as extensive as those that obtained up North. In fact, the list of Shakespeare plays from which students were to choose two for study was particularly comprehensive: *A Midsummer Night's Dream, The Merchant of Venice, As You Like It, Twelfth Night, The Tempest, Romeo and Juliet, King John, Richard II* and *Richard III, Henry V, Coriolanus, Julius Caesar, Macbeth,* and *Hamlet*. It is easier to say what was left out rather than what was included: while perhaps no one would expect *Timon* or *Titus Andronicus* to have been included, one might well wonder about the exclusion of *Antony and Cleopatra*—and *Othello*. Of course, with the data I have, it is impossible to know with any certainty whether the omissions betray a culturally charged resistance to the staging of miscegenation that they seem to hint at. But if Shakespeare was the vehicle of race knowledge, it is surely possible that some potential counterknowledges were better kept out of sight.

* * *

I've already suggested that there were local perturbances in how Shakespeare was adopted in the wake of the College Board. In an age before standardized testing, and equally before the post–World War II emergence of university bureaucracies, much educational policy seems to have been driven by university presidents; indeed, testing policy and "great men" seemed to be in homology with the Gilded Age robber barons to whose needs for an educated workforce reform and regularization of the schools was sometimes overtly addressed. As I've noted, it was Charles William Eliot, the president of Harvard from 1869 to 1909 (and before that, professor of analytical chemistry at MIT) who first gave impetus in the 1870s to the educational reform that would allow for vernacular literature—that is, literature in English—to come to prominence alongside classical languages in entrance requirements. It was the president of Columbia University, Nicholas Murray Butler, whose influence in New York City educational circles first set the College Board exams as entrance requirements for several New York universities in 1901 (these were the first universities in the nation to require them, a state of affairs that continued for almost a decade). It was not until the University of Virginia appointed its first president in 1904, Edwin Alderman, that it began to specify examinations resembling those being required at the other institutions I've considered. And it was the first president of Stanford University,

David Starr Jordan, who designed the very content of the entrance examinations for students interested in enrolling in this new university. His somewhat idiosyncratic deployment of Shakespeare—as, potentially, a vehicle for the exploration of eugenicist concepts—was reflected in the content and makeup of the exams he seems to have personally administered as part of his efforts to recruit students.

Like Howard and the University of Virginia, Stanford was not a part of the College Board, nor would it become one for many years. Even so, Jordan was influenced by Eliot's New Education model, as well as the proximate example of the University of California, Berkeley, and his prior experience at Midwestern land-grant institutions. Jordan's sense of the ends to which education might be put were instrumental; as befits someone chosen by the Stanfords to found a new university, he was frankly open to pleasing the representatives of business. Indeed, given his sense that one had, in effect, to be "Greek-minded" to derive knowledge from Greek classics, and that modern men were not necessarily nor advantageously so, it is possible that knowledge of Shakespeare was, for him, not coterminous with a vernacularized form of cultural capital.[37] I do not mean, of course, that it did not matter if students did not know Shakespeare's texts, nor that knowing the right ones gave one a better chance at entrance to Stanford and other universities; the moment when particular texts would be replaced by any texts, specific knowledge by a test of skills to be applied to any texts, was in the future. Rather, I mean to suggest that even as Jordan was examining students' comprehension of a given passage it appears he was also, at times at least, using Shakespeare as a kind of proving ground for "modern" ideas about race, not unlike some of the primers that Elson has examined.

While examinations administered at Stanford by the turn of the century evince the same interest in *Macbeth* to be found in the Northeast, its earliest tests for admission appear more idiosyncratic. Witness the examination question for May 1893, designed to admit students in the new university's second year. Part A of the opening examination, which tests for English, introduces the following exchange:

> *First Speaker:*
>
> Mislike me not for my complexion,
> The *shadow'd livery* of the burnish'd sun,
> To whom I am a neighbor and near bred.
> Bring me the fairest creature *northward* born,
> Where *Phoebus'* fire scarce thaws the icicles,
> And let us *make incision* for your love,
> To prove whose blood is reddest, his or mine.

I tell thee, lady, this *aspect* of mine
Hath *fear'd* the valiant: by my love I swear
The *best-regarded* virgins of our clime
Have loved it too: I would not change this hue,
Except to steal your thoughts, gentle queen.

Second Speaker:

In *terms of choice* I am not solely led
By *nice* direction of a maiden's eyes:
Besides the *lottery of my destiny*
Bars me the right of voluntary choosing:
But if my father had not *scanted* me
And hedged me by his *wit*, to yield myself
His wife who wins me by what means I told you,
Yourself, renowned prince, *then stood* as fair
As any comer I have look'd on yet
For my affection.

Students were asked to identify the exchange, naming the speakers, the situation, and the play, as well as to gloss the italicized words and phrases. While *The Merchant of Venice* was, as we have seen, already a culturally familiar text and one that moreover could easily be lent to racialized discourse, Jordan's particular choice of Morocco's courtly speech to Portia nevertheless appears remarkable. Despite the passage's rhetorical interest, its subject matter, marked as it is by a declaration of exceptional identity, seems unlikely to lend itself to a broad audience that might be interested in the management of the passions, the usual purpose of extracts found in McGuffey's and elsewhere in the primer tradition. Nor could Morocco's eloquence on his own behalf, meant to counter Portia's presumable resistance to being wooed by an African, be enlisted on behalf of "race knowledge" as had the straightforward racism of Antonio's meditation on Jews. Jordan showed a notable interest in this minor character; in the 1897 entrance examination, students are asked: "By what line of argument does the Prince of Morocco persuade himself to choose the golden casket?"

Similarly, in the examination question for May 1895, applicants are presented with Shylock's speech denouncing Antonio as a Christian, referring both to his tribe and his "sacred nation" (a phrase that students were particularly asked to gloss, along with "usance" and the phrase "there where merchants most do congregate"); in 1898 students were asked: "Was Shylock treated unjustly? Give the reasons for your answer." This question appeared in the same examination where students were also asked to explain the following passage from *Merchant*, again paying particular attention to italicized words: "The Duke cannot *deny* the *course of law:* For the commodity that *strangers have With us in Venice*, if it be denied, *Will much impeach the justice of the state.*"

Jordan, a noted icthyologist, was also well-known as a eugenicist. To be sure, Jordan was no crude racist: he hoped that evolution would cause human society to develop past the point where slavery was anything but repellent, and he seems to have engaged directly, amicably, and more than once with San Francisco's large assimilated Jewish population. At the same time, Jordan was the author of such studies as a 1902 volume entitled *The Blood of the Nation: A Study of the Decay of Races Through the Survival of the Unfit.*[38] "Blood" was for him, "while technically incorrect," nevertheless a potent metaphor for the work of heredity and indeed a "symbol for race unity" (9). In this treatise he proclaimed "the superiority of the Anglo-Saxon" (29) and averred that "wherever an Englishman goes, he carries with him the elements of English history. It is a British deed he does, British history he makes. Thus, too, a Jew is a Jew in all ages and climes, and his deed everywhere bears the stamp of Jewish individuality" (9).

Although Jordan never specifies a positive content for his tautological statement "A Jew is a Jew," it requires no great stretch of the imagination to read his focus on Shylock's utterances as eliciting from applicants an engagement with eugenicist premises concerning raced, Jewish identity. By the same logic, the emphasis on Morocco's "shadow'd livery" in the 1893 examination lends itself at once to affirming the reality of racial difference, of the matter of "blood," and to the possibility of revaluing it positively, at least insofar as Morocco's emphasis on his worth and Portia's response to him are concerned.[39] In the wake of Delia Bacon's and Ignatius Donnelly's autodidiactic efforts to recast Shakespeare as Francis Bacon, the "father of English Science"—that is, to place the texts of Shakespeare's plays in the ambit of the scientific knowledge in the late nineteenth century—Jordan seems to have offered a more authorized and even, within the parameters of the pseudoscience of eugenics, progressive recalibration of the tendency to read Shakespeare as a font of racialized knowledge.[40] The possibility glances at my initial claim about Shakespeare's centrality and the way his texts lent themselves to new ends—ends that, if my surmises prove accurate, are clearly related to historically congruent discourses about race and national identity, as they are worked out through educational practices.

* * *

As Jordan's questions about *The Merchant of Venice* and the play's absence from the curriculum of the City College of New York suggest, there are myriad factors at work in the new privileging of some Shakespearean plays over others in this period of formation for the pretertiary, public canon. It may be speculated that some Shakespearean texts, once central to the rhetorical and indeed even forensic tradition when introduced as fragments, are deemed less able to accommodate questions that ask for critical reflection or aesthetic assessment. As Mary Trachsel has argued, the College Board became more and more concerned with students' ability to demonstrate a specifically literary (and institutionally congruent) form of knowledge, a demonstration that, in turn, necessitated the reading of whole plays rather than selected speeches aimed at performance.[41] This may be why *King John* and *Henry VIII*, extracts from which once had regular currency in McGuffey's and other versions of the nineteenth-century educational-oratorical tradition, began to drop out of currency, in favor of *Macbeth* above all.[42] Another reason may well have been their connection to British history, a connection all the trickier to negotiate in an educational climate where the demand to produce citizen-elites was tied to a recursive Anglocentrism defined by root stock rather than by a continuing political alliance with Britain as a nation-state. Even as a discrete discourse of literary aesthetics emerges, however, as the examination demands a shift away from the demonstration of rhetorical and compositional skill and toward summoning forth a type of written performance presumably remote from the moral taxonomies of the primer, *Julius Caesar* and *The Merchant of Venice* manifest a certain staying power. Thus, answering a 1903 examination question necessitates an understanding, however rudimentary, of character: "Compare the mental struggle of Brutus and the conflict in Shylock's mind between avarice and the desire for revenge" (quoted in Trachsel, 85). Needless to say, the form of the question does not preclude an adversion to racial stereotypes, nor, for that matter, to the tropes of patriotic zeal.

However, some plays must have been dropped for reasons that had less to do with the analytical priorities of formalized literary study and the emerging profession of English than with the role Shakespeare played as avatar of national identity, now understood not so much in terms of patriotic duty as in terms of racialized boundaries. Witness both the persistence of *Merchant* and the all-but-total absence of *Othello*, now generally regarded as one of Shakespeare's most exquisite constructions in language, from the turn-of-the-twentieth-century college examination and curriculum materials I have studied, Northern as well as Southern. As with *King John* and *Henry VIII*, selections from *Othello* had been a staple of schoolhouse oratory, and McGuffey students had studied the expressive capabilities encoded in, among other selections, Othello's final speech, apparently without regard to the race of the speaker (which, as I've suggested, may well have been suppressed in extract). Yet when it comes to the initial college selections with which I have been concerned, interest in the play is scarce, virtually nonexistent. This might seem the more surprising given that Elaine Brousseau has described *Othello* as "Shakespeare's American Play," a staple of the nineteenth-century stage.[43] Or, more precisely, of the minstrel theater, where, as Alexander Saxton has argued, the burlesquing of racial difference is part of the construction of white nationhood.[44]

It is naturally hard to account with certainty for the omission of *Othello* from the limited collegiate examinations and curricula I have surveyed. The College Board's lists were influential, but hardly all-determining: witness the appearance of the play in the texts set for Harvard's own examinations in 1882 as well as in the Columbia curriculum of 1898.[45] And if the absence is motivated, Howard University may well have bypassed the play for reasons wholly different from those that obtained at, say, the University of Virginia. Even so, given the interest in race identity and race knowledge that appears intermittently in contemporary educational materials, and given as well the growing unease in the wake of the Civil War about interracial desire and its consequences, it seems that the movement from oratorical selections to whole plays might have rendered *Othello* a peculiarly volatile text. The word "miscegenation" emerged in American legal discourse starting in 1863, replacing the older term "amalgamation"; in juridical opinions of the time, *Othello* became a touchstone for, as William Lamartine Snyder termed it in the title of his 1889 study, the "legal perplexities of wedlock in the United States."[46] Debate also focused on whether Shakespeare could possibly have meant to endorse a union so contrary to sense—a sense, that is, exquisitely, even paranoically, calibrated to the affective possibilities of a nation in which slaves were no longer chattel. And such erotic paranoia was by no means a purely Southern phenomenon: the U.S. district court entry that introduced "miscegenation" to the realm of legal discourse in America in 1863 occurred in the Southern District of New York, that is, in the New York City that was so significant when it came to institutionalizing College Board protocols—and which in that same year was riven by anti–Civil War Draft riots, during which eighteen black citizens were lynched, five forced into drowning, and seventy more disappeared and were presumably killed.[47]

The burgeoning discourse concerning the criminalization of "mongrel marriages" coincided with the fact that *Othello*, publicly unobjectionable to white educators when previously encountered in decontextualized oratorical extracts or to white citizens in parodic minstrelsy, was not featured in the College Board's initial efforts to modernize—and homogenize?—admissions requirements. It must also be remembered that the board's emphasis on Shakespeare reinforced the enshrining of the playwright as the bearer of highbrow, because Anglo-Saxon, values that Levine has described as occurring at this same historical moment. In this regard, it is tantalizing to wonder even about the fetishistic prominence of Shakespeare's less obviously problematic Scottish play, especially in light of the parallel emphasis given to Sir Walter Scott's novels in College Board reading lists. A New York University dissertation, published in 1916, notes that Scott's writings and Shakespeare are useful texts for teaching "race heritage" in the public schools.[48] Absent a significant amount of further information, caution must be used in pushing this suggestion too far: did no English history serve such a purpose? Did *Macbeth* constitute a text at once useful for the inculcation of literary quality and for the representation of "race" as well as gender to an educational discourse interested in such matters?

* * *

The new demands made of old propositions position the secondary school canon as a residual formation, a bit of cultural sedimentation that continues to function to fulfill the aims of an older regime even as it does a different form of productive work in a newer one. The more familiarly discursive demands of early twentieth-century questions may attest, that is, to the new power of English departments to establish a humanist-text-based literacy as the benchmark for university performance.[49] But aesthetics, precisely because it is foregrounded as a new dominant, demands the at-least partial annexation of a prior dispensation whose aims were more overtly interpellative, more clearly directed at using Shakespearean excerpts to draw the strict boundaries of citizenship. It is not that different Shakespeare plays were never brought in to serve the new purposes of formalist competence; rather, it is that a few of the old plays return, again and again, as though to guarantee the ideological legacy of primary literacy a continued, if submerged, life.

Above all, too, it is the recognition that what may once have been a dominative practice does not persist as such under historically variable conjunctures. That the early years of the twenty-first century are not identical to, or even isomorphic with, the state of affairs that obtained one hundred years earlier is really not open to question. While more recent academics have pursued the opposite notion, critically attending to the uses to which Shakespeare has been put in the manufacture of hegemony, or, alternatively, to the Right's assault on the expansion of the university literature curriculum, it has not noticed that Shakespeare persists as an inescapable part of the curriculum that precedes it.

On one level, to say as much is simply to suggest that education only built on the general knowledge constituted by nineteenth-century primers such as McGuffey's readers, within which selections from Shakespeare were already to be found. Yet however popular they were, those readers were allied with an irregular system of education that seldom, if ever, led to high school or college. In other words, in order for Shakespeare to be understood as public culture at the present moment, the texts have to have been displaced from their prior role in education—or, perhaps, to be positioned as lost, as rarefied, elite, and implacably opposed to the mass forms then in emergence. That positioning is, as I've suggested, highly familiar.

If the bygone administrations of the College Board gave rise to a form of subjectivity elite at its inception because it depended not only on the possession of sufficient cultural capital to acknowledge aesthetic effects but also of the leisure to read, and the monetary capital to acquire, whole plays rather than extracts, that is no longer precisely the case. Given the all-but-mandatory nature of a university education now for employment in many routine clerical jobs, and given as well that some estimates indicate that 40 percent of the U.S. populace will have had some college education in the very near future, the gap that we reify between college on the one hand and primary- and secondary-level education on the other needs denaturalizing, since reading the educational system as an articulated continuum made so by historically distinct forces will better enable a materialist analysis of Shakespeare in the schools and hence in American life.

Despite frequent concerns with the purported elitism of academic practice to which the only antidote appears to be an engagement with mass-cultural figurations, most academics concerned with the study of English (scholars of composition and rhetoric importantly excepted) have had nothing to say with respect to the educational practices with which we are indeed in a position of comparative, and unexamined, privilege. Beneath our critical radar has been the production of Shakespeare in educational venues other than our own, yet another instance of what I have termed "extramural" Shakespeare. Here it is the proximate object that stands in no easy because inversely specular relation to university practice; without the hydraulics of carnivalesque inversion, the history of Shakespeare in the schools has passed by and large without notice, as without consequence for our labors and interpretive ends.

Concomitant with that history, however, is the growth of a market in, rather than for, Shakespeare, one driven by pedagogical agendas but also in excess of them, as the near-eternal proliferation of new editions of Shakespeare—some with critical materials, some with selections from contemporary texts, a preferred form for every pedagogical imperative—attests.

Part of the market in Shakespeare, however, is not legitimately—officially—pedagogical but illegitimately so. I have already touched on the study guide in the preceding chapter: such substitutes for the "real" text are, in a nonjudgmental dispensation, iterations of a famously unstable canon, merely alternative performances of the Shakespearean. And then there is the subset of publications that concerns itself with the heavy business of rendering the ineffable inaccessible, that deems Shakespeare as susceptible of simplification for those of ironically little wit—"for Dummies" or "Idiot's Guides."

For all the irreverence of the titles, however, such productions apparently leave the veneration of Shakespeare untouched, as though a self-mockingly acknowledged inadequacy covered over a desperate longing to be admitted to the mysteries left unslaked by the compulsory encounters of high school. A "real" "dummy"—someone who for complex socioeconomic reasons had not attained a high school degree and whose knowledge of Shakespeare would therefore be fugitive—would, I venture to guess, feel too accurately interpellated by the faux-insulting title for those heretofore exempt from the market in books by and about Shakespeare to find use in such volumes. However important the market continues to be as an arbiter of educational practices (via the economics of textbooks and the prevalence of study guides) and as a rival to those practices (notably, through material ancillary to Shakespeare films, as I'll argue in the next chapter), its more direct productions, including televisions parodies, advertisements, and the like, depend on a Shakespearean substrate that is itself the product of a prior educational familiarity, of an interpellation the more interesting for its evident incompleteness, which is to say the refractoriness of those who have ostensibly been hailed by Shakespeare.

But the market in Shakespeare is not confined to print, as has been variously acknowledged by such scholars as Richard Burt and Barbara Hodgdon. And my own discussion of the necessary analytical priority given to education as an agent of mass induction into the ranks of the Shakespeareanized has already noted the importance of such other mass forms as film, a trend inaugurated by Vitagraph that persists, albeit in altered form, well into the present, as the example of *Looking for Richard* inevitably suggests.[50] But it is also the case that competing discourses reveal that by the end of the twentieth century, the mass-educational project was under siege, or, alternatively, was undergoing a structural recalibration that sought to bring education itself more directly under the aegis of market forces: hence school vouchers, the for-profit university, school consultancy firms that assumed the management of public schools in lieu of the state or local municipality, and even the increasing commercialization of homeschooling products. No wonder then, if the culture industry, in promoting certain Shakespeare films for classroom consumption, seeks to cut out the middleman educator.

CHAPTER 4

The Shakespeare Film, the Market, and the Americanization of Culture

The conjunction of Shakespeare and film is about as old as the medium itself. That said, the questions that might be asked about the conjunction depend upon the historical moment being considered. Uricchio and Pearson have suggested that early cinema positioned Shakespeare as a central figure of Anglo-Saxon patrimony for non-Anglophone immigrants deemed in need of enrollment in the national imaginary; in this, cinema's work is not so different from that undertaken contemporaneously, albeit in a significantly different register, by the College Board.[1] As I've suggested in the preceding chapter, the College Board has bequeathed us a Shakespeare who is an inalienable part of the educational apparatus, one whose subsequent presence pervades ever-lower levels of schooling: hence my argument that Shakespeare is now a part of American public culture. But even if the specter of the pedagogical continues, at times, to attach to Shakespeare on film, it stands to reason that a century or so after the medium and the playwright first came together, the discourse about both demands repositioning for what it reveals about the mutations of the cultural field in which we might place Shakespeare, since the emergence of mass culture as such and as the other of elite culture.

Consider, for instance, the premillennial Academy Award for Best Picture in 1999 to John Madden's *Shakespeare in Love*: with it, the Motion Picture Academy of America seemed to have made official a long-sought rapprochement between high and low, Shakespeare and film. Indeed, from the mid-1990s through to the end of the century, scarcely a month passed without a new Shakespeare-oriented project being scheduled or publicized. Kenneth

Branagh, already responsible for three such films, entered into a deal in 1998 with Intermedia Films to produce several plays for cinematic distribution, with each production not to exceed an hour and a half in running time; an adaptation of *The Taming of the Shrew*, *Ten Things I Hate About You*, was released in the spring of 1999; and Julie Taymor, the director of *The Lion King* on Broadway, released a *Titus Andronicus* that was, according to the April 1999 issue of *Vanity Fair*, "a triumph of avant-garde gore."[2] Although as recently as 1984, Richard Burton had stated that Shakespeare films were "box-office poison," based on more recent evidence, at least, it appeared they had finally turned into something more widely and commercially palatable.[3]

Given my focus on extramural Shakespeare in this study, it is crucial to ask why Shakespeare should have become so popular with the culture industry at the end of the twentieth century. My speculation about commercial viability seems to suggest that the undeniable increase in the number of films indexed a burgeoning public gusto for Shakespeare. Yet the fact of these films' appearance demands juxtaposing evidence of box-office appeal (where, that is, it exists) with the economic and ideological conditions that might have brought together Shakespeare, on the one hand, and the film industry, particularly the U.S. film industry, on the other, at this particular conjuncture. After all, the production agendas of the modern global cinema can scarcely be modeled by the simple law of supply and demand, even given Hollywood's dubious penchant for turning yesterday's success into today's formula and the handy fact that Shakespeare's scripts are essentially in the public domain, and so comparatively quick and cheap to develop. In light of Burton's remark, it is perhaps an irony that Shakespeare has a legible place in the tense priorities of commodity culture, where his name stands as a free-floating signifier for quality: consider Terence Hawkes's resonant "meaning by Shakespeare."[4] (Or consider a shopping bag from Trader Joe's, a chain of food stores, that features Shakespeare's visage—eyes blocked out, the better to pretend to disguise him—and the legend "A famous name we cannot reveal" over a narrative about its high-quality private-label goods.) Even if a given Shakespeare film is not a box-office success, then, the prestige of involvement might compensate filmmakers and subsidizing producers for any unsatisfactory profit margins.

To talk of immaterial compensation, however, is necessarily to engage with cinema's particular flexibility in serving as a site of ideological production: Hollywood in particular has been demonized by social critics who consider its mass representations the agents of moral collapse, even as the city has been decried as the leading edge of elitism. Such critics have also been notable among those bemoaning the apparent eclipse of Shakespeare by mass culture in the academy: hence the 1996 media furor to which I referred in the preceding chapter, occasioned by Georgetown University's ceasing to require that English majors take Shakespeare. The many excoriations of what was, after all, only a local curricular decision, one already quietly adopted by many colleges, indicates that in certain valorized segments of public discourse, Shakespeare has come to represent stable literary (and, by extension, ideological) values held to be under siege because of academic practice, which mirrors the mass audience's irresponsible fascination with Hollywood and other forbidden objects.[5] Given the general esteem with which *Shakespeare in Love* was regarded after its release, it is thus nicely ironic that a series of intensely familiar propositions about Shakespeare-as-author were being purveyed by a medium—film—presumed antithetical to the very values Shakespeare has been held to embody. (Falsely presumed, that is: as my prior references to Uricchio and Pearson's work on Vitagraph cinema make clear, at the emergence of the mass-cultural project as such, Shakespeare belonged on-screen, the better to serve as a vehicle of uplift to the widest number of people.)

This conjuncture of events suggests that the Shakespeare film explosion of the 1990s was uniquely well positioned to take the heat off the culture industry for its putative excesses and, incidentally, to repair the defects of the fall—by which I mean not only recent acts of apostasy in the academy, but potentially also the lack of enthusiasm toward Shakespeare felt by much of the U.S. population, to which *Looking for Richard* bears potent witness. By this token, the Shakespeare film seems to operate according to the familiar bromide: it is a sugar-coated pill for "the masses" (a term as anachronistic as its referent is elusive), even as the bottom line suggests that it is a loss leader for the accountants. While such mystifications probably reveal a number of persistent fantasies appropriate to analyzing the recent bardolatrous glut, I'd like to get at the issue another way: by examining the category "Shakespeare film" itself. Behind its connotative front, it has worked as a highly interested counter in recent discussions of the films, demanding nothing so much as acquiescence with the happy fact of proliferation—and obscuring the fact that even within the *medium* of mass culture, a number of divisions have emerged, revealing competing propositions not only about Shakespeare's place in the United States but also about the extent to which film is meant to "serve" a given play-text, and through it a fantasy of audience that is never far away whenever Shakespeare and the cinema come together. Should the adaptation of *The Taming of the Shrew*, for instance, which, like *Clueless*'s version of *Emma*, is translated to the demotic of the modern U.S. high school in which both texts are now frequently taught, be considered categorically indistinguishable from Taymor's production, featuring the much-lauded and classically trained Anthony Hopkins as Titus, and located in a postmodern Roman mise-en-scène that suggests Derek Jarman's *Edward II* in its temporal indiscriminacy? Is it enough that mall movie and art cinema have the apparition of Shakespeare in common for us to forget all the differences in direction, style, language, cast, audience—not to mention budget, production, and distribution—that would mark them as importantly distinct? Indeed, as I have argued, the contrary. Just as reading Kurosawa's *Throne of Blood* and *Ran* as evidence of Shakespeare's infinite translatability elides what is *not* Shakespearean in Kurosawa's Japanese films, so the false genre called "the Shakespeare film" seems to insist on the stability of Shakespeare as a sign and on the transparency of the film industry as a screen upon which Shakespeare is projected.[6] In the process, what is occluded is the possibility that the films, precisely as *films*, have constituted part of an important public referendum on Shakespeare's value and function at the end of the twentieth century.

As I've noted elsewhere in this study, Shakespeare was the object of one such referendum at the beginning of this century, when the formation of discourses of "highbrow" and "lowbrow," of the elite aesthetic object that signified access to higher education and the myriad forms of mass-cultural entertainment, first came into play, even as film proved newly useful for fostering immigrant consciousness of the Anglo-Saxon heritage of the United States. Given the pervasiveness—indeed the dominance, according to cultural studies scholars such as Michael Denning—of mass culture, that by-now reflexive division of the cultural field is all but exhausted as an analytic, even as the economic relations that brought the division its material potency continue to mutate.[7] Almost despite itself, Pacino's documentary reminds us that most U.S. subjects experience a mixture of resistance toward and intimidation by Shakespeare even as their educational exposure to the texts increases in scope. Nevertheless, the alienated reading and writing practices by which they first come to those texts have been less indicative of the inhibiting force of the elite as a category than an indictment of educational fantasies about high literacy, assimilation, and upward mobility on the one hand, and Shakespeare's "universal lovability" on the other—fantasies with which, as my analysis of *Looking for Richard* might indicate, cinema has often collaborated. At any rate, the social transformations that gave rise to the College Board and that have typified industrialized modernity have ultimately rendered Shakespeare a "tutelary deity" in the U.S. classroom, particularly at the secondary level, and so in the U.S. imaginary, within a more general and idealist dispensation that once deemed the study of literature an enabling form of distinction.[8] The recent cinematic phenomenon with which I'm concerned, however, represents a struggle over Shakespeare's place in U.S.

culture that is occurring extramurally, outside academic circles. While there has been much crucial work scrutinizing the role Shakespeare is asked to play in hegemonic formations, its direct effect on public discourse in the United States is at best hard to assess: academics surely do not commission, fund, or motivate Shakespeare films, and far too often they do not even conceptualize such films as economic, as opposed to ideological, agents.[9]

What is not hard to assess, however, is the recent dominance of the market in arbitrating questions of value capitalism was once content not to control directly. In such a regime, it may not be sufficient to have Shakespeare serve as a loss leader. Witness the film industry's targeting of the education system, a market long dominated by the generally expensive BBC/Time-Life video releases of the 1970s and 1980s. Publicity materials for *Looking for Richard* (whose box-office revenues were not particularly impressive) evince Hollywood's efforts to expand its audience—and in some sense to supplement, even supplant, trained educators—by offering to provide exercises to be used in class along with a video of the film, thereby redoubling the film's tendency to didacticism. That the culture industry, understood as a business, has begun its march on such heretofore neglected arenas suggests the way to characterize the referendum for which the films constitute effective evidence: as a contest between increasingly triumphal (at least before the stock market crash) market forces and literature as a regressive formation exempt from direct market instrumentality. While such regressive formations around the aesthetic tend to dominate in the U.S. imaginary (hence the Georgetown controversy), that such a struggle was staged in a cinematic forum changes the questions and makes the commodity status of filmed Shakespeare itself both a register of the debate and a marker of the terms of success, especially given the increasingly global cinematic market that extends from the United States outward.

Hence my interest in two 1996 productions: Kenneth Branagh's *Hamlet* and Baz Luhrmann's *William Shakespeare's Romeo + Juliet*, in distribution, in the United States and elsewhere, at approximately the same time.[10] Their simultaneity on the one hand and their marked differences as filmed commodities on the other, make it possible to consider them as embodiments of the extramural struggle over Shakespeare I've described. Kenneth Branagh's lavish and prestigious film embodies an increasingly regressive notion of cultural capital that is, in the United States and rather like Branagh himself, associated with the specifically literary legacy of Great Britain and with Shakespeare as an embodiment of originary (that is, Anglo-Saxon) cultural capital. In this regressive dispensation, the obvious value of *Hamlet* demands that it be filmed with reverence and that purely economic considerations take a back seat to creating a cinematic master-text. In contrast, Baz Luhrmann's film (like *Shakespeare in Love*) gives Americans a Shakespeare without tears, a Shakespeare devoid of the conventional trappings of "quality cinema" and an elite theatrical or literary tradition. The text's domestication to the aesthetics of U.S.-derived mass media signals the consonance between Shakespeare and the economic agendas of cinematic commodity culture. In each case, a proposal about Shakespeare, either as burnished (and imported) cultural good, or else as locus of excitement and irony already naturalized to the United States, informs and is subtended by the test of the market. As I have suggested, what is at stake is the possibility of a new national articulation around Shakespeare.

The comparative analysis that follows represents only a gesture at the specific financial underpinnings of the two films. A more comprehensive study of filmed Shakespeare in the United States, and ultimately in global commodity culture, would take seriously the fiscal maneuvers necessary to bring any Shakespearean adaptation to the screen: it would remember how both the market for such films, and all questions of funding, are changing historical phenomena, and recognize the increasing importance of the United States for all cinematic productions; it would factor in the role of transnational production coalitions in attempts to make niche-marketed cinema viable; it would learn more about how budgets are secured in relation to casting decisions; it would study how distribution deals are crafted in relation to larger studios, with the increasingly global market for cinema in mind; it would investigate whether and how video-rental revenues are projected and factored in, in advance of production; finally, it would read all local phenomena in the light of changing global trade policies (e.g., the General Agreement on Tariffs and Trade [GATT]) concerning film as a cultural product.[11]

Of course, the fiscal practices of the film industry offer only a starting point for understanding the larger business of Shakespeare—the financial resources that go into reproducing, publishing, disseminating, and professing the poems and plays, dispersed over a variety of practices and institutions—that make it possible for us to continue to debate his significance. Studying these quite literally material aspects of the Shakespeare industry would reveal at least as much about his shifting place in the United States in these perimillennial years as any curriculum controversy. And, if one takes Terence Hawkes's hint that "Bardbiz [is] merely the continuation of American foreign policy by other means," such revelations might, like Hollywood itself, have more than local, and more than ideological, influence (Hawkes, 153).

*   *   *

My point of departure concerning the film versions of the plays that proliferated at the end of the twentieth century is the naturalistic narrative lines along which they have often been constructed. As James N. Loehlin has usefully indicated, "[t]he realist Shakespeare film is characterized by the sort of mid-range naturalistic acting, cinematography and editing that is used in most Hollywood films. The characters are presented as 'real people,' in plausible makeup and costumes, and the film relates the narrative straightforwardly, without calling attention to the medium."[12] While earlier films, such as Olivier's *Henry V* and *Hamlet*, invoke the conventions of the stage or the sound set (or else those of art film as art, via highly self-conscious camera work), many Shakespeare-inflected films since then seem to have accepted that film is a "natural" medium for presenting the plays, debates about adaptations notwithstanding.[13] Shakespeare films may not be able to count on the ordinariness of television, the sense, according to Graham Holderness, of a medium completely interpenetrated with everyday life, present almost by default.[14] Nevertheless, like most films in distribution, such Shakespearean productions put a semblance of the ordinary on offer— even if a subset of the audience demands that those watching a Shakespeare movie follow the protocols of live theater, rather than of moviegoing. Indeed, that some spectators approached Branagh's *Hamlet* with the same reverence they would bestow on a live performance indicates the connection to be found between cinematic realism and correspondingly "ordinary" (which is to say conventional), even retrograde, propositions about the intrinsic value of the Shakespearean scripts on which these realist Shakespeares are based. In this sense, the disposition toward Shakespeare undergirding the category of "Shakespeare film" that I want to call into question seems most in operation when the audience conventions that hold true for film in general are not—when, that is, audiences expect Shakespeare films to be special cases of the cinema.

Kenneth Branagh's *Hamlet*, which follows on his film debut as *Henry V* (1989) and his subsequent production of *Much Ado About Nothing* (1993), will be my primary evidence for this case. The two earlier films clearly established Branagh as the cinematic successor to Laurence Olivier—which is to say, as the crossover actor, the classically trained British star who, when he moves from stage to sound set, carries along with him the prestige both of originary country and elite genre, and who in a U.S. context therefore operates as a guarantor of quality cinema. But however much the first films marked Branagh as a precocious and prematurely autobiographical phenomenon in the United States, neither *Henry* nor *Much Ado* signifies sufficiently as a canonical masterpiece. Not so with *Hamlet*, the consecrated vehicle for the reproduction of an influential model of male subjectivity and the presumable center of the Shakespearean canon in the public imaginary, both here and abroad.

Not surprisingly, the cultural importance generally ascribed to this text, which is sustained by cinematic as well as theatrical and critical history, has left ample traces on Branagh's film. His *Hamlet* is innovative in detail; nevertheless, it reveals Branagh's fidelity to modes of representation that are both reactionary in ideological terms and a contradiction in terms of the market for Hollywood-inflected realist cinema, to which it owes its primary aesthetic allegiance. Clearly, Branagh's at-times gratuitous casting reveals his investment in the nexus of value that is the Hollywood star system: witness the number of big-name American actors in minor parts, who are as likely there to secure funding as to represent the universality of the Shakespearean dispensation. Moreover, Branagh's directing serves to focus audience attention on his own performance, a performance that offers many instances of what Theodor Adorno has called "regressive fetishization"—moments, that is, whose only cogency comes from their nature as set pieces designed to generate a momentary affective response, rather than from their integral relation to a sustained narrative, experience, or interpretation of the play.[15]

Perhaps the most egregious instance of such a set piece occurs as Hamlet looks at Fortinbras's troops arrayed against the Polacks. When the movie was in theatrical release, it was the last scene before a much-anticipated intermission; it still marks the end of the first disk in the two-disk DVD release. With its swelling music and slowly craned camera rising up and framing Hamlet against soldiers in formation (a perhaps-deliberate echo of the rousing patriotism of the Crispin's Day speech in Branagh's more cogent film), this moment might manage to extort sentiment even from a spectator interested in reading the ambiguity of Hamlet's ever-diminishing form against the ever-louder triumphalism of the music. The crescendo that accompanies "My thoughts be bloody or be nothing worth!" propelled viewers into the light of the auditorium, having halted the action by implying that Hamlet's meandering quest for revenge has finally crystallized into resolve. When the lights dimmed again, however, that impetus was revealed (as the fidelity to script must inevitably reveal it) as purely sensational, beholden (like the chandelier-swinging, or the visually impressive yet illogically simultaneous eruption of Fortinbras's soldiers from behind the mirrored doors whose chambers don't communicate with one another) to a momentary cinematic effect that is for Adorno the sign of Hollywood's power to imprint the commodity aesthetics of mass culture on all comers, especially reproductions of the classics.

Yet however much his direction reflects the values of mainstream Hollywood cinema, Branagh's much-remarked-upon insistence that his *Hamlet* be filmed from an uncut script militates against the logic of the film market, which increasingly demands action-packed, and hence

Figure 2 *Hamlet.*

export-friendly, products rather than magniloquent four-hour epics.[16] On the evidence of Branagh's practice, Shakespeare's *Hamlet* is a sign of exceeding preciousness: hence the play around the monumental inscription of the dead king's name that serves as both a title-card and a parting shot. When, at the end of the movie, the inscription "HAMLET" is gradually obscured, the sequence suggests not just the beginning of Fortinbras's reign but the film's triumphal relation to its object: this comprehensive version having reached its end, *Hamlet* is done (for?) and need never be done again.

Despite the strong weight of performance practice throughout history, for Branagh, not one word of the play can be lost without peril. Nor, apparently, can inference or recitation pass without being inserted into the cinematic plenum, without, that is, being illustrated: thus the movie provides scenes from the fall of Troy, the panic of Hecuba, the private recollections of Ophelia. That at times the film seems to illustrate Hamlet's narrative moments emphasizes its author's position as a *literary* icon, rather than, say, purely as a dramatist—which is precisely, of course, how most of the U.S. populace comes to the plays. (Hence my students' ardent defense of Branagh's cinematic extravagance: more *Hamlet* has meant, for them, more clarity about a text that cannot at any moment or on any point be taken for granted.)

Thus Branagh's apparently perverse, and apparently counterproductive, notion of copiousness is not so innocent of market logic after all, if by that

Figure 3 *Hamlet.*

phrase one signifies a double appeal: at once to the earnest student looking for a reliable trot and to the niche occupied by fairly literate fans of cinematic adaptations of nineteenth-century novels, the presumable addressees for the "Shakespeare film" in all its unreconstructed glory. The conservative amplitude of the script, for instance, is well served by the anachronism of its setting in nineteenth-century Europe, with Blenheim Palace made to stand in for Elsinore. In this regard, Branagh's *Hamlet* approximates the period and style of Masterpiece Theater and Merchant-Ivory productions, aligns itself with them in interpellating a U.S. audience interested in, and comfortable with, British-inflected representations of texts from the distant (but not too distant) past. Given the attention to luxurious settings and interiors that characterizes these films, this time before might be called "the upholstered past," made for ease and relaxation, a past that is domesticated, effortlessly knowable.[17] The nineteenth-century setting enables the audience to recognize a cultural fantasy of both history and Shakespeare as all-inclusive: via the liberal and anachronistic palliative of color-blind casting, Branagh neutralizes the historical imbrication of the nineteenth-century nation-state in imperialist formations, and turns the court of Elsinore into a fiction of millennial diversity.[18] (That actors of color are given comparatively few speaking parts reveals the impoverishment of this dispensation.)

Like the BBC and Merchant-Ivory productions I've mentioned, indeed, like *Shakespeare in Love*, Branagh's *Hamlet* therefore participates in a belated discourse of bourgeois prestige, where movie attendance demands, at the very least, an investment in a prior tradition of high (verbal) literacy, a competence entirely befitting the conservatism of Branagh's interpretation itself, despite his articulated desire to render Shakespeare accessible to all. If dominant cultural formations around the pre-eminence of the aesthetic artifact work to maintain their hold through reproduction, then this *Hamlet*, like some of the other films that appeared in the 1990s, serves to sustain elitism in the apparently paradoxical form of a mass-cultural artifact. The splendors of the mise-en-scène Branagh has deployed provide a precise counterpart for the film's status as a visual rendition of traditional literary capital, and thus, it seems, an effective reassurance to recent polemicists that Shakespeare is still a locus of familiar (and pedagogical) value.

And yet this traditional capital is a form of wealth not always valued by the largest segments of the current market, among them the youth market, at whom several other Shakespeare films I mentioned were aimed. Branagh's difficulty in getting the film funded—and the promise, recorded in his introduction to the filming diary for *Hamlet*, to cut it drastically for home distribution—betray the persistent return of the sentiment with which I began: Shakespeare and the movies don't mix. Given his film's grosses in cinematic release, it seems that Branagh's attempt to revivify the discourse of humanistic cultural capital is one his distributor, Castle Rock Entertainment, might well have found less than economically compelling.[19] The discourse that ratifies *Hamlet* is too attentive to an audience doomed to recede as the exchange value of a specific model of high literacy recedes for it to succeed in any but the niche market I have described. Branagh's *Hamlet* might, via its own auteur's efforts, propose a Shakespeare recognizable, even appealing, to those who opposed Georgetown University's decision to cease requiring a course devoted to the author. Indeed, it might even be considered as an interesting supplement by the film industry to the perceived deficiencies of higher education—be read, that is, as evidence that the market has become interested in resecuring cultural dominants perceived to be under siege, as I indicated in connection with *Looking for Richard* earlier in this study. But in itself the film can only account for the value of a cultural good to those who, in one form or another, are already disposed to ascribe value to that good.

Branagh's subsequent deal with Intermedia Films seems to have dissolved after the 2000 appearance of *Love's Labour's Lost*. So prominent and useful a Shakespearean entrepreneur has not entirely disappeared from the scene, especially given the comparative profitability of both *Henry V* and *Much Ado About Nothing*: along with Home Box Office (HBO) Productions and BBC Films, in 2006 he produced a version of *As You Like It* set in nineteenth-century Japan for American cable television, which seems to have been broadcast only once, in 2007.[20] That in itself is unusual: HBO usually repeats its original programming several times. Moreover, unlike many other HBO-commissioned films, it was also never commercially released to movie theaters in the United States. Taken along with the initial restriction of Branagh's Intermedia releases (including *Love's Labour's Lost*) to less than half the running time of *Hamlet*, and the apparent dissolution of that Intermedia deal, the obscurity of Branagh's most recent Shakespeare production indicates the relative failure of his grand and marmoreal comprehensiveness and hence the insolvency of bourgeois Shakespeare in the years around the new millennium.

* * *

Branagh's bourgeois Shakespeare is, at base, recognizable as the Shakespeare of residual Anglophilia. When he claims that "the man [Shakespeare] is for everyone"—and then undergirds that claim by prominently featuring U.S. comedians such as Billy Crystal and Robin Williams—his directorial broadmindedness turns the film itself into a spectacle of postimperial British largesse eager to extend itself ever further into the U.S. imaginary.[21] But is Shakespeare still Britain's to control, especially as a cinematic commodity? Consider in response Baz Luhrmann's brilliantly polished, exciting, and troubling *William Shakespeare's Romeo + Juliet*, whose Hollywood-action-picture-inflected energy cannot but stand in stark contrast to Branagh's more stately, more stereotypically British, film. Set in a fictive and run-down Verona Beach but filmed comparatively cheaply in an economically depressed Mexico City (and jointly produced by companies in Australia and Canada as well as in the United States), *Romeo + Juliet* offers a siting of Shakespeare more appropriate for, and symptomatic of, the neocolonialism of the global youth market that emanates from the United States outward. As most readers might suspect, Luhrmann's film has proven far more profitable than Branagh's: approximately two-thirds of its estimated budget of $14.5 million was recouped in its opening weekend in the United States. Indeed, that the Internet Movie Data Base provides some indication of European grosses and that it documents rental revenues in excess of $22 million attest to the fact that Luhrmann's movie has been positioned as something of a phenomenon.

Some of the reasons for its comparative success are not far to seek. Luhrmann's direction clearly locates *Romeo + Juliet* in cinematic, rather than literary, history (it alludes to Hollywood Westerns in the brawls between Montague and Capulet, for example) in more structurally and thematically relevant ways than does Branagh's film. And the quick-cut editing, the soundtracks, and the movie's fashionable costuming are obvious components of its success, insofar as they already indicate the movie's exuberant capitalization on the prevalent mass aesthetics of a global youth market.

Much more could be said about how the film reworks as well as exploits the codes of mass cinema. But this kind of attention obscures how it functions as a commodity, how it stokes mainstream desires while apparently wearing its "Shakespeare" with a radical difference. Particularly striking is the way the film glamorizes its essentially conservative invocation of racial, ethnic, and gender diversity. Unlike *Hamlet*, *Romeo + Juliet* has major parts played by actors whose nonwhiteness is significantly foregrounded; however, the way in which they are exoticized resonate better with U.S. policy retrenchments around affirmative action and minority rights in the post-Reagan years than with any genuinely progressive casting agenda. Despite the possibility that Leonardo DiCaprio functions as an object of attraction across genders, it is Mercutio, played by Harold Perrineau, an African American actor, who is assigned principal responsibility for any homoerotic subtext in his relationship to Romeo.[22] This is shown most spectacularly in his drag performativity, but it is also revealed by his terminal encounter with Tybalt, whose taunting, enraging query about "consorting" with Romeo is staged so as to become the verbal equivalent of gay baiting. It is also troubling that a character played by a black actor is additionally responsible for illustrating the downside of pharmaceutical stimulation: his "Queen Mab" speech repositions a potentially inspired poetic fantasy as hallucinatory and incoherent raving. (In contrast, Romeo's poeticizing is shown to be controlled and self-conscious, inscribed in a notebook and then validated as poetic by the uncomprehending plainspokenness of Dash Mihok's Benvolio.)

Even if the obvious collision of raced body and illicit activity is read as a durable figment of the white imaginary, as edited and scored (the music signals "trouble"), the scene does not invite a reassessment of its hoary staging of the black junkie so much as pile one form of othering, of outlawry, onto another. Harold Perrineau is an arresting, talented actor; however, like Des'ree, performing at the Capulet ball, or Quindon Tarver, the young choir boy who sings "When Doves Cry," he isn't allowed to steal the film so much as give it piquancy, entertainment value, "color." Similar arguments could also be made concerning John Leguizamo's Tybalt, whose Latin menace, conjoined with his implicit homophobia, are played off against the comparatively decent, tremulous, and Anglo-Saxon– or Celtic-seeming Benvolio; or about Paul Sorvino's operatic wife-beating grandee Capulet.[23] In contrast to many of their friends and relatives, the matching complexions of DiCaprio's Romeo and Claire Danes's Juliet suggest young love as a kind of haven for the epidermal elite of North America, caught in a hothouse of untrammeled and exotic passions.

Yet in presenting the ruling houses of Montague and Capulet as competing corporate entities in iconic skyline shots, Luhrmann images that the fantasmatically ripe and overdone violence is somehow related to capitalism rather than to blood and family, as in the original, or to race, as its spectacular casting suggests. It is clear enough that capitalism may provide a ready equivalent for the mixture of power, rivalry, and privilege that subtends the original enmity between Montague and Capulet—and, further, that racism and capitalist violence might be historically conjoined. Still, that the competing families are also corporate entities is not, at first glance, of much consequence for the diegesis: obviously, for all of Shakespeare's vaunted ability to offer up structures of feeling for emergent capitalism, he cannot have predicted the particular form of its violence, even if his language scripts the advertising billboards that crop up throughout the film. But if for Luhrmann capitalism seems significant only insofar as it adds to his image repertory, the production of his film cannot escape being embedded in its logic. The looming corporate presences on the skyline of Verona Beach—both corporate names, and, like "Trump," twin signs of well-funded egotism—therefore become my way into an analysis of how the commodity status of this particular Shakespeare film, and a good measure of its appeal, are secured by exploiting the benefits of location. After all, part of the reason Luhrmann chose Mexico City for the setting of this film was that, given the country's recent economic crises, "everything was for sale" there, as at least one magazine story had it.

Or on sale: the Hollywoodized film industry, like many other Northern enterprises, confronts the comparatively high labor costs of U.S. centers by working in locations where such costs can be kept down. While Toronto is a preferred venue for many film and television ventures that seek a generic metropolis as backdrop, the producers of *William Shakespeare's Romeo + Juliet*, it seems, have followed the lead of other types of industries in looking to the global South to minimize production costs and maximize profit, to a place where, by Hollywood standards, everything is for, or on, sale. Michael Denning has remarked in passing that Mexico has long stood as "Hollywood's other"; the Mexico that enables *Romeo + Juliet* to be produced affordably, however, and that the film in turn puts on display, is less purely and mythically primitive, more the secondary and disadvantaged partner in the North American economic relations structured by the shibboleth of the free market and dominated by U.S.-based formations such as NAFTA.[24] Evidence that Mexico is being positioned to function as the neocolonial outpost of its more highly capitalized neighbor to the north may be read in the insistence among reviewers and publicists that the movie's fictional venue be likened to Venice Beach or to Miami—to some place, that is, within the United States. Of course, that the characters speak English might be one argument for the imaginative translation; but insofar as having Italians speak English didn't bother Shakespeare, it seems less than convincing here as a reason. Rather, the displacement insists on the preeminence of the United States as a site for economic and hence cultural production, and this has consequences for the movie's positioning of Shakespeare.

The surplus value for *Romeo + Juliet*—its comparative success as a film commodity at the moment of its appearance—that Mexico City makes possible is extracted from the exoticized bodies of performers to whom I've already alluded: Leguizamo's Tybalt and Perrineau's Mercutio, in particular, endow the movie with the stylistic effects of its aspirations to the global postmodern.[25] This argument cannot engage meaningfully with the actual working conditions under which the movie was made: exactly how, for instance, shooting in Mexico kept costs down. But it can at least consider the diegesis as a symbolic guide. In bringing the narrative together with film's status as commodity, I want to draw on Marx's theory of surplus value to reveal how signification is secured in the manufacture of a cultural good that, like *Romeo + Juliet*, capitalizes on the benefits of an increasingly worldwide production system. It is the "exoticism" of Mexico City itself, the atmospherics provided by its hallucinatory pollution and its monumental statues, totems of Catholic devotion that loom at least as large as the family signs, that makes possible a productive accretion of value around this version of Shakespeare. This local color revalorizes *William Shakespeare's Romeo + Juliet* as a product designated for knowing, and Northern, consumers of postmodern kitsch, ironists with respect to a system of belief that, exteriorized, acquires status as a marker of style.

Thus the cinematic mise-en-scène reveals a canny sense of how to adapt multiculturalism for stylistic purposes that require no concession to understanding the complexity of racial or ethnic formations, a tendency already borne out by the casting. Consider the movie's proliferation of religious iconography, which constitutes perhaps the most striking element of its visual style, and which is the scenic counterpart of its significantly raced bodies. I have already mentioned the thrilling faux totalitarianism of the immense religious statues around which the action seems to pivot. But the indigenous Catholicism of Mexico has been mined for greater contributions to the look of the movie. The Madonnas, angels, candles, and florid bleeding hearts emblazoned on shirt and chest all serve to index the "passion" to be found in the script, and thus to supplement its suspiciously pallid and Anglicized "star-crossed lovers," whose underplayed performances were widely praised for a realness constituted precisely in relation to the excess that characterizes the rest of the movie. These iconic elements in their original siting are strongly associated with Latin American devotional practices to be found, presumably, in the very Mexico City where filming took place. In the film, however, they have been deracinated from context and character investment and set loose to signify the mainstreaming of a stylized and ironic consumption of global difference.

In her discussion of the way Latin American iconographic material has become transmogrified into trendy knickknacks, Celeste Olalquiaga notes that such iconography is originally meant to materialize an impalpable and, indeed, ineffable spiritual experience, whose very tackiness becomes an inverted measure of the sublime it records.[26] Yet the perspective that passes judgment on artifacts in terms of the decorum of elite art (even when that art is devotional) already presupposes a distancing between assessor and object, a failure to share the framework of devotion, and a consequent substitution of a slumming aesthetics removed from the emotive intensities of Latin Catholic religious practice. As Olalquiaga notes, "Ethnicity and cultural difference have exchanged their intrinsic values for the more extrinsic ones of market interchangeability" (39). To put it more precisely, in the regime of kitsch, objects associated with specifically nonmarket rituals of exchange have come to supply cheap commodities by whose means an ironic sensibility can be secured. In *Romeo + Juliet*, Latin American Catholic paraphernalia constitute an extradiegetic compliment to this ironized spectator, offering, instead of the bourgeois aesthetics of Branagh's *Hamlet*, the sophisticated bricolage of the multicultural market, on offer to the young consumers toward which the movie and its tie-in products seem principally to have been addressed.

The distance between such objects and those in their ambit that is the precondition of kitsch is modeled throughout the diegesis. When the very Anglo-seeming Juliet kneels to pray amid a wealth of angels, for instance, or when neon crosses proliferate in her tomb, the tableaus are visually arresting, but they are not to be read as meaningful articulations of either faith or character; they cannot be used to consolidate a "reading" of a Juliet steeped in Latinity, or to provide verisimilar evidence of Verona Beach's generally fervent Catholicism. These possibilities map out a paradox. On the one hand they depend on a more orthodox understanding of the ends, both aesthetic and interpretive, that Shakespearean instantiations ought to serve, by asking for a focus on character. On the other, to the extent that they thoroughly Latinized *Romeo + Juliet*, they would demand a *dislocation* of such traditional sensibilities and a movement toward the radically different Shakespeare that the film apparently puts on offer. Rather than engage with either possibility, however, Luhrmann's direction, unlike Branagh's, never presents Shakespeare as a straightforward focus of reverence; equally, however, it does not propose the text as a site for a genuinely critical engagement.[27] Rather, what the film's icono-fetishism reflects is the extent to which the vicarious experience proffered by kitsch can be extended even in the direction of (cinematic) Shakespeare. Taken to its logical conclusion, this would be to read the Shakespearean itself in *Romeo + Juliet* as something alien to the principal subjects addressed by the film, an object given value through the process of market exchange. In a word, Shakespeare would be little distinguishable from kitsch.

* * *

Should Baz Luhrmann's *William Shakespeare's Romeo + Juliet* be read primarily as a Shakespeare film? In light of the preceding analysis, this appears a perverse question, given the title's trumpeting of authorship: unlike Branagh's *Henry V*, where Shakespeare's name was suppressed from all advertisements, Luhrmann's film clearly revels in the connection.[28] That Shakespeare's name was not perceived to be a further selling point for a film directed by and starring a British actor then little known to a wider public may explain *Henry V's* laconic title; after all, so soon after Burton's remark that Shakespeare is poison at the box office, why should Branagh have made the risk to commercial success greater than it already was? By this logic, then, it would follow that *William Shakespeare's Romeo + Juliet* was already so assured of a market that it could risk affiliation with what Branagh's initial film feared to look upon.

Given that Luhrmann, whose only previous U.S. release was the critically acclaimed but hardly blockbuster *Strictly Ballroom*, was far from a household name at the moment of the second film's release, and given, too, the smart idiosyncrasies of this particular film, its distributors could hardly have been so assured, despite whatever audience guarantees DiCaprio and Danes might have seemed to provide. If the title *William Shakespeare's Romeo + Juliet* is indeed a marketing strategy, it represents a far more sophisticated sense of audience, and consequently of the film's position in the market, than was the case with Branagh's *Henry V*. Here, the relation between film and title, and hence between script and author, is one of both affiliation and disavowal: while nowhere is the connection to Shakespeare hidden—indeed, the script is comparatively faithful to Shakespeare—the very style of the film seems to deny relation. Deny it, that is, if one's sense of what a Shakespeare film ought to be like is extrapolated from *William Shakespeare's Romeo + Juliet's* cinematic antecedents, from a reserve of ideological propositions about literacy, pedagogy, mass popularization, and the work the Bard must be seen to do, the difference he must be asked to mark from consumer culture.

What I am not saying, I hope, is merely that Luhrmann's film gave us a Shakespeare for the 1990s: my suspicion in 2000, when an earlier version of this essay was first published, that his success will not be duplicated by other youth-oriented Shakespeare productions has been borne out, a fact that ought to put paid to continuing arguments about cinematic capacity to make the dramatist "relevant." Besides, if anecdote can be a nonce substitute for ethnography, Luhrmann's conception generated some resistance among the usual audiences for Shakespeare films: several colleagues can echo my experience in being asked by generally well-educated (and generally, although not exclusively, middle-aged and white) people whether we found the film offensive, which I take to be at least partly that audience's projection onto the academic of a fixed bourgeois aesthetics naturalized to the Bard. But what gives this particular film its provocative hold on other types of spectators can be read in the editing—not simply because of the pace it establishes, but because of the repeated collisions it stages between text and referent, which in this analysis might stand in for the collision between "Shakespearean" aesthetics and those of cinematic commodity culture, fabled (and pilloried) for their glamorization of violence. Take, for instance, the textual "swords" that are insistently represented by guns: the bracing anachronism is reinforced by tightly focused shots on those menacing, gleaming weapons, totemic icons of American movies.

The camerawork at these early moments, which by metonymic focus establishes the world of the diegesis, cannot but force the issue of incongruity between what is said and what is seen, between what literary tradition demands as visual cue and what film, as a medium, proffers in (self-conscious?) response.[29]

In the broadest possible sense, *William Shakespeare's Romeo + Juliet* works at such an incongruity. Throughout, what is said is certainly Shakespeare's language (although not conventionally recognizable as such), but what the film puts on offer is anything but "Shakespearean," by which I mean the conventionally historicist expectations activated by a film like Branagh's *Hamlet*. Indeed, even what is spoken comes under suspicion, precisely because it is not uttered in the orotundities mocked by Kevin Kline in *Looking for Richard*: the prosaic articulations of the cast were sometimes deemed by film critics to rob the play of its poetry, as though the paradoxical effect of Luhrmann's own species of textual fidelity were to consolidate by negation the essentialist quality of Shakespearean language. This reaction occurred despite the fact, as I have already argued, that the film gives us to understand when a speech is "properly" poetical and when it is to be understood

Figure 4 *Romeo + Juliet.*

otherwise. In establishing its own conventions about Shakespearean language, *Romeo + Juliet* puts aside the classic and theatrically inflected tradition of acting styles characteristic of Shakespeare films such as Branagh's and those of his predecessors, in favor of representing such language as, in the main, everyday speech, akin to the speech of advertising or of ordinary, even banal emotions. Such nondeclamatory vocalizing actually manifests the subsumption of a recognizably Shakespearean "voice" under the regime of the cinematic: what is seen—the gun, the bleeding heart, the star—cannot but be more important than what is said (if not sung) or by whom the script was produced. The priority of the visual—or, given the commercial success of the soundtrack, the musical—over a nicely deflated linguistic register insists on a new American identity for Shakespeare, one that a reverent Hollywood star like Pacino would be hard-pressed to duplicate.

Rather than claim that *William Shakespeare's Romeo + Juliet* is a Shakespeare for now based on any simple-minded and inevitably temporary sense of its "relevance," then, I propose instead that the film gives us a masterful accommodation of Shakespeare to the U.S. horizon, that it marks perhaps the first time that the dominant aesthetics of Hollywood are fully set loose to do their work on a text and author which, though naturalized already to the U.S. framework by educational and research institutions, tend to be reproduced as other, and as anterior to those institutions yet proper only to them. What, indeed, does it mean to claim that Shakespeare is "at home" in the United States? Certainly it does not mean, as Al Pacino seems to have believed in making *Looking for Richard*, ignoring the ideological apparatuses, mass education principal among them, that have already made Shakespeare pervasive here: in fantasizing that U.S. audiences only need to see Hollywood stars use Method acting to grapple with a British deity to be brought to worshipful attention, Pacino errs as readily as Branagh. Rather, given the millennial dream that we have witnessed the end of history with the demise of the Cold War, and the heretofore persistent fantasy that the predicted global triumph of the free market may precisely be read as the success of the American economic plan, to make Shakespeare at home in the United States is to render him, too, a direct apparatus of the market.[30]

In his exceptionally useful account of Shakespeare's institutionalization in the United States, Michael Bristol has argued that the Americanization of Shakespeare that began with John Adams in the late eighteenth century represents "a massive transfer of authority and cultural capital [from Britain] to American society."[31] This transfer of assets has not prevented an ideologically motivated and adventitious recourse to Shakespeare as Anglo-Saxon "race knowledge," as witnessed by the previous chapter. But it has also been accompanied by an increasingly flexible recasting of received tradition, notably the relationship between financial capital and the cultural capital to which Bristol alludes, which is to say between a "vulgar" but undeniable marker of class, and its shadowy, if metonymic, counterpart. Under current U.S. economic conditions, when part-time jobs in the humanities indicate that even academia has reconfigured labor for the age of flexible accumulation, possessing a wealth of literary knowledge seems more a guarantor of downward mobility than a muted and enabling echo of the prestige of money and birth. Luhrmann's *William Shakespeare's Romeo + Juliet* repositions Shakespeare for the realities of this millennial market, where, as I have argued concerning its religious iconography, surplus value is secured by means of what seems a familiar U.S. gambit: neocolonial outsourcing.

* * *

William Shakespeare's Romeo + Juliet is undeniably a smart and seductive text, even for a reader who insists that it not be interpreted as a found object. Consider only how the fleeting glimpses of advertisements in Shakespearean language seem already to adumbrate the preceding analysis. They tantalize as parodies of contemporary advertising's opportunistic appropriations of the Bard as a sign of excellence: remember that Trader Joe's shopping bag. At the same time, those very advertisements take seriously the film's necessary proposition that Shakespeare scripts the discourse of the diegetic everyday, which is to say, the discourse of its own fictional representation of public culture. To acknowledge these and other such complexities, to note the film's capacities to generate sophisticated readings, is to heed the way it interpellates a number of ideal readers: *William Shakespeare's Romeo + Juliet* has something for the semiotically inclined college professors who (despite the shame of it in some quarters) love mass culture, as well as for

Figure 5 *Romeo + Juliet.*

the DiCaprio fans who saw the movie five or six times; that is, for those who foreground the Shakespearean connection and those who, potentially, might disavow it, read past it, even see it as kitschy. But to say as much is also to acknowledge that *Romeo + Juliet* fulfills the role of the film commodity with particular expertise—at least, for one with a script by Shakespeare produced at the end of the century.

For these purposes, it simply does not matter that the film has the capacity to ironize the very formations around millennial Shakespeare that it supersedes. There was a time when, it seems, irony was considered to be the basis of an oppositional political practice, when, as Roland Barthes expresses it in *Mythologies*, "sarcasm [was] the condition of truth." I wonder whether such a modeling of distance ever did have the effectivity he claimed for it: Barthes himself scripted a sad fate for the leftist mythographer, cut off, alienated from the center of culture and from those whose consciousness she or he would attempt to re-form.[32] Nevertheless, it needs no ghost to tell us that cynical distance has gone mainstream. Like the English majors many of us have trained as resistant, canny spectators, debunkers of cultural myths who are now working in the advertising industry, irony has become a part of the sales repertory of capitalism. When the global force of free-market policy sets itself the task of vanquishing alternative cultural logics, it can even sell Shakespeare.

But it cannot sell the Bard for long; perhaps it does not want to. The efflorescence of Shakespeare films in the 1990s did not constitute the emergence of a growth industry but rather followed precisely the hyperaccelerated, novelty-seeking agendas typical of Hollywood cinema in an age of global capitalism. Not only did Branagh not continue to produce Shakespeare films; neither did Luhrmann, although the logic of my analysis might seem to suggest that he or someone following in his wake should have done so. My point, however, was not to prognosticate the future but rather to suggest one concrete way in which Shakespeare, as a public object with a historically variable relationship to mass culture could, under the right circumstances, emerge from the cloak of the pedagogical from which he seems difficult to alienate, and into the direct light of market relations.

There are, of course, myriad other ways this suggestion might have been pursued, which would complicate my schematic separation of education from market forces. Witness the vigor with which numerous publishers have attacked the textbook market, from comprehensive one-volume editions of Shakespeare to selections based on genre or popularity; from single plays published with a wealth of contextualizing documents or important critical debates to student-oriented summaries of scholarship on a given subject pertinent to Shakespeare studies; and on to publishers once best-known for producing cutting-edge scholarship but now more heavily focused on monographs suitable for course adoption. If, as I suggested in chapter 2, SparkNotes has refashioned the student study guide for an era of student-centered collaborative learning, what growth market there is in academic publishing also puts the student at the putative center of address—and of consumption. This forceful reinstallation of Shakespeare in the schoolroom might seem paradoxical given the recent spate of biographical works aimed at the general (i.e., nonclassroom) reader, of which Stephen Greenblatt's *Will in the World* is the best-known example. Seen another way, however, Greenblatt's book, and others like his, might be taken instead to indicate the extent to which academics have come to recognize—or fantasize about—the public character of Shakespeare.

But as my analysis of Pacino's documentary has already indicated, that public (at least some segments of it) is not quite at the point of address imagined for them by academic—or, for that matter, celebrity—fantasy. If some subjects, like Pacino's walkers in the city, aver a wholehearted, even gleeful, resistance to bardic messianism, others occupy a more elusive because more contradictory space. Evidently possessed of sufficient cultural capital to know Shakespeare well enough to offer bemused critique, as perimillennial, postmodern subjects, they articulate their relation in terms of skepticism and distance, a homology, if a depoliticized one, of the very suspicion of the Bard's cultic power intrinsic in cultural materialism as well as in Luhrmann's film. At least as exemplified by Ira Glass's discourse on *This American Life*, which I discuss in the next chapter, such removal confirms that Shakespeare and elites are no longer in a one-to-one correspondence.

And yet, almost despite itself, the public radio broadcast introduces another possibility, which represents the countermove in the dialectical analysis I have been at pains to pursue. While Shakespeare is demystified, even ironized, by one segment of the broadcast, his texts retain the capacity to represent an alternative, utopian dispensation even when they are overcoded with cultural noise about Shakespearean value. (It is perhaps no accident that *This American Life*'s episode focuses on a production of *Hamlet*). Such social dreaming cannot, of course, substitute for concrete political action; moreover, it is easy enough to dismiss the moments when, as I will claim, it is being expressed as merely a familiar ideological *re*-mystification. But since the possibility for another account of Shakespeare must rest, in part, on a willingness to hear and think otherwise, it is to the analysis of that difference that I now turn.

CHAPTER 5

Social Dreaming and Making Shakespeare Matter

Thus far I have been at pains to suggest that it is only by attending to the way in which institutions such as the pretertiary school and the latter-day culture industry have served as privileged and even competing sources of dissemination that we can truly begin to locate Shakespeare extramurally, in perimillennial public culture in the United States. Moreover, it has been my contention that we must begin to speak of Shakespeare as public—that is, as a discursive object whose imaginative extensions belie the obsolete modernist division of culture into high and low, and whose material presence far exceeds any straightforward description. It is only in doing so that we can jettison the anachronistic and obfuscating assessment that Shakespeare remains principally the province of elites who, one hundred years ago, sought to ally him with hegemony and a racialized patrimony in the face of new immigration patterns, and whose legacy is presumed to persist virtually uninflected. As this study has tried to suggest, the subsequent work of the twentieth century has been to extend the reach of Shakespeare into the secondary school and even farther into the mass-educational apparatus, where familiarity with at least a handful of the plays has fueled a series of formations, from NEA initiatives to documentary and film adaptations. Even these cinematic conjurations of Shakespeare seldom escape what I've called the pedagogical imperative, however much they define themselves as antidotes to the schoolroom. At the same time, the growing alliance between education and market forces suggests a way in which some, at least, of the Shakespeare films of the 1990s aim to supplement, perhaps even rival, the state-sponsored national educational system that gave rise to mass familiarity with Shakespeare in the first place.

But I want to conclude with a recognition that Shakespeare in perimillennial culture cannot truly be understood without acknowledging the persistent power of his name and his texts to represent an alterative dispensation, despite the ideological ballast with which he is fraught and despite the air of the classroom that cannot but attach itself to this so-called elite figure above all. In support, I could point to signs of lively engagement with the plays to be found online, from nonacademic discussion boards to fan fiction.[1] Although much that is valuable might be gleaned from such sources, Constance Penley's study of slash fiction produced by fans of *Star Trek* offers an exemplary caution and corrective to those interested in examining communities in whose interactions they are not otherwise ongoing participants.[2] Such analysis can seem parasitical regardless of intention, a problem long familiar to anthropologists, ethnographers, and cultural studies scholars. Additionally, attention to e-fandom would seem to place Shakespeare in some zone of exemption from more concretely institutional representations, whereas my argument is that Shakespeare's roots in the American classroom ,which lends him the aura being anterior to or removed from everyday culture, mean that extramural formations are always hybrid, a combination of schooled fantasy and its local and quotidian transformations. More to the point, the relationship of amateur formations to more official (and inertial) ones cannot be calibrated in advance. Although the fact that such a fan culture exists confirms my argument about Shakespeare's pervasiveness in its most basic form, I suspect my mediated representation of it would say more about academic fetishizations of the popular than the possibility that even in the most overcoded, fraught situations, Shakespeare might represent an imaginative alternative yet worth attending to.

That said, a prison performance group enacting *Hamlet*, the focus of this chapter, represents that kind of an overcoded and fraught site for the study of Shakespeare, the more so in that in the understanding of many Americans, prison culture is almost inevitably a materially as well as ideologically mediated experience of otherness. Moreover, the problem of mediation is redoubled by the fact that my analysis concerns a public radio broadcast for *This American Life,* "Act V," that offers to represent the effect on inmates in the Missouri Eastern Correctional Center of preparing for a production of the final act of *Hamlet* in 1999.[3] Given my concern with how Shakespeare is conjured up beyond the walls of the academy, it might seem that I have shed the confines of one potentially restrictive and claustral institution only to multiply its totalizing effects elsewhere. Prison theater programs, within which Shakespeare looms large, are not compulsory—indeed, one general feature is that participation is voluntary but also contingent on the inmate's good behavior while incarcerated. Nevertheless, on first inspection they offer almost parodic imitations of the ethical-pedagogical imperatives long associated with the Bard in mainstream discourse, particularly when it comes to pretertiary education. For the world at large, it has been a cliché that Shakespeare is not only good, he is good *for* you, in a way meant to transcend the limits constituted by dominant social relations. It cannot but seem, therefore, that a prison Shakespeare program must write the redemptive possibilities of bardolatry even more hyperbolically, so that Shakespeare becomes the ticket not merely to personal goodness but to a transformation of the self administered with such magical completeness that personal and hence institutional emancipation—parole—must surely follow.

Inevitably, some residue of the transformational narrative I have just described so skeptically must linger, albeit invoked with more caution, a greater understanding of the material limits of Shakespeare's conjuring power and of the leverage provided by individual consciousness, than tends to be the case when prison Shakespeare becomes a subject of public interest. My aim here is to reclaim Shakespeare as a repository for social dreaming, the dispensation toward revolutionary transformation associated with the utopian Marxism of Ernst Bloch. Bloch's philosophical disposition led him to value even fleeting traces of a radically egalitarian future in the present, and it has been characterized by Jack Zipes in terms of its "non-synchronicity": that disposition has generally been out of step with Western Marxist discourse (including the forms that influenced both cultural studies and cultural materialism) as well as with life on the ground, which seldom if ever warrants statements of such optimism, such "learned hope."[4] Perversely enough, that is what renders him so useful for my purpose. Being out of whack with the times—Bloch's recognition that hints of a better world glimmer up under the most dismal circumstances, where they signify even if doomed to flash unfulfilled—makes it the easier to distinguish my claim that Shakespeare constitutes an important public reserve for utopian dreaming from the more typical positions I've outlined, which are marked by temporal as well as ideological expediency. As should by now be obvious, interest in prison Shakespeare has often been riven with suspect investments all the more telling for their superficially anodyne character: the narratives of redemption promulgated by agents of consensus depend for their success as narratives on precisely *not* recognizing the extent to which broad-scale educational programs, which documentably diminish prison recidivism, have been more and more the targets of a prison-industrial complex driven by the profit motive, as well as by a juridical climate that tends to affirms the utter irredeemability of offenders through such mechanisms as the three-strike rule. In such scenarios, prison stagings of Shakespeare retain an old claim to serve as alibi for the interests of the powerful, regardless of whether or not teaching the plays "does good" for concrete incarcerated subjects.

My analysis does not depend, however, on the specificity of what actually transpires in prison Shakespeare programs, although they are the subject of increasing scholarly as well as intermittent general interest.[5] Without direct, sustained, and hands-on access to its on-the-ground complexity, not to mention the sheer difficulty of such work, it would be presumptuous of me to attempt to characterize the material project. But *This American Life* offers a redaction of that work to its listeners, a redaction in which Shakespeare operates as both alibi and excuse. In the end, the broadcast is less about a Shakespearean performance for which a criminal history is posited as the ultimate form of Method acting than about the lives fragmentarily recorded in its service, lives that might otherwise go unremarked upon; nevertheless, it is because of Shakespeare's most famous play, *Hamlet*, that the broadcast makes its claim on the attention in the first place. In fact, mediation turns out to be the point, both when it comes to the fact of the episode's existence and to the peculiarities of its enunciation. Because the access *This American Life* provides to "big-house Shakespeare" and to the inmates in its ambit is refracted through the discursive institution of public radio, the show thereby creates a different sort of object for analysis: a hybrid born at the intersection of media, the culture of high literacy, criminal and juridical state apparatuses, and what remains of the public sphere in this perimillennial epoch.

As that might suggest, equally to the point is the fact that my own interest in "Act V" is not reasonably open to the particular charge of academic parasitism. Inevitably, my attending to the show makes me an auditory voyeur, listening unseen to carceral responses shaped by editorial intervention and offered in service of revelation—of knowing, *perceiving*, something. That position is, however, technically open to anyone: hence the importance of recognizing the broadcast as one surviving element in the public sphere, with all the limitations, and residual advantages, that such a formation implies.[6] The privilege of anonymity radio bestows is endlessly reiterable; but so, too, is the possibility of limited relation offered in this specific case, as I hope to suggest. Insofar as I am an educated listener with some dispensation to listen to (even if I do not always think well of) public radio programming, I comprise part of the audience at whom the broadcast is more specifically directed. If that means I must recognize how *This American life* interpellates me, at least I do not come to it imagining I inhabit a position of complete exteriority. And even if the framing portions of "Act V" expect its listeners to share an ironic distance from Shakespeare or a privileged experience of the plays, it is also important to acknowledge that relations of power occur as much on the receiving end as on the productive one, that as an auditor and an analyst I construe meaning preferentially and in contradistinction.

As a transactional space, then, my meditation on "Act V" is as complex and partial as it is mixed. To some, I'm sure, that renders it fatally compromised, destined not to escape a sentimental wish to read past the operations of power. But to allow analysis to rest with acknowledging those operations is as good as to admit that regardless of conjuncture, there is no going beyond ideology when it comes to extramural Shakespeare—a stance the more peculiar since it is precisely such a "going beyond" that we critics take on as our right, even as, potentially, we deny the possibility that others less credentialed in skepticism might be capable of the same moves. As I have noted, in the past, progressive critics have focused on identifying Shakespeare with cultural capital, thereby stressing Shakespeare's exchange value even as the critics' own complex investments in his texts—their freedom to *use* them, as it were—have proceeded more dialectically. All that I will be suggesting here, in effect, is that the same privilege to use and invest in Shakespeare (or, of course, not) be extended to those, like the inmates, whose comparatively belated access comes at some expense under undeniably fraught circumstances, and is displayed in public. Hence my claim—call it an insistence—that it is precisely through the broadcast, almost despite itself, that the best evidence for my point about the possibility of a better world, for the prisoners as well as for the listeners who are brought into imaginary propinquity with them under the sign of Shakespeare, can be gleaned.

And to make this claim, as I have perhaps already intimated, is also to insist that the old habit of calling out positions like the one I am articulating as compromised is as outdated as the sense that no more remains to be said about Shakespeare's public function than that he is the property of elites. Thinking conjuncturally necessitates jettisoning old a prioris where they do not serve the purpose and inventing alternatives that might better reflect the changed moment. If, to echo the provocative title of Courtney Lehmann's book, "Shakespeare remains," the ability of bard formation to persist against any critical articulation, whether it be of the residual fetishist of high culture, the cynical postmodern, or the critic of ideology, is not to be underestimated.[7]

* * *

During the heyday of cultural materialism, Alan Sinfield compared Shakespeare to the public airwaves—the very medium of transmission and a national birthright that, if understood properly, would have little to do with cultural capital and everything to do with a progressively ecumenical cultural politics.[8] And yet the airwaves themselves have become an increasingly strained and peculiar metaphor for public property in the United States, especially since Federal Communication Commission [FCC] decisions in favor of media agglomeration and the concomitant development of highly profitable monopolies have rendered much of broadcast radio homogeneous, completely unreflective of and unresponsive to the needs of the local. Programming diversity has become available only via subscription services such as Sirius and XM: tellingly, these two services have merged as of this writing. Perhaps more important, the growing prominence of cross-platform media content has rendered the digital environment the successor regime to the world of broadcast media; hence the residual idea of journalistic media as constituting a public sphere. Though Jurgen Habermas's concept of that sphere was, with some mutation and with a sense of a falling-off as market forces pushed their way to the fore, adapted from newsprint culture to describe the performances of mass-media sources of news and opinion that emerged in the last century, digital culture cannot readily follow in their wake.[9] Not only have the older media generally lost audience shares to the newer forms; no one formation has become hegemonic or is immediately likely to, and thus the likelihood of constructing *an audience*—which is to say, a unitary group of subjects functioning as a mass public and linked imaginatively to one another through temporary broadcast means—is small. The critical fanfare accompanying emerging digitality aside, what forms of collective consciousness will durably precipitate out of new media as yet await rigorous description.

In the increasingly pinched and even obsolescent iteration of the bourgeois public sphere constituted by broadcast media in the twenty-first-century United States, public radio—understood not as pure descriptor but rather as a proper name—occupies a contradictory place. For one, that name cannot but associate it with PBS, the televisual Public Broadcasting System that began broadcasting in 1970. The connection is more than nominal: although they are organizationally and fiscally distinct, both are products of the Public Broadcasting Act of 1967, whose aim was to form an institution, the Corporation for Public Broadcasting, dedicated to creating programming suitable for educational purposes and funded in part through the state and in part through audience contributions. Earlier in its history, PBS was known for its commitment to presenting cultural products marked out as elite or otherwise signaling "quality": hence such series as *Live from Lincoln Center, American Masters, the BBC/Time-Life Complete Shakespeare,* and, above all, British television products such as *Masterpiece Theatre,* with its alluring representations of what I have, in connection with the Branagh *Hamlet,* termed the upholstered and inevitably Anglophilic past. Some of that programming persists under the newly shortened title *Masterpiece*. But its gradual supplanting, especially during funding drives, by nostalgic productions of reunited pop groups from the 1950s, 1960s, and 1970s, and by shows dedicated to increasing personal wealth, are yet further indices of the diminishing value of once-prestigious cultural products in the current economic conjuncture, within which the market has become its own end: to put it bluntly, they do not bring in the money. When bracketed with public television's shift, then, public radio's own declining commitment to classical-music programming would suggest an enervated force, and hence the possibility of an equally declining market share that would trope the ebbing of the specifically class-inflected bourgeois public sphere.

In fact, the opposite is true for public radio. Its news programming has always had a comparatively broad and steady audience. But it is relatively new—and highly successful—cultural programming of the sort that *This American Life* exemplifies that marks public radio's movement away from received high-cultural values and toward a quasi-demotic discourse that could never be mistaken for populist. The show is distinguished not so much by the wide range of subjects it covers as by the voice in which it speaks, largely attributable to host Ira Glass and not dissimilar from those of other public radio "stars" of recent coinage—figures who, like David Sedaris and Sarah Vowell, have broken out into minor celebrityhood and, as cult authors, have linked public radio with the realm of letters and literature. Like many of their peers, they neither wear causes on their sleeves nor engage with the iconic high-cultural objects of a prior dispensation. Rather, they tell stories, offering drily witty meditations born of a performative disengagement from passion and high seriousness—and, almost equally, from aesthetic texts or experiences like Shakespeare's plays or, for that matter, the realm of political or civic engagement. Their tone is ironic, their concerns generally personalized. The wry performativity of these commentators seems carefully calibrated to a broadcast world now long conditioned by the Reagan-era demand for equal time and an NPR charged in recent years with liberal bias: since everything seems to take place under erasure, it would be hard to make a case for the affirmative value of any given articulation. It is telling that although I assume these speakers share at least some of my values, it is not always clear what the basis for my assumption might be, at least in the first instance.

But of course, what seems familiar and intelligible is the tone, reminiscent of the postmodern ironies of graduate school subjects in the humanities, among whom pop culture constitutes the default frame of reference: hence the appeal of *This American Life* to a demographic not always identical with that for public radio news programming.[10] In keeping with the stance of studied devaluation, Glass does not speak with the invariable eloquence of an older generation of radio broadcasters, whose vocal polish constituted the habitus of the profession. Glass's utterances instead seem extemporaneous, off the cuff: they remind me of the gropings and imperfections of ordinary speech without being themselves reducible to it. The infrequent moments when he stumbles are of a piece with the apparent artlessness of his discourse: his not an art that hides art in the traditional sense of making effect look uncontrived, but rather one in which the labor of coherence and the occasional failure to accomplish it are hallmarks. No room is left for doubt that Glass is an educated man; his performance, however, suggests an almost volitional gap between his evident cultural capital and the self who performs, a self who seems to mistrust the high polish of earlier commentators and to expect that his audience will, too. Hence my claim of a quasi-demotic discourse that is, if colloquial, also not particularly populist.

It is a performance with some consequences for "Act V": as my reference to the leisure-time productions of selfhood found in graduate programs suggests, the stance seems to betoken a well-hidden residuum of progressive politics at the same time it guarantees a distance—sometimes performative, sometimes, quite authentic-seeming—from the cultural fetishes of a prior dispensation. Among them is an unreflexive allegiance to Shakespeare. If anything, *Hamlet* is in need of remystification for the listeners interpellated by the broadcast, since it is initially represented as something of a puzzlement, a strangely exotic object despite its presumed familiarity. But it is not a remystification played entirely straight—played, that is, simply to serve, as mystification almost always does, the interests of a class-inflected power that relies on Shakespeare as an ideological prop. This remystification works to opposite effect: presumably, without it, Shakespeare would have scant relevance to the audience of *This American Life*.

* * *

The apparent distance from Shakespeare manifested by the program's opening appears to confirm my thesis that Shakespeare, on the one hand, and cultural and political power, on the other, have already effectively been dissevered, leaving Shakespeare merely as the fetish or millennial dream of those few who represent a residual formation and who haven't yet learned the dry and knowing pleasures of irony.[11] In this regard, "Act V" constitutes the dialectical counterpart of the NEA's "Shakespeare and American Communities": if official Washington has recently been busy ameliorating what it has hypostasized as the gap between Americans and Shakespeare in the determined service of the nation-state, then *This American Life* seems to want that gap to be even wider, or, in keeping with academic revalorizations of the popular I've been arguing against, believes it already to be so.

Thus Glass's opening words, which frame "Act V" for the audience of *This American Life*: "OK, here is something we did not expect. Check this out." That casual, unmotivated "OK" establishes the tone: the conversational word stands in for a formal opening address while suggesting a prior familiarity, even an ongoing conversation, with members of the program's audience. Hence, presumably, that "we": whom does it comprehend? The staff of *This American Life*, certainly, but potentially also the audience further sutured in intimate relation with the host. As I've hinted, behind that informality is a great deal of cultural (and racial?) capital, enough that it's hard to consider that "we" is a stand-in for an abstractly universal, mass, public, even allowing for the ideological character of the latter; for all that, as I've averred, the position of auditor is open to anyone, it seems clear that the default addressee is a college-educated listener inclined to a similar irreverence. What "we" are being invited to check out is the fact that *Hamlet* gets put on a great deal: clips are played from productions across the country, from amateur and professional companies, even children's theater camps, all adduced to demonstrate both the popularity of the play and the inexplicability of that popularity. This much is evinced by Glass's subsequent indication that Hamlet's central dilemma, which depends on having had one's father murdered and on contemplating the commission of another murder in turn, offers little for "most of us to relate to."

If *This American Life* is any indication, it's no longer commonplace to espouse the universal applicability of Shakespearean tragedy; *Hamlet* is instead deemed "kind of a weird play." Despite, or perhaps because of, the evidence of its widespread popularity, Ira Glass establishes an effective distance from the all-but-compulsory veneration due Shakespeare's master text that pervades much of American culture. Beyond Glass's somewhat portentous words and the title of the episode, the play as play—as dramatic or aesthetic text, or as object fraught with cultural significance—does not much seem to interest him: Hamlet is a "guy," the play full of a lot of "stuff" that has to be taken at best metaphorically if it is to be understood at all. It's possible Glass is miming the casual indifference of the high school student who would rather not be made to care about, connect with, the play (until, that is, his move to metaphor). Even if that is the case, though, the performance, which cannot be taken at face value, offers an ironized positioning but little different in absolute value from the critical dispensation typical of ideology critique I've been contesting throughout this study. If, as political critics of the 1980s and 1990s generally asserted, Shakespeare is only the property of bygone elites and only the locus of mystification, then distance, boredom, and even suspicion seem the only responsible or appropriate responses to his name. Ideological outrage thus becomes a subspecies of indifference, rather as I've suggested sarcasm is the Barthesian subset of postmodern irony when it comes to Luhrmann's version of Shakespeare.

Even so, given what I've already written in chapter 2 concerning the outmoded discourse of backward-looking elites who continue to insist on the transformative power of encountering Shakespeare, that Glass refers to "us" as excluded from seeing something in Shakespeare would, in the first instance, seem contradictory. But that is where the question posed by some subset of "us" enters in: while Glass is clearly apportioning off the staff of *This American Life* and, ultimately, their imagined audience from the prisoners about whom listeners are going to hear, the segmentation also bespeaks the gap between the sensibilities of this newer audience for public radio and those associated with inveighing against Georgetown University's curricular dethroning of Shakespeare in the 1990s. "Most of us" are far indeed from sharing the reflexive piety of an earlier and hegemonic formation that posited Shakespeare as a pious social good. Equally, however, as public radio listeners we are also far from sharing the ready dismissiveness toward Shakespeare documented on the street in *Looking for Richard*, or, for that matter, from the average high school student. Deeming *Hamlet* "kind of a weird play" is doubtless an evaluation, but one that implies not so much a repudiation of the weight of cultural demand that attaches to Shakespeare's name as an informed and even bemused skepticism toward a particular drama.

And it also implies the privilege to proffer such skepticism without either explanation or apology. Glass's casual aversion to weirdness cannot but remind us of the possible difference in class sign between public radio's imagined audience and the chosen avatars of American indifference Pacino fantasizes about reaching. If Pacino's film embodies bardic messianism to make Shakespeare a more publicly palatable object to those who either have not heard the call or who have somehow failed to be thus interpellated, Glass's framing suggests that it seeks to address those who perhaps might have heard and understood that call and yet found it wanting, at least performatively and temporarily. What renders *Hamlet* so bizarre is never explained directly, but it is implied, urged, by the problem of relation and referentiality, of those not subtended by "most of us." Glass continues: "What would the play be like if it were actually performed by murderers and other violent criminals? What would *they* see that the rest of us do not? ... [T]he answer is, a lot."

For those other subjects, neither "most" nor "rest," excluded from Glass's category yet the focus of the episode's attention nevertheless, familial murder, indeed murder of any kind, is something it is apparently quite possible "to relate to." And it is the idea of "relating" that renders Glass's—and, subsequently, Hitt's—representation of Shakespeare so volatile and so useful for my purposes. Relation (in the sense of "relating to a text") is, as academics know, the sign of a pedagogical strategy endlessly in search of an imaginative purchase on the subject position of a student who cannot but perceive the gap separating herself from a text some 400 years old; while it persists in many a secondary school, as a strategy in the academy it has been displaced by more theoretical accounts of meaning-making, cultural materialism among them. As a critical practice, it is somewhat abject. Here, however, relating becomes an experiential nexus that seems to make the prisoners who are the object of the broadcast better at "seeing" an unnamed something, presumably something essential, in a play that is for the rest of us but merely inexplicable—not only remote in time, space, circumstance, and language, but in the demand for relation itself that attends upon it.

Maybe, however, a weird play is merely one in need of quickening, of having a good story told about it: *This American Life* is above all a show that tells such stories. The ironic attitude I've explored suggests the possibility that Shakespeare might be made newly interesting if detoured through a realm of otherness, heightened by the testimony of a personal experience of violence few of the show's auditors might wish to share with the characters in the play. After all, Glass indicates that this might be the most "evocative" production of the play being put on that year, an assessment Hitt echoes in beginning his report with a brief list of the myriad times he has seen the play (perhaps an intentionally pretentious one, given that he includes a Swedish-language staging by Ingmar Bergman—in Brooklyn). The story to be told, then, concerns the reporter's astonishment in finding (deciding?) that inmates who have been convicted of violent, troubling crimes might bring their histories to their analysis of the characters they play. As he puts it: "hanging out" with this group of "convicted actors," he finds he "doesn't know anything about *Hamlet*."

The statement is preposterous on the face of it. Despite his rhetorical nullification of his own habits and elective affinities, Hitt's claim to discern in the prisoners' staging a superior rendition must precisely depend on knowing a great deal about *Hamlet*, maybe even on a connoisseur's pleasure that seems at some remove from the performative disengagement I've already discussed (why else, after all, attend a production in a foreign language by a famous director?). And yet the nullification is, in effect, what aligns him with Glass: in suggesting the apparent failure of his cultural capital to yield sufficient return, Hitt also implies the possibility of exhaustion with the work of accumulating it, of paying homage to a sterile demand.

Until, that is, he encounters those actors with convictions. While performance is famed for its immediacy (and Method acting particularly celebrated for making the understanding of character a sort of inside job), it is not exactly performance as such that Hitt valorizes in his reportage from the correctional center. Rather, it is an unintellectualized authenticity apparently brought to *Hamlet* by the inmates and warranted by their sins of commission, which yields an intensity, a value-added affect, then transmitted to the reporter and others in attendance. "Act V" rather obscenely turns crime and punishment into a hands-on equivalent for what is, after all, a *schooled* approach to characterization: Hitt describes inmate James Word's "channel[ing] Laertes [...] in a way that should make any Method actor cringe with jealousy." In thus valuing the inmates' living the part (or, rather, having *already* lived it) so that it can speak through them, be "channeled" by them, Hitt marginalizes the work of comprehension performance also demands: the efforts, also recorded in the broadcast, of taking in a language so refractory and unfamiliar, that signifies what the inmates do not live and have not lived or had prior educational access to. That work of taking on is more than a means to an end, but here it merely seems to render possible the revivification of the play for a privileged someone on the outside who can't otherwise relate to *Hamlet* or who is made jaded by repeated exposure. It makes, that is, for a good story.

That *Hamlet* is newly quickened with meaning under these extreme conditions leads to a commutative possibility: inmate life is significant only insofar as it is coextensive with (or perhaps legitimated by) a production of *Hamlet*. So much might perhaps be expected: public radio did, after all, bow to pressure in 1994 and cancel convicted killer and journalist Mumia Abu-Jamal's occasional series "Live From Death Row," which had originally been commissioned to provide its listeners with unusual access to the conditions of those awaiting execution. And perhaps that cancellation might lead one to anticipate the fact that "Act V" offers no complex understanding of how criminality is constructed; how and when it is raced, classed, and gendered; how to think about and reflect on its categorical imperatives. Hitt does note that the inmates who hope to be cast members are half white and half black in number; he also indicates that many have not finished high school, and that "To be or not to be" is all the Shakespeare they have previously encountered. Even so, he goes out of his way to model an almost exoticizing distance for his auditors: one participant is described as a "retired postal employee and devout Wiccan"; another reads lapidary magazines. There is also a gratuitous reference to a former participant who was "an Amish pedophile—but that's another story." Initially we get little sense of what crimes his interview subjects have committed and how long their sentences are: as a result, they are presented to us as specimens embedded only in the matrix of the prison as it exists at that moment, and even then almost exclusively in relation to the theater project.[12] In keeping with this dispensation, Hitt at one point asserts he sees his interviewees first and foremost as actors; when they speak, their age is often the only personal information they are heard to disclose.

Yet his assertion is necessarily undermined by the very fact of the broadcast. Why, after all, make the trip to witness Act V of *Hamlet* at the Missouri Eastern Correctional Center if it wasn't because the actors were prisoners? Why begin discussion of his first day by talking about the "screamer" he is given upon entering—a device to alert a guard immediately should he be endangered? Later, however, Hitt confesses that the men have refused to discuss their crimes with him, preferring to keep them in the past; his desire to know them (perhaps to fix them in place, keep the boundaries secure?) leads him to consult public records, where he finds many have committed truly heinous acts, some of which he describes on-air, lingering particularly on an act of sexual violence committed against a child the same age as his. Hitt notes feeling betrayed by this discovery, a response revealing an extraordinary capacity for willed ignorance—or else a rather arbitrary and procrustean approach to his subjects. Yet he also grudgingly acknowledges that in his quest to know the level of their culpability he has betrayed their trust in him as well.

By the time Hitt gets to that point, however—which is to say, by the time the show is more than half done, a transition that it marks by a formal break in the program—the gap that separates the prisoners from the audience is already under contest. I do not mean to suggest, of course, that mediation disappears or that the power to turn a scrutinizing lens, or rather microphone, on them does not matter: far from it. That Hitt has gone as far as he has in violating his interviewees' privacy suggests, at the very least, that his investment in them has come to exceed the Shakespearean pretext that motivates his broadcast: so much is signaled by the fact that when the episode resumes, it focuses on an inmate who uses the text to understand his past, rather than the converse. But Shakespeare does not disappear. Instead, the fact of Shakespeare unsettles the broadcast and becomes the medium through which the question of identification, as textual practice and as a revenant from an abeyant liberalism, gains unexpected power.

* * *

The disjuncture between what "Act V" avows and what I take to be the work of the program itself forces a reconsideration of the politics of interpretation with which I began this study. Hitt's rhetorical evasiveness seems to suggest that the very identification between player and role that compelled his interest in prison Shakespeare has wound up threatening the secure distance between himself and his interviewees upon which depends his privilege to deploy them for his own ends. Taken alongside the parallels between the Glass's own falsely naive repudiation of identificatory reading, "Act V" causes me to wonder whether such estrangement from Shakespeare's totemic power—which includes estrangement from the literary discourse of identification—no longer functions as a politically progressive move, as it might have during the heyday of cultural materialism, but rather has become the new dominant among the privileged subjects of postmodern cynicism. When Jonathan Dollimore noted that Lear's move to pity "houseless poverty" was not so much an affirmation of the human condition as such but of the extreme circumstances under which (and only under which) such pity could be generated in those with power, he was offering a salutary reminder of the necessity of reading the text without idealist illusions, especially given the structural privilege Shakespearean tragedy accords to characters for whom material immiseration is seldom the need to be reasoned about.[13] Such dialectical insights depend for their force on the reader's separating herself from Lear, on refusing the gesture of identification that more or less effortlessly leads to unearned assertions about the universality of suffering—the sorts of things that are always adduced under a hegemonic dispensation calculating its own interests into the sum total of reasons to study Shakespeare in the first place.

We are right to be skeptical of such flabby generalizations, to resist hypostasizing them. But "Act V" suggests that, in demanding imaginative extension, literary and dramatic identification might exert a pressure to reconsider what forms of Shakespearean attention could serve this conjuncture, this point in American cultural politics and in our national history with Shakespeare. To say as much is to reflect on a perimillennial American culture within which neoliberal and libertarian positions, which from an affective standpoint are little different from quasi-organized selfishness, continue to write themselves ever larger in political discourse even as they inveigh against those whom a winner-takes-all economy has made into losers—and against the "elites" who only sometimes stand on behalf of those losers.[14] So growing a retrenchment from a sense of imagined community has left progressive critics to articulate a despair that any kind of public sphere, however flawed and however limited its historical instantiation, can be recuperated.[15] Under these circumstances, a critical practice skeptical about fellow-feeling as a reflexive response to Shakespeare might need to give way to one that insists such things as sympathy—as relations with those beyond our immediate ken—are still possible, that a community, a nation-state, with them can still be imagined, reclaimed, as a long-term project with its own dreams of political transformation. And, that recognition, in turn, forces me to consider whether the work needed to read for identification is not so much about writing the self large (hence the twinned challenges of "relating" and of the grandiose yet atomized subjectivity of neoliberalism) as about challenging the boundaries of self, the better to change the nexus of imaginary social relations and to experience unfamiliar subject positions and, perhaps, pleasures heretofore deemed rarefied: as Richard Dyer has suggested, to know "what utopia would feel like rather than how it would be organized," even if only for a moment.[16]

But potentially, of course, for more than that, as the end of the broadcast makes clear, while marking the boundary between utopian possibilities and the more earthbound narratives within which incarceration and transformation—the original impetus for the penitentiary as an institution—are bound up. Many of the prisoners taking part in the production of *Hamlet* will ultimately be up for parole, a moment of critical assessment that finds a precursor in the cast party that follows the play's public performance, where actor-inmates mingle with journalists and outside supporters, and that coalesces with the play itself as performance of publicly admissible subjectivity, as Hitt suggests:

> In a high-security prison, though, when a play is over, it's over.... The guards had informed everyone that they'd have about ten minutes for the cast party; like any play all the work was for this moment: to get to the end of the last performance successfully. And now that it's here these few minutes are shot through with a kind of melancholy. In the side room—everyone sees him—is the guard waiting to strip-search them back into the yard. He wears a dull expression on his face and rubber gloves on his hands. But that would be ten minutes from now; there is still time for pretending.
>
> According to the prison commissioner, 97% of the people locked up today will someday join us on the outside.... A few [...] of the cast have parole board hearings coming up, to decide whether they've changed enough and should be allowed to mingle with us on the outside. To that extent, this whole night, including the cast party, is just another rehearsal.

Leave aside what is both surreal and obscene in prison life as we are allowed to understand it, an observational doublet underlined by a respectful review of the prison performance from an attendee who claims of the performance that "a four hundred year old text is restored to freshness." Of greater weight is the fact that Hitt's words reveal that the inmates know they are being watched, evaluated, assessed for traces of recuperability. Their relation to *Hamlet* is, potentially, what enables them to reestablish a relation to the civil society whose penal instruments have sent them there; more importantly, it is what enables them to be *seen* to do so. Or heard: there is no effacing the role that Hitt's narration plays in conjoining dramatic production with the question of transformation and parole for an audience beyond the immediate community. One might deem any such performance coercive, and no doubt there are coercive elements in all rehabilitation programs, for all their dependence on voluntary association. And of course the same may be said of *This American Life*'s insertion of itself into the site of exchange between the prisoners and the theater program, especially given that Agnes Wilcox, who founded the program and who directs the inmates in the production under scrutiny, is all but supplanted as privileged interlocutor by the radio correspondent. Yet the function of Shakespeare in both productions—public radio's no less than the prison's—is far from exhausted by this recognition.

Rather, by the end of the broadcast, I am haunted by the ease with which my own occasional resistance to the distancing *of This American Life and* to its invocation of Shakespeare has threatened to obscure the fact that something productive might be happening in the prison. In not naming it, in calling it *something*, I aim to keep the sense of its lability in play, a sense to which the editing of the broadcast itself contributes in raising the specter of parole as connected to Shakespeare but refusing to satisfy the desire to hear of a particular outcome, deferring the matter instead onto the broader question betokened by Hitt's closing words about parole and rehearsal.[17] Shakespeare constitutes a necessary material condition, something akin to the airwaves: without him, it seems, those broader questions might never be heard to emerge.

But nonetheless, Shakespeare is also an arbitrary vehicle. It is crucial to recognize that the inmates who variously respond to Shakespeare's language might, in the end, be moved by any language that revealed for them the simultaneous, unexpected possibilities of identification *and* difference—or that generated for them the forms of material attention that are the precursor to and the practical extension of literary relation. (Witness the fact that Wilcox works with them on other dramatists besides Shakespeare.)[18] Although Glass and Hitt suggest that the coalescence around murder is what the prisoners share with their text and what makes them better interpreters of it than "the rest of us," the inmates themselves seem more fascinated with the access the play grants them to a new repertory of emotions, discourse, and modes of self-representation—when, that is, they not made to respond to Hitt's own efforts to suture player and play on the basis of criminal history:

> *Waller*: "My name is Danny Waller, I'm forty-four years old. The character that I've played was the ghost of Hamlet's father. The reason I chose that when I first read the script, the words jumped out at me, and they made me feel things that I haven't felt before."
> *Hitt*: "What in your experience drew you to those particular words?"
> *Waller*: I took a man's life, and I felt he was talking to me through that, that he wanted me to know what I put him through. [Reads the speech that begins: 'I am thy father's spirit doomed for a certain term to walk the night...' and moves to 'Thus was I sleeping...sent to my account with all my imperfections on my head.'] It was pretty much the same way with him. He was, he was taken before his time."
> *Hitt*: "So when you read the character, do you feel like, who's talking when you say those lines?"
> *Waller*: "I'm the body up there, but the words are coming from mostly William Pride, the man that I killed, he's mostly the one talking."

If, as Neils Herold has averred in his discussion of the documentary *Shakespeare behind Bars*, the prison constitutes a "textually saturated environment," traversed by the letter of the law and countertraversed by Shakespeare's words, it must be acknowledged that "Act V" constitutes yet another layer of textuality: it would be naive to imagine that the interviews provide unmediated access to the real.[19] Hitt's interventions cannot help producing some normative version of the prison subject for public consumption, a prison subject made all the more interesting through his presumably spontaneous embrace of the Shakespearean as the source of conscience. Demonstrating empathy for one's victim, as Waller does, may come in handy for such purposes, as would seeing the play as an introduction to the world of great literature, a sentiment one could easily imagine endorsed by those who opposed Georgetown University's elimination of a Shakespeare requirement for English majors. Consider in this regard the words of Bratt Jones, one of four actors who share the part of Hamlet:

> I think this has taken me to being sane for just one day. Just one day I'm sane enough, you know? If you don't keep exercising your mind, then you start to lose it... This gives me the opportunity to see a society beyond what I'm used to. I'm familiar with rap music and videos and big butts on the TV and all that but let me come back to something that I'm not

familiar with. Let me get into something else. That did open up my eyes to reading Sylvia Plath and Frost and Wordsworth and different other people.

That literature enlarges the sense of self, that it stretches the mind—these are overfamiliar tropes; I wonder how many of us, particularly politically inclined critics on the left, would consider positing them in so bald a form in our scholarly productions and, for that matter, even in our teaching. They have become as delegitimated and suspect as the other part of Jones's statement, which rejects popular culture as shallow and which thereby stands as the obverse of a critical practice that has insisted such products are as textually meaningful as any consecrated high-cultural text and, precisely because the former are "popular," perhaps more so.

Hence my earlier reversion to the idea of what is abject in Shakespeare criticism. It is tempting to dismiss Jones's sentiments as ventriloquism of a repressive cultural dominant, or as the by-product of a broader interpellation represented by the theater project as a whole and by Hitt's editorial shaping. Indeed, such a dismissal could, under the right conditions, be preferable to critical arrogance, which assumes that all articulations have equal status and are equally knowable. Gayatri Spivak has famously written of her skepticism that intellectuals can ever understand the political intentions of those structurally beneath them in the ensemble of social relations: in claiming that "the subaltern cannot speak," Spivak argues that ideological presuppositions inevitably cancel out any confidence even sympathetic intellectuals might have that subjects deprived of privilege can be heard to signify clearly.[20] The slippage she analyzes, occasioned by representation understood as (textual) presence and representation understood in a more overtly political sense, ought, if taken to its logical conclusion, undercut any claim I might make: her words would suggest that it is solely my desire that the mediated forum that is *This American Life* offers access to subjectivities whose own conditions of self-expression—and rights as citizens—are, despite their inevitable compromise, available for critical recuperation.

But Lata Mani's rejoinder to Spivak offers the possibility of a practical counterstrategy.[21] In analyzing accounts of sati provided by colonial administrators who viewed widow-burning as barbaric and who pitied the women they believed were forced into self-immolation, Mani demonstrates that reading against the grain of those administrative narratives enables one to attend to slight dissonances in representation; as she argues, these dissonances constitute the traces of those bygone widows' agency, a sense of their independence from the imperial discourses of horror and condescension to which they were otherwise captive, as well as from any simpleminded idea that they had capitulated to "tradition." The analogy between the prisoners in "Act V" and the subjects of colonial narratives is, at best, imprecise. As I've noted, invoking a postcolonial context has been an intermittent characteristic of recent work on Shakespeare and American culture; it has even been intriguingly deployed by Herold to describe the performance experience of prisoners doing Shakespeare, who constitute the periphery to more hegemonic and more "central" instantiations of Shakespeare in the hands of the powerful, such as the former Reagan official Kenneth Adelman and his Shakespeare-for-corporate-leadership program, "Movers and Shakespeares." But without precision and without a clear sense of its material limits, this critical practice risks extravagance and exoticism.

Nevertheless, I allude to the debate between Spivak and Mani not to suggest we map colonial relations onto the United States as a substitute for an attention to class, as has often been done, but rather to propose that the imaginative extension provided by Shakespeare with which I am concerned needs to be met by an imaginative extension on the part of the critic. Whether Mani is strictly accurate in finding evidence of the widows' choices in the records she mines is less to the point than the fact that her informed strategy represents a principled rejection of methodological and political pessimism. Underneath the temptation constituted by pessimism lies a sure danger that is the obverse of what *This American Life* is purveying: if Hitt's rhetorical strategy is to imaginatively erase the gap between him/us and the prisoners, only to reassert it by probing into their criminal histories, a dismissive reading from an academic also reinstates those prisoners in a realm of pure difference that better serves academics than it does the situation under scrutiny. The difference here may not be purely anthropological or imperial; even so, it relegates the prisoners who are interviewed to one of two unacceptable positions. Either they are little better than the "cultural dupes" scholars of cultural studies have taught us to be skeptical about—structurally deprived subjects who consume ideology because they know no better.[22] Or else they are doomed to signify and yet be ignored because of the contaminating effects of mediation, read past in the service of critiquing that ideology.[23]

Hence the need to recognize two simultaneous conditions: at the same time we must recognize the tug of power and the possibility of mystification, we must also acknowledge that the prisoners' words as recorded need to be taken seriously, and, tactically, at least, at face value. That Jones speaks of wanting to know something *new*, whether Shakespeare or, for that matter other writers, something that has not been "familiar" to him before, nicely captures the sense of what I wish to convey. His longing is not for the exchange value of cultural capital; it is for language he can use—and be seen to use, As I have argued, to read those words as merely symptomatic of hegemonic formations is to deny subjects like him working under a series of constraints—political, economic, juridico-discursive—any access, however incomplete and however apparently compromised by institutional agendas, to self-determination and self-understanding, which is to say, to the conditions of autonomy with which I began: to make his own history, if not under the circumstances of his own choosing. And that is why the fortuitousness of Shakespeare as a provisional liberatory agent must be counterbalanced against the necessity of understanding Shakespeare as pervasive in U.S. public culture. It is only because Shakespeare—as opposed to, say, Milton or Morrison or, for that matter, Plath or Frost—is the fetish object that he is that this intervention has whatever purchase it has beyond the prison. Any other writer might not have already had a sufficient claim on the public imaginary to bridge the divide between inside and outside, those who do "big-house Shakespeare" and those who might be brought to ponder it.

And that purchase extends to the problematic broadcast itself. By the end of the show, it has become clear that, despite its framing of the hour as dedicated to what inmates can tell *us* about *Hamlet* (a framing that cannot but seem colonialist), we have not been offered a glimpse of Shakespeare's play as a resonant text about criminality and illuminated by criminals, as Glass and Hitt have led us to expect. Rather, what comes into prominence is what it means to detain and punish—and how those acts define, and are defined by, public (and public radio's) discourse on the limits of a civil society. A reading, only partly cynical, would note the pitifully restricted imaginative capacities ascribed to the audience, and presumably shared by the show's producers: in a show whose agenda is to tell stories, would no one listen to the voices of prisoners if the show were not about a production of *Hamlet*?

But another way of thinking about it suggests itself, one that sees through the one-dimensional utopianism of social planning against which Jameson has written.[24] It is through the pervasiveness of such institutions as Shakespeare that a lot of social discourse—thinking and dreaming—can take place. And, unlike other institutions that have defined and circumscribed their lives, Shakespeare seems to have given the prisoners a sense of the possibilities of enlargement, in all the resonant and complex meanings of that word. Given the repressions of mandatory sentencing—three strikes and you're out—and the ever-growing prison-industrial complex, having Shakespeare materialized in this way and in this location is, at the moment, no small matter.

Such dreams, hemmed around by institutional and representational constraints and located in individual consciousnesses rather than collective action, are no durable substitute for full-scale social transformation. And whether or not my argument about the decline of Shakespeare's mythological power is correct, there is a built-in limit to what representations can make happen. But transformative thought has to start somewhere; indeed, it can gain a hold on many places, as Ernst Bloch has suggested:

> Everybody's life is pervaded by daydreams: one part of this is just stale, even enervating escapism, even booty for swindlers, but another part is provocative, is not content just to accept the bad which exists, does not accept renunciation. This other part has hoping at its core, and is teachable. It can be extricated from the unregulated daydreams and from its sly misuse, can be activated undimmed. Nobody has ever lived without daydreams, but it is a question of knowing them deeper and deeper and in this way keeping them trained unerringly, usefully, on what is right.[25]

* * *

I want to close by offering a few observations about the necessity of reading as I have just done, and more broadly about the idea of Shakespeare as public object. The first question that must be addressed is whether, in the service of a critical agenda, I have merely recast a liberal fantasy of universality in terms only glancingly progressive. Tony Bennett, for instance, deemed utopian readings as setting off "harmless firecrackers," and Frederic Jameson has strenuously protested against the tendency to read utopia without the violently struggled-for and large-scale social rupture that it seeks to summon forth.[26] But I am also conscious of the need for retrenchment: utopian readings would indeed be toothless soundings of light and noise if I were also arguing that merely having critics read texts differently made anything momentous happen. Ideology critique was born of a particular moment in Marxist cultural discourse, where the acknowledgment that language was productive of consciousness made it possible to believe that intervening in the process of textual reproduction, isolating its historical and political unconscious, was material *political* practice. It would be no wonder if reading texts affirmatively were open to the same charge and subject to the same conjunctural limitation.

Obviously, I am far from the first to foreground the possibility of reading Shakespeare in light of utopianism; Hugh Grady and Kiernan Ryan, for example, have offered persuasive analyses that draw on the principle of hope as pertinent to a reading of the plays.[27] In discussing Fredric Jameson's reading of Western Marxist critics Walter Benjamin, Herbert Marcuse, and Ernst Bloch, Ryan argues against political readings concerned merely with reproducing a hermeneutics of suspicion. He calls for a simultaneous recognition that none of these critics "had any difficulty discerning in the great art of the past vivid premonitions of a dispensation whose advent we still await" (228). Thus he echoes Bloch's own sense of the role of such art: "Every great work of art thus still remains...impelled towards the latency of the other side, i.e. towards the contents of a future which had not yet appeared in its own time" (Bloch, 127).

What is at particular issue at the moment is the comparative trouble the term "great art" can still cause in an institutional nexus. And for good reason. Anyone reading this study is likely well familiar with debates concerning the canon and the question of its representativeness, both aesthetically and politically. What needs pushing against is the way in which those debates are traversed by questions of materiality and defined by institutional practices. The very call to assess a select number of texts as peculiarly durable in their essence, and furthermore to claim that that essence lies in the crystallization of a Jamesonian "future unconscious," is likely to generate discomfiture, since these claims both depend on and reinforce a mystified model of value. To put it simply, texts like Shakespeare's would have, for complex reasons, already been accorded the mantle of greatness long before Jameson, Raymond Williams, or even Bloch, for that matter, sought to locate the source of that greatness in linguistic or generic structures amenable to Marxist discourse.[28] One need not be in the habit of pursuing symptomatic traces to wonder how utopianism in this generic, text-centered guise can be reconciled with the evidence, marshaled during the heyday of cultural materialism, of Shakespeare's imbrication in hegemonic formations, where much indeed is made, and continues to be made, of the greatness of his art. As I've tried to suggest in the preceding analysis of "Act V," a critical strategy isomorphic with what it seeks to negate needs at least to call attention to the problem of its mirroring.

My mention of Raymond Williams is fortuitous here, since his role in crystallizing the cultural studies project at Birmingham has influenced the emergence of mass-cultural studies and popular practices as an alternative to the pedagogy of, and a vestment in the aesthetics of, the canon as the sum total of value. Mass-culture study of Shakespeare has eschewed the problematical aura of great art and more or less followed in the wake of a Benjaminian optimism about the demystifying effects of industrially inflected multiplicity: popular forms are held to carnivalize the high seriousness of elite objects like Shakespeare and to aid in the process of their desecration and demystification, as I've previously noted. Yet however appealing and pervasive, this familiar argument depends for its force on the continued remystification of Shakespeare from above, posited against rebellion from below, which is to say, on a contest between cultural registers that chooses Shakespeare as its privileged ground. To put it more simply, the carnival continues only if the means by which relations of power are contested remain unchanged—and if they keep Shakespeare close to the heart of ideology.

As I've been at pains to suggest, however, it is not at all clear that this contestatory model of culture has become anything more than figural in recent years. The so-called culture wars notwithstanding, the energy in conservative diatribes is, as I've noted in chapter 1, increasingly focused on Hollywood as the new center of elitism. This focus not only ratifies mass culture as the principal site for the production of a national-popular imaginary, it leaves high-cultural formations of elitism behind as a front of engagement. Even the corollary argument that mass culture constitutes a force of optimistic democratization has come under scrutiny from progressive critics: as Susan Buck-Morss has recently demonstrated, the twentieth century has witnessed the rise and fall of populist tropes concerning the dreamworld of mass culture, within which Shakespeare, however appropriated to subvert received cultural hierarchies, has no special or enduring priority.[29]

In other words, the study of popular forms has proven a less-than-sure antidote to the problematic of capitalism, or at least of the front that engages the class struggle as via a suspicion toward the canon. This failed embrace of popular forms and taste means, among other things, that a discourse of aesthetic durability might come to serve a different function than the acquisition of restrictive cultural capital, and the maintenance of privilege, with which it has been aligned. And this is where I swerve from my utopian predecessors even while I share their insistence on the political force of hoping for a better future. Rather than locate the sense of futurity in the texts "themselves" (a phrase that suggests that all semantic meaning is not historically and institutionally contingent), I've argued for examining non-academic formations around Shakespeare even when they perpetuate positions and beliefs that might, at first glance, seem outmoded and even abject. Not, as I hope I have already made clear, in order to valorize the popular as a realm of pure difference—such a stance risks an enervated sentimentality about "the people" masquerading as an embrace of democratic populism—but, rather, to combat both received cultural hierarchies and the endless differentiation of taste characteristic of market relations, to acknowledge what discussions of popular Shakespeare have so far failed to take in: that the course of the twentieth century has been the course of the dissemination of Shakespeare as an author. His plays, far from constituting a form of elite property "appropriated" by alternative modalities, by disempowered subjects who must steal him from the powerful, are for all intents and purposes now as much a part of U.S. public culture as any other subject in secondary education, for good or for ill. As a result, they exceed all attempts to fix them in a binary heuristic between high and low.

Equally inescapable, I would aver, is a dialectic around nonacademic response to Shakespeare, a dialectic shaped by the apparently and ineluctably pedagogical ambit that generates our national understanding of Shakespeare's compulsory lovability and that more broadly generates the conditions for what is possible with and around Shakespeare. If Shakespeare has been constituted by the mutations of pedagogy from an essential property of bourgeois cultural capital into a universally lovable object deemed beneficial to all regardless of class, such a demand has left the nonacademic public exposed to Shakespeare but two possible responses: accede to the demand—or reject it. Love it or hate it, in other words. But owing to the asymmetry characteristic of the pedagogical, it is only *loving* Shakespeare that is, or can be, learned. Anything else—repudiation, dismissal, dislike—is deemed natural, even if (because?) "authentic."

Another way of putting it is, of course, ignorant. To that extent, the demand to love Shakespeare necessarily maintains the residual overtones of class-inflected taste. To become part of Shakespeare's public, to shed "ignorance," is to accede to the lingering demands and investments of high literacy: hence the pedagogical imperative that has attached to Shakespeare in the twentieth century, which takes as its agenda that Shakespeare is a kind of aesthetic spinach, good and good *for* you, if only you will learn to take it in properly. And more and more, one *must*. Such a stance is so naturalized as to go without acknowledgment, except by academics who have overmuch focused on their own possession of cultural capital. And yet what the stance fails to imagine is that *dislike* of Shakespeare is also a social fact rather than a natural inclination, a form of class reproduction whose effects are in and of themselves hard to valorize.[30] Shakespeare names a site so overcoded with cultural agendas that an innocent reaction is all but impossible: very few people indeed come to Shakespeare "for the first time," as it were. As I have tried to suggest, the claim that Shakespeare is rarefied and difficult is, these days, more often to be found in mass-cultural formations than in academic ones—but it goes without saying that Americans have gone to school on mass culture as well. If, for Al Pacino, having someone aver that Shakespeare "sucks" is an occasion for remedial work, it is possible to see in that irreverent remark the adoption of an attitude tendentiously associated with a "people's" culture that proudly stands against schoolroom lessons even when they are being offered out of school.

What I am trying to suggest is that dislike of Shakespeare is also matter of practical consciousness, perhaps even a residual one. And in the preceding chapters I have striven, not to offer an argument about the importance of changing that practical consciousness, but to argue for understanding the conditions under which it may, may not, or even can be changed—of limit-cases and liminal experiences. And of when it may be seen as changed, a perspective that acknowledges understanding that Shakespearean value is not only overcoded and arbitrary, but meaningful insofar as assent to it is concerned. Bratt Jones, the prisoner interviewed by Jack Hitt who finds meaning in Shakespeare rather than in rap, has already been so positioned by antinomies of value that it requires an extreme critical tact for an auditor to hear what he has to say.

This series of questions brings me back to the second of my terms: "public," which is both an analytical component of this study, a tool, and a shorthand whose blandly descriptive facade needs to be troubled. When I invoke the term "public culture," I am not simply renaming Jurgen Habermas's influential term or claiming it for a quasi-autonomous realm of production divorced from the political—even if I do take on board the criticisms, voiced by Nancy Fraser and others, of the regulatively race-, class- and gender-bound nature of his formulation and of the consequent need to reposition debate categorically, given an American discourse geared ever more restrictively toward a fantasmatic meritocracy of the individual as over against the group.[31] In his useful analysis of the subject of publics, for instance, Michael Warner distinguishes between the bourgeois public sphere, in which the contingencies of (inevitably privileged) personhood are dissolved or, in his word "negated," and its successor, that of the mass public, in which the contingencies associated with gendered or raced excess uncontained by bourgeois proprieties and having no place in them come to dominant the field. He little acknowledges that social relations might be one site for the formation of what he usefully calls "counterpublics," even as he redefines the question by referring to a "mass public," a citizenry incorporated and corporatized by media form and spectacle.[32] But that "mass public," and its unnamed successor regime, might precisely be part of the problem. As John Frow, Michael Hardt, and others have noted, the social conditions needed for a functioning democracy—for a public sphere that, despite the criticisms to which it has justly been subjected, is a necessary adjunct to democracy—are in crisis.[33] As mass forms of communication are superseded by a plurality of platforms and a plurality of forms of address, the very material conditions for a nation as imagined community fall into abeyance. Thus the articulation between the "public sphere" and "public culture" cannot be clear-cut: if I am correct that culture is not the leading edge of social relations in the perimillennial United States but rather an alibi for more material forms of domination, the relationship of culture to any efforts to resuscitate the sphere of political discussion cannot be guaranteed merely by a shared concept.

At least as an initial premise, I am after something a little simpler. Following in the wake of the journal of the same name, I adopt the term "public culture" as a resolution to the analytical difficulties occasioned by hierarchical alternatives. As Carol Breckenridge and Arjun Appadurai have written:

> Why use the adjective *public* for cultural forms that appear to be well described by so many other, more familiar ones like popular, mass, folk, consumer, national, or middle class? The term *public* is not a neutral or arbitrary substitute for all these existing alternatives. Nevertheless, it appears to be less embedded in such highly specific Western dichotomies and debates as high versus low culture; mass versus elite culture; and popular or folk versus classical culture...
>
> This leads to the second reason for the use of the term *public*. The term *public culture* is more than a rubric for collectively thinking about aspects of modern life now thought about separately. It also allows us to hypothesize not a type of cultural phenomenon but a zone of cultural debate. We now speculate that this zone may be characterized as an arena where other types, forms and domains of culture are encountering, interrogating and contesting each other in new and unexpected ways.[34]

Although Breckenridge and Appadurai are writing in particular of South Asian cultural forms, the term "public culture" has taken on a wider currency, in keeping with the authors' sense that much of what was once described in national and categorical terms needs to be thought about as "a zone of debate." This zone is especially apposite when it comes to perimillennial Shakespeare. If, as I have striven to demonstrate, Shakespeare has been dissevered from the historical relation that his texts have had to elites, the texts persist, naggingly, promisingly. To meet the demands, aesthetic as well as political, of a new conjuncture, we might begin by finding new uses for Shakespeare in public.

Notes

Introduction: Shakespeare in Public

1. The remark about Charlie the Tuna is owed to Michael Bristol, whose *Shakespeare's America, America's Shakespeare* (New York: Routledge, 1991) provided the original impetus for this study. For the civilizing effects of Shakespeare and Shakespeare in American culture, see Bristol; Kim Sturgess, *Shakespeare and the American Nation* (Cambridge: Cambridge University Press, 2004); and Lawrence Levine, *Highbrow/Lowbrow: The Emergence of Cultural Hierarchy in America* (Cambridge, MA: Harvard University Press, 1988). Levine's account certainly identifies an important phenomenon, albeit one more influenced by immigration patterns and the development of mass forms of entertainment than he allows for. However, Levine leaves the impression that there was no discernible elite discourse on Shakespeare contemporaneous with the popular performances he describes. Yet the documentary record amassed by Peter Rawlings in *Americans on Shakespeare 1776–1914* (Aldershot, UK: Ashgate, 1999) makes clear that Levine is describing a comparative tendency rather than an absolute break.
2. An incomplete list would include Jonathan Dollimore, *Radical Tragedy: Religion, Ideology, and Power in the Drama of Shakespeare and His Contemporaries* (Chicago: University of Chicago Press, 1984); Jonathan Dollimore and Alan Sinfield, eds., *Political Shakespeare: New Essays in Cultural Materialism*, 2nd ed. (Ithaca, NY: Cornell University Press, 1995); John Drakakis, ed., *Alternative Shakespeares*, (London: Methuen, 1983); Terence Hawkes, *Meaning by Shakespeare* (London: Routledge, 1992); Graham Holderness, ed., *The Shakespeare Myth* (Manchester: Manchester University Press, 1988); Jean Howard and Marion O'Connor, eds., *Shakespeare Reproduced: The Text in History and Ideology* (New York: Methuen, 1987); Ivo Kamps, ed., *Shakespeare Left and Right* (New York: Routledge, 1991).
3. For postcolonial Shakespeare, see for instance Thomas Cartelli, *Repositioning Shakespeare: National Formations, Postcolonial Appropriations* (New York: Routledge, 1999);. Ania Loomba and Martin Orkin, ed., *Post-Colonial Shakespeare* (London: Routledge, 1998); Craig Dionne and Parmita Kapadia,

eds., *Native Shakespeares: Indigenous Appropriations on a Global Stage* (Aldershot, UK: Ashgate, 2008). For Shakespeare, film, and new media, see Linda Boose and Richard Burt, eds., *Shakespeare the Movie: Popularizing the Plays on Film, TV, and Video* (London: Routledge, 1997); Richard Burt, *Unspeakable ShaXXXspeares: Queer Theory and American Kiddie Culture* (New York: St Martin's Press, 1998); Richard Burt, ed., *Shakespeare After Mass Media* (New York : Palgrave Macmillan, 2002); Thomas Cartelli and Katherine Rowe, *New Wave Shakespeare on Screen* (Cambridge: Polity, 2007); Courtney Lehmann and Lisa Sparks, eds., *Spectacular Shakespeare: Critical Theory and Popular Cinema* (Madison, NJ: Fairleigh Dickinson Press, 2002); Douglas Lanier, *Shakespeare and Modern Popular Culture* (Oxford: Oxford University Press, 2002). For performance, see Barbara Hodgdon, *The Shakespeare Trade: Performances and Appropriations* (Philadelphia: University of Pennsylvania Press, 1998); W.B. Worthen, *Shakespeare and the Authority of Performance* (Cambridge: Cambridge University Press, 1997). It should go without saying that these lists are far from comprehensive.
4. John Joughin, ed., *Shakespeare and National Culture* (Manchester: Manchester University Press, 1997).
5. Steven Greenblatt, *Will in the World: How Shakespeare Became Shakespeare* (New York: Norton, 2004). Greenblatt's popular success has occurred in the wake of Harold Bloom's similarly directed volume, *Shakespeare: The Invention of the Human* (New York: Riverhead Books, 1998).
6. Michael Warner has a trenchant analysis of the call for transparent writing on the part of academics as a misrecognition; see *Publics and Counterpublics* (New York: Zone Books, 2002), 125–158.
7. For more on how the idea of the popular functions in academic discourse as an outside to academic work, see Denise Albanese, "The Popular Mechanics of Rude Mechanicals: Shakespeare and the Walls of Academe," in *Shakespeare Studies 2004*, ed. Susan Zimmerman (Madison, NJ: Fairleigh Dickinson University Press, 2004), 295–321.
8. Ernst Bloch, *The Principle of Hope* (1959), 3 vols., trans. Neville Plaice, Stephen Plaice, and Paul Knight (Cambridge: MA: MIT Press, 1986).

1 Reframing Shakespeare for the Millennium: American Culture, "Elites," the Academy—and Beyond

1. See also Laura Ingraham, *Shut Up and Sing: How Elites from Hollywood, Politics, and the UN Are Subverting America* (Washington, D.C.: Regnery Publishing, 2003).
2. For a documentary introduction with a very useful and detailed timeline, see Richard Bolton, ed., *Culture Wars: Documents from the Recent Controversies in the Arts* (New York: New Press, 1992).
3. Dana Gioia, transcript of interview with Tavis Smiley, "Dana Gioia on the National Endowment for the Arts' Upcoming 'Shakespeare in American

Communities' tour," National Public Radio (NPR), May 7, 2003 (available from LexisNexis Academic).
4. Roger Kimball, "Goodbye Mapplethorpe, Hello Shakespeare," *National Review Online,* January 29, 2004; for similar sentiments, see William Safire, "A Gioia to Behold," *New York Times,* March 8, 2004, A19; and Thomas S. Hibbs, "Thankful for the NEA?" *National Review Online,* November 26, 2008.
5. National Endowment for the Arts, *Shakespeare in American Communities* (July 2008), publication downloadable at www.arts.gov. The quoted material appears on p. 3.
6. *Shakespeare in American Communities,* 3–4. In fact, "Phase Two" of the initiative is explicitly titled "Shakespeare for a New Generation."
7. Gioia, quoted in Bruce Weber, "Stratford-upon-Main-Street: Shakespeare to Tour, Thanks to the NEA," *New York Times,* April 23, 2003, E1; for an analysis of the founding of the Folger Library, see Michael Bristol, *Shakespeare's America, America's Shakespeare* (New York: Routledge, 1990).
8. *Shakespeare in American Communities,* 4. And hence the highly publicized joint endeavor in 2004 between the NEA and the Defense Department to bring *Macbeth* to U.S. military bases as a part of "Shakespeare in American Communities": conjoining these two ideologically and materially significant institutions suggests a propagandistic role for the Bard while confirming "the troops" as another kind of national fetish.
9. http://www.nea.gov/news/news03/ShakespeareAnnounce.html (accessed June 14, 2010). I note in passing that the foundational narrative that once explained the project has shifted over time; the initial Web pages (which have since been taken down) stressed performance over education, but the press releases, which are all that remain of those inaugural moments, put education and performance on equal footing.
10. http://www.arts.gov/national/shakespeare/About.html (accessed January 7, 2010).
11. There is likely a displaced political argument here: the coastal cities of the Northeast and the West are widely seen as coextensive with liberal values, the province of "elites" in the tendentious form recognizable in the Santorum quotation.
12. Roland Barthes, *Mythologies* (1957), trans. Annette Lavers (New York: Hill and Wang, 1973), 145–148.
13. Richard Hoggart's 1957 study *The Uses of Literacy* (New Brunswick, NJ: Transaction Publishers, 1992) has been foundational in this regard, although the position is now also firmly established in composition and rhetoric studies.
14. Max Horkheimer and Theodor Adorno, "The Culture Industry: Enlightenment as Deception," in *The Dialectic of Enlightenment* (1947), trans. John Cumming (New York: Continuum Books, 1976), 120–167; Clement Greenberg, "Avant-Garde and Kitsch" (1939), in *Art and Culture: Critical Essays* (Boston, MA: Beacon Press, 1961), 3–21; Dwight Macdonald, "Masscult and Midcult," in *Against the American Grain: Essays on the Effects of Mass Culture* (New York: Random House, 1962), 3–75. For a useful analysis of intellectuals' attitudes to

popular culture, see Andrew Ross, *No Respect? Intellectuals and Popular Culture* (New York: Routledge, 1989).
15. Graham Holderness, "Preface: 'All This,'" in *The Shakespeare Myth*, ed. Graham Holderness (Manchester: Manchester University Press, 1988), xi–xvi; xii.
16. That such readings seldom addressed the question of reception with any specificity, nor considered the circumstances of their production, is problematic; it leads back to a critique of reader-response models within cultural studies much larger than the present study.
17. Witness Thomas Cartelli's *Repositioning Shakespeare: National Formations, Postcolonial Appropriations* (New York: Routledge, 1999) and Christy Desmet and Robert Sawyer, eds., *Shakespeare and Appropriation* (London: Routledge, 1999).
18. Thus the Web site aftersherrielevine.com appropriates Levine's own versions of Evans, and makes the .jpg files available to anyone who wants them. Clearly, this system of reproduction and distribution eliminates concerns about originals, copies, and ownership: the images, precisely because they are tagged as digital images, enter a public realm.
19. Douglas Lanier, *Shakespeare and Modern Popular Culture* (Oxford: Oxford University Press, 2002).
20. Peter Stallybrass and Allon White, *The Poetics and Politics of Transgression* (London: Methuen, 1983).
21. Sharon O'Dair, *Class, Critics, and Shakespeare: Bottom Lines on the Culture Wars* (Ann Arbor: University of Michigan Press, 2000). I read O'Dair's study after I published the "Popular Mechanics" essay and so was unable then to note that O'Dair also draws on the phrase from *Midsummer's Night's Dream* to figure a similar relation between those in the know and those outside its dispensation, and hence between inside academic walls and outside them.
22. The phrase "ideological dupes" had some currency in cultural studies debates about whether consumers of popular culture were unwitting victims of manipulation or whether responses to such texts were more knowing and complex. It can readily be extended to suggest that any investment in elite culture by those not "born to it" must perforce be a matter of indoctrination. For a more complicated historical analysis of the relationship between working-class readers and Shakespeare, see Andrew Murphy, *Shakespeare for the People: Working-Class Readers 1800–1900* (Cambridge: Cambridge University Press, 2008). I am not aware of any similar study concerning the United States.
23. This position is widespread in cultural studies work of the 1990s, but it is most often associated with John Fiske. For an economical version of the argument, see John Fiske, "Cultural Studies and the Culture of Everyday Life," in *Cultural Studies*, ed. Lawrence Grossberg, Cary Nelson, and Paula Treichler (London: Routledge, 1992), 154–173.
24. John Frow, *Cultural Studies and Cultural Value* (Oxford: Clarendon, 1995), 60–88.
25. Fredric Jameson, "Reification and Utopia in Mass Culture," *Social Text* 1 (Winter 1979): 130–148.

26. Thomas Cartelli has described Levine's account as informed by "democratic nostalgia": see *Repositioning Shakespeare*, 44. Alan Sinfield has suggested that Levine overschematizes a struggle between elite and popular Shakespeares, which was resolved nevertheless in favor of the former's domination over the latter; see *Faultlines: Cultural Materialism and the Politics of Dissident Reading* (Berkeley: University of California Press, 1992), 264–265.
27. Hence Joseph Papp's casting of African American actors in Shakespeare during the civil rights era was seen as part of a revolutionary political moment; see Helen Epstein, *Joe Papp: An American Life* (New York: Da Capo, 1996). The issue is also taken up in chapter 2.
28. This is not to deny that *Madame Butterfly* (for example) participates in the maintenance of gendered Orientalist fantasies. But Orientalism, like opera, has strong roots in the European aesthetic tradition.
29. Pierre Bourdieu, *Distinction: A Social Critique of the Judgment of Taste* (1979), trans. Richard Nice (Cambridge, MA: Harvard University Press, 1984); John Guillory, *Cultural Capital: The Problem of Literary Canon Formation* (Chicago: University of Chicago Press, 1993).
30. Michèle Lamont, *Money, Morals, and Manners: The Culture of the French and the American Upper-Middle Class* (Chicago: University of Chicago Press, 1992).
31. Raymond Williams, *Keywords* (New York: Oxford University Press, 1985). The term "elite" has been analyzed in a volume designed to take up where Williams left off. See Tony Bennett, Lawrence Grossberg, and Meaghan Morris, eds., *New Keywords: A Revised Vocabulary of Culture and Society* (Oxford: Blackwell, 2005). The entry for "elite" mainly concerns itself with elite theory in sociology; see 99–102.
32. For an analysis of the word "popular," see Morag Shiach, *Discourse on Popular Culture: Class, Gender, and History in Cultural Analysis, 1730 to the Present* (Stanford, CA: Stanford University Press, 1989), 17–34.
33. All definitions and citations for "elite" and "aristocracy" are taken from the *Oxford English Dictionary* (2nd ed., 1989; accessed May 27, 2010).
34. The *OED* also intermingles its citations to the sense of "elite" I have foregrounded with several specifically botanical usages, for example, "a tree selected for seed collection or vegetative propagation on account of some specially good property it may possess" (1953).
35. All subsequent quotations from Eliot will be taken from the 1962 reprint of a text originally published in 1948; see *Notes Towards the Definition of Culture* (1948; reprint, London: Faber and Faber, 1962).
36. See, for Max Weber, the famous essay "Classes, Status Groups, and Parties," first published in 1922; available in *Weber: Selections in Translation*, ed. W. G. Runciman, trans. Eric Matthews (Cambridge: Cambridge University Press, 1978), 43–56.
37. Tom Bottomore, *Elites and Society*, 2nd ed. (New York: Routledge, 1993), 8.
38. For statistics and the European state, see Michel Foucault, "Governmentality," in *The Foucault Effect: Studies in Governmentality*, ed. Graham Burchell,

Colin Gordon, and Peter Miller (Chicago: University of Chicago Press, 1991), 87–104; Alain Desrosières, *The Politics of Large Numbers: A History of Statistical Reasoning*, trans. Camille Naish (Cambridge, MA: Harvard University Press, 1998). For statistics and colonial populations, see Ann Laura Stoler, *Race and the Education of Desire: Foucault's History of Sexuality and the Colonial Order of Things* (Durham, NC: Duke University Press, 1995).

39. Indeed, I am far from the first to suggest the ambiguity of the sign "elite"; see, for instance, James H. Meisel, *The Myth of the Ruling Class: Gaetano Mosca and the "Elite"* (Ann Arbor: University of Michigan Press, 1962), esp. v-vi; 5–6.

40. For a useful definition of neoliberalism, see John Frow, "Cultural Studies and the Neoliberal Imagination," *Yale Journal of Criticism* 12, no. 2 (1999): 424–430; see also David Harvey, *A Brief History of Neoliberalism* (Oxford: Oxford University Press, 2005).

41. John Guillory, "Literary Critics as Intellectuals: Class Analysis and the Crisis in the Humanities," in *Rethinking Class: Literary Studies and Social Formations*, ed. Wai Chee Dimock and Michael Gilmore (New York: Columbia University Press, 1994), 107–149.

42. The difference might further be explained by the fifteen years intervening between his analyses and my own, as well as by the incommensurability in our institutional placements.

43. Stanley Aronowitz, "The Last Good Job in America," in *Post-Work: The Wages of Cybernation*, ed. Stanley Aronowitz and Jonathan Cutler (New York: Routledge, 1998), 203–223.

44. In addition to Bourdieu, see Michel Foucault, *Discipline and Punish: The Birth of the Prison*, trans. Alan Sheridan (New York: Vintage Books, 1995); Louis Althusser, "Ideology and Ideological State Apparatuses," in *Lenin and Philosophy and Other Essays*, trans. Ben Brewster (New York: Monthly Review Press, 1971), 127–186; Barbara and John Ehrenreich, "The Professional-Managerial Class," *Radical America* 11, Part 1 (March-April 1977): 7–31; 11, Part 2 (May-June 1977): 7–22.

45. Richard Ohmann, *English in America: A Radical View of the Profession* (New York: Oxford University Press, 1976). See also his *Politics of Letters* (Middletown, CT: Wesleyan University Press, 1987).

46. Stephen J. Brown, "The Uses of Shakespeare in America: A Study in Class Domination," in *Shakespeare, Pattern of Excelling Nature: Shakespeare Criticism in Honor of America's Bicentennial from the International Shakespeare Association Conference, Washington, DC, 1976*, ed. David M. Bevington and Jay L. Halio (Newark, DE: University of Delaware Press, 1978), 230–238; the quoted material appears on 235.

47. A similar point might be made about Michael Bristol's *Big-Time Shakespeare* (New York: Routledge, 1996), which is motivated by popular resistance to the arguments in *Shakespeare's America* to essentialize Shakespearean durability: as though it were the texts "themselves" that endure, rather than institutions that find in those texts, which would otherwise fall into desuetude, a reservoir of value subject to reiteration and preservation.

48. Marjorie Garber, "Shakespeare as Fetish," *Shakespeare Quarterly* 41, no. 2 (Summer 1990): 242–250.
49. For a trenchant analysis of how English departments in particular have been subject to economic exigencies, see Cary Nelson and Stephen Watt, "America's Fast Food Discipline," in *Academic Keywords: A Devil's Dictionary for Higher Education* (New York: Routledge, 1999), 55–58.
50. Bill Readings, *The University in Ruins* (Cambridge, MA: Harvard University Press, 1996), 2.
51. See Richard Hofstadter, *Anti-Intellectualism in American Life* (New York: Knopf, 1963).
52. David Harvey, *The Condition of Postmodernity* (Oxford: Blackwell, 1989), 147–197.
53. As, indeed, am I, for whatever self-disclosure is worth to my argument.

2 Pacino's Cliffs Notes: Looking for Richard's "Public" Shakespeare

1. *Looking for Richard* (1996), directed by Al Pacino. Twentieth Century Fox. Available as a digital download from Amazon.com or iTunes.
2. For an analysis of Pacino's body in relation to Method acting, see Barbara Hodgson, "Replicating Richard: Body Doubles, Body Politics," *Theatre Journal* 50, no. 2 (1998): 207–205; for an elegantly condensed argument about Pacino and performance that has several points in common with the present chapter (particularly in its attention to the movement from Old World to New), see Thomas Cartelli and Katherine Rowe, "Shakespeare and the Street: *Looking for Richard*," in *New Wave Shakespeare on Screen* (Cambridge: Polity, 2007), 98–102.
3. Papp's productions in the Delacorte Theater often featured actors who were already well-known and destined to become even more so, such as Morgan Freeman, Sam Waterston, and Meryl Streep.
4. See Thomas Cartelli, "Shakespeare and the Street: Pacino's *Looking for Richard*, Bedford's *Street King*, and the Common Understanding," in *Shakespeare, the Movie, II: Popularizing the Plays on Film, TV, Video, and DVD*, ed. Richard Burt and Lynda Boose (London: Routledge, 2003), 186–199.
5. I am not certain of the location of the church: filming took place in New York (especially in and around the Cloisters), Montreal, Stratford-upon-Avon, and the then-uncompleted Globe in London.
6. See W. B. Worthen, *Shakespeare and the Authority of Performance* (Cambridge: Cambridge University Press, 1997), 95–150.
7. Information about the casts of Papp's productions can be found at the Public Theater Web site: http://www.publictheater.org/celebrating/past.php (accessed January 10, 2010).
8. See also Denise Albanese, "Black and White, and Dread All Over: The 'Photonegative' *Othello* and the Body of Desdemona," in *A Feminist Companion to Shakespeare*, ed. Dympna Callaghan (Oxford: Blackwell, 2000), 226–247.

9. Or so the International Movie Data Base (imdb.com) entry for Pacino indicates.
10. All transcriptions, and hence all errors, are my own, although I have also consulted a transcription of the entire film available at http://www.script-o-rama.com/movie_scripts/l/looking-for-richard-script-transcript.html (downloaded August 1, 2006). The ellipses are for clarity.
11. John Simon, *John Simon On Theater: Criticism 1974–2003* (New York: Applause Books, 2005), 140–142; the quoted passage appears on 140.
12. Marjorie Garber, "Shakespeare as Fetish." *Shakespeare Quarterly* 41, no. 2 (Summer 1990): 242–250.
13. Tyler Cowen has suggested that an expanded cultural marketplace has benefits for all, but as befits the school of rational choice economics to which he belongs, questions of moral value are strictly bracketed out: see *In Praise of Commercial Culture* (Cambridge, MA: Harvard University Press, 1998).
14. See, for instance, Harry Berger, Jr., *Imaginary Audition: Shakespeare on Stage and Page* (Berkeley and Los Angeles: University of California Press, 1989); and Barbara Hodgdon, "The Critic, the Poor Player, Prince Hamlet, and the Lady in the Dark" in *Shakespeare Reread: The Texts in New Contexts*, ed. Russ McDonald (Ithaca, NY: Cornell University Press, 1994), 259–293.
15. In fact, Pacino conducts a few interviews with what appear to be British scholars sitting in their book-lined studies. The credits reveal these "scholars" to be the actors Barbara Everett and Emrys Jones, largely unfamiliar to American audiences. I am not sure whether Pacino means this to be a sly joke.
16. When I mentioned to Lawrence Levine that I was going to be writing about study guides and Shakespeare, he characterized them in this spirit as "genuine popular culture."
17. SparkNotes, *The Tempest, by William Shakespeare*, contributors Susannah Mandel, Adam Stewart, Brian Phillips, Patrick Flanagan, John Crowther, and Justin Kestler (New York: Spark Publishing, 2002), 17–18.
18. By way of anecdotal illustration, I was told by a graduate student who taught high school English in a conservative Northern Virginia school district that he would stay away from using Baz Luhrmann's 1996 film *William Shakespeare's Romeo + Juliet* in his classroom because he knew local parents would object to its treatment of sexuality and "promotion of drug use."
19. The people who've volunteered to me that they enjoyed *Looking for Richard* are not the sort who'd ever say publicly that Shakespeare "sucked." Mostly, they are earnest students and college-educated nonacademics who presumably share a favorable dispensation to their object anyway.
20. William Uricchio and Roberta Pearson, *Reframing Culture: The Case of the Vitagraph Quality Films* (Princeton, NJ: Princeton University Press, 1993).
21. For Olivier, see Denise Albanese, "School for Scandal?: New Media *Hamlet*, Olivier, and Camp Connoisseurship," *Renaissance Drama* 34, ed. Jeffrey Masten, Wendy Wall, and W. B. Worthen (Evanston, IL: Northwestern University Press, 2005), 185–208; for the BBC/Time-Life Shakespeare, see J. C. Bulman and H. R. Coursen, eds., *Shakespeare on Television: An Anthology*

of Essays and Reviews (Hanover, NH, and London: University Press of New England, 1988), especially Graham Holderness, "Boxing the Bard," 14–18.

22. This is not to say that their attitude has not been shaped or reinforced elsewhere: mass entertainment, for instance, has a long history of burlesquing Shakespeare for his unapproachability and incomprehensibility, which Douglas Lanier has usefully detailed in *Shakespeare and Modern Popular Culture* (Oxford: Oxford University Press, 2002).
23. Helen Epstein, *Joe Papp: An American Life* (New York: Da Capo, 1996), 119–133.
24. Jason Zinoman, "First Thing We Do, Let's Seat All the Lawyers," *New York Times,* July 11, 2004.
25. Pierre Bourdieu and Hans Haacke offer a series of nuanced and astute observations on the relations between art, politics, and state- and market-sponsored institutions in *Free Exchange* (Palo Alto, CA: Stanford University Press, 1995).

3   Shakespeare Goes to School

1. The March 2007 conference at the Folger Shakespeare Library, "Shakespeare in American Education, 1637–1932," was perhaps the first attempt to cover the subject systematically and historically; it brought together scholars of English and American literature, theater, and education. A small portion of this chapter was presented at that conference; other parts of it, based on my ongoing research, touch upon subjects presented by various scholars there, although my orientation and source materials are different. My interest in this topic, and in the role of the College Board in particular, was spurred by Arthur N. Applebee's *Tradition and Reform in the Teaching of English: A History* (Urbana, IL: National Council of Teachers of English, 1974). I wish to acknowledge my general indebtedness to Applebee, both for this invaluable study and for suggestions he made for future research in the time leading up to the conference at the Folger.
2. I owe the clarity of this claim to Elizabeth Renker, whose survey of Shakespeare's place in the curricula or colleges and normal schools for the Folger conference suggests the distinction.
3. I am aware of the tendentious character of this generalization. Even if most Americans finish high school, significant numbers still do not: for instance, the minimum age at which an individual can leave formal schooling is sixteen.
4. This generalization does not include the significant minority who attain GEDs, where "functional literacy" rather than that mediated by literary texts is demanded.
5. Lawrence Levine, *Highbrow/Lowbrow: The Emergence of Cultural Hierarchy in America* (Cambridge, MA: Harvard University Press, 1988), and Kim Sturgess, *Shakespeare and the American Nation* (Cambridge: Cambridge University Press, 2004).
6. Mary Trachsel, *Institutionalizing Literacy: The Historical Role of College Entrance Examinations in English* (Carbondale, IL: Southern Illinois University Press,

1992), 29. Trachsel's analysis seems politically outdated, given its uncomplicated sense that professional standards, now as well as then, function simply as exclusionary practices; nevertheless, I am indebted to her insights on standardization and the role played by the growth in research faculties in English.
7. Joseph Quincy Adams, "The Folger Shakespeare Memorial Dedicated April 23, 1932: Shakespeare and American Culture," *Spinning Wheel Magazine* 12, nos. 9–10 (1932): 212–215; 229–231. The quoted passages occur on 230.
8. William Watkins, *The White Architects of Black Education: Ideology and Power in America, 1865–1954*, foreword by Robin D. G. Kelley (New York: Teachers College Press, 2001); Michael Fultz, "African American Teachers in the South 1890–1940: Powerlessness and the Ironies of Expectation and Protest," *History of Education Quarterly* 35, no. 4 (1995): 401–422; Fultz, "Teacher Training and African American Education in the South 1900–1940," *Journal of Negro Education* 64, no. 2 (1995): 196–210. For a brief, provocative discussion of attitudes to schooling in America as conditioned by the needs of laborers, see Stanley Aronowitz, "Against Schooling: Education And Social Class." *Social Text* 22, no. 2 (2004): 13–35.
9. For informal schooling, see Joseph F. Kett, *The Pursuit of Knowledge under Difficulties: From Self-Improvement to Adult Education in America, 1750–1990* (Stanford, CA: Stanford University Press, 1994).
10. Benedict Anderson, *Imagined Communities: Reflections on the Origin and Spread of Nationalism*, 2nd ed. (London: Verso, 1991).
11. For Southern taste in Shakespeare, where there is evidence of a long history of performance in such cities as Annapolis and Williamsburg, see Philip C. Kolin, ed., *Shakespeare in the South: Essays on Performance* (Jackson: University of Mississippi Press, 1983). For a more temporally limited account of Shakespearean performance in the West, see Helene Wickham Koons, *How Shakespeare Won the West: Players and Performers in American's Gold Rush 1849–1865* (Jefferson, NC: McFarland, 1989).
12. William Holmes McGuffey, *New Sixth Eclectic Reader* (Cincinnati: Wilson and Hinkle Co., 1867).
13. Dorothy Sullivan, *William Holmes McGuffey: Schoolmaster of the Nation* (Rutherford, NJ: Fairleigh Dickinson University Press, 1994), 149. I owe to Jonathan Burton my sense of the difference in levels between the Fourth and Sixth Readers; see the transcripts of his interview for the Folger-produced radio series "Shakespeare in American Life'" at http://www.shakespeareinamericanlife.org/transcripts/burton1.cfm (accessed May 30, 2010).
14. Henry William Simon, *The Reading of Shakespeare in American Schools and Colleges: An Historical Survey* (New York: Simon and Schuster, 1932), 28; 30–31.
15. Dorothy Sullivan has noted that the Sixth Eclectic Reader discussed by Simon was actually not "directly attributable to either of the McGuffey brothers" (Alexander had collaborated with William) but rather to educators associated with the publishing firm that had picked up the volumes; see *William Holmes McGuffey*, 211.

16. In a paper presented at the Folger conference, Jonathan Burton demonstrated how in McGuffey's selection from *The Merchant of Venice* the lines have been elided and edited so as to efface Portia's transgendered impersonation in the pivotal trial scene: the speaker is identified only as "Judge." It seems likely that such silent repositioning is typical.
17. Ruth Miller Elson, *Guardians of Tradition: American Schoolbooks of the Nineteenth Century* (Lincoln: University of Nebraska Press, 1964), 283. The lists Simon provides also support her claim concerning the pervasiveness of Brutus's speech at the death of Caesar.
18. George B. Churchill, "Shakespeare in America" (address delivered at the annual meeting of the German Shakespeare Society, April 23, 1906), in *Americans on Shakespeare 1776–1914*, ed. Peter Rawlings (Aldershot, UK: Ashgate, 1999), 418–448. The quoted passage occurs on 420.
19. The fact that *Cymbeline* and *The Tempest*, with their similar defenses of a natural aristocracy over the efforts to change that nature through nurture,, also joined the repertory at the same time as these political plays, cautions against reading the theater solely as an inspiration for democratic practice—or, alternatively, against presuming that the textual contradictions valorized by reading practices such as ours can be cast backward in time. But unlike those other plays, *Julius Caesar* has persisted as an educational touchstone.
20. In analyzing the differing reception given in the North and the South to Edwin Booth's postbellum *Richard II*, Catherine M. Shaw has provided useful evidence that the assassination of Lincoln by Booth, and the parallels to Caesar, were not remote from the popular imaginary; see "Edwin's Booth's *Richard II* and the Divided Nation," in *Textual and Theatrical Shakespeare: Questions of Evidence*, ed. Edward Pechter (Iowa City: Iowa University Press, 1996), 144–163. See also John Andrews, "Was the Bard Behind It?" *Atlantic Monthly* October 1990, 27; Andrews, "Shakespeare and the Lincoln Assassination" *The Shakespeare Newsletter* 42, no. 2 (1992): n. 213.
21. The essays in *Shakespeare in the South*, which cover Maryland, Virginia, Charleston, New Orleans, Mobile, Mississippi, and Houston, suggest that very few performances of *Julius Caesar* were staged in the region. While inference from a necessarily limited evidential basis is hazardous, it is nevertheless tantalizing to speculate about the role of the play in demarcating Northern versions of the nation from Southern.
22. Ruth Warren, "The Popularity and Influence of Shakespeare's English and Roman Historical Plays in America from the Beginnings to 1950." Unpublished M.A. thesis, College of the Pacific, 1955.
23. See, for example, Scott Newstok, "'Step aside, I'll show thee a president': George W. as Henry V?" (http://www.poppolitics.com/archives/2003/05/George-W-as-Henry-Vh; accessed January 11, 2010).
24. Thomas Derrick, *Understanding Julius Caesar: A Student Casebook to Issues, Sources, and Historical Documents* (Greenwood Press Literature in Context Series) (Westport, CT: Greenwood Press, 1998), 106–129.

25. S. G. Goodrich, *The Fourth Reader for the Use of Schools* (Cambridge, MA: Folsom, Wells, and Thurston, 1839; quoted in Elson, *Guardians*, 84.
26. Alan Sinfield, "Give an account of Shakespeare and Education, showing why you think they are effective and what you have appreciated about them. Support your comments with precise references," in *Political Shakespeare: New Essays in Cultural Materialism*, ed. Jonathan Dollimore and Alan Sinfield, 2nd ed. (Ithaca, NY: Cornell University Press, 1995), 134–157.
27. For information about the AP English Literature curriculum, see *English Course Description: English Language and Composition/English Literature and Composition May 2007, May 2008* (College Board AP: www.collegeboard.com/student/testing/ap/sub_englit.html; accessed January 10, 2010). It should be noted that the course of study for language and composition, which often stands in for freshman composition, stresses non-fiction such as biography, criticism, and science writing and excludes fiction, poetry, and drama.
28. Peter Roberts, *Shakespeare and the Moral Curriculum: Rethinking the Secondary-School Shakespeare Syllabus* (New York: Pripet Press, 1992). Roberts, who has taught at a New York City private school, sent out a survey to "English Department chairpersons" (at private secondary institutions) nationwide: his data reveal that more and different plays are taught, and often more demanding editions used, than tends to be the case in public schools, where the immense public resources tied up in comprehensive textbooks often exert an inertial pull on the curriculum and hence on what plays will be taught year after year.
29. Witness the 2007–2008 guidelines for AP English Literature: Shakespeare is but one of a vast number of authors whose texts might be studied in a course eligible for college-level credit.
30. David Starr Jordan, "The Building of the University," in *The Voice of the Scholar: With Other Addresses on the Problems in Higher Education* (San Francisco: Paul Elder and Company, 1903), 28.
31. Levine, *Highbrow/Lowbrow*, 169–177; William Uricchio and Roberta E. Pearson, *Reframing Culture: The Case of the Vitagraph Films* (Princeton, NJ: Princeton University Press, 1993), 17–40.
32. To this extent, the tests stand in broad support of Levine's argument that Shakespeare became increasingly associated with the "highbrow"—wealthy individuals of Anglo-Saxon heritage—whose interests most elite colleges were overwhelmingly dedicated to serve in the years under discussion.
33. For the first two years (1898–1899 and 1899–1900) after the five boroughs were constituted into a single administrative unit and put under the supervision of the New York City Board of Education, a report produced for the superintendent of schools that reproduced qualifying examinations for school principals and teachers yields some insight into the centrality of *Macbeth* at all levels of teacher training. A 1899–1900 examination for a high school teacher, for example, asked the applicant to interpret passages, explain metaphors, and "Describe [his] method of treating the play of 'Macbeth' in a literature class, stating aims and collateral work." *New York City Superintendent of Schools Annual Report, 1899–1900* (New York: Board of Education, 1899), 156–157.

34. For a more complete listing, see Arthur N. Applebee, *Tradition and Reform*, Appendix III, 275–277.
35. Thomas R. Price, *The Construction and Types of Shakespeare's Verse as Seen in Othello* (New York: Press of the New York Shakespeare Society, 1888).
36. According to Applebee, the following year, 1893–1894, is when a precursor to the College Board, the Committee of Ten, meets at Vassar to establish entrance requirements in English literature apart from composition; see *Tradition and Reform*, Appendix I, 271.
37. "We find that Greek-mindedness is necessary to receive from the Greek all that this noblest of languages is competent to give. We find for the average men better educational substance in English than in Latin, in the Physical or Natural Sciences than in the Calculus." David Starr Jordan, "The Building of the University," 28.
38. David Starr Jordan, *The Blood of the Nation: A Study of the Decay of Races through the Survival of the Unfit* (Boston, MA: American Unitarian Association, 1902).
39. In the absence of students' responses to these prompts, I can only hazard contextualized guesses, and it must be underscored that they are but guesses.
40. Delia Bacon, *The Philosophy of the Plays of Shakespeare Unfolded* (Boston, MA: Ticknor and Fields, 1857); Ignatius Donnelly, *The Great Cryptogram: Francis Bacon's Cipher in the So-Called Shakespeare Plays* (New York and London: R. S. Peale and Co., 1888).
41. Mary Trachsel, *Institutionalizing Literacy*, 70–103.
42. For evidence that *King John* might have been read as an aid to citizenship, consider the words of Virginia Mason Vaughan in 2000: "[The] opening scene...suggests that legitimacy is a constructed category, that it depends on the consent of various political constituencies...*King John* is concerned with the formation of a national consensus"; see Virginia Mason Vaughan, "*King John*," in *A Companion to Shakespeare's Works, Volume II: The Histories*, ed. Richard Dutton and Jean E. Howard (Oxford: Blackwell, 2003), 379–394. The quoted material appears on 382.
43. Elaine Brousseau, "Now, Literature, Philosophy, and Thought, Are Shakspearized: American Culture and Nineteenth Century Shakespearean Performance, 1835–1875." Ph. D. dissertation at the University of Massachusetts, Amherst, 2003, 17.
44. Alexander Saxton, *The Rise and Fall of the White Republic: Class Politics and Class Culture in Nineteenth-Century America* (1990), with a new foreword by David Roediger (London: Verso, 2003), 165–182.
45. Applebee, *Tradition and Reform*, Appendix III, 275.
46. William Lamartine Snyder, *The Geography of Marriage: Or, Legal Perplexities of Wedlock in the United States* (New York: G. P. Putnam's Sons, 1889). A passage from *Othello*, in which Brabantio wonders whether Desdemona can be "half the wooer," serves as an epigraph on p. 64 and introduces an argument asserting that mixed-race marriage is disgusting and against popular taste, but that it ought nevertheless not be subject to legal prosecution.

47. While the riots were undoubtedly racial in part, they also manifested a class valence: richer draftees were able to buy themselves out of service. In addition to the approximately 100 black people who died, it is estimated that up to 2,000 poor white male rioters were also killed. See Luc Sante, *Low Life: Lures and Snares of Old New York* (New York: Vintage, 1992), 350–354.
48. Frank Forest Bunker, "The Functional Reorganization of the American Public School System." Ph.D. dissertation, New York University, 1913 (Washington, D.C.: Government Printing Office, 1916).
49. See Gerald Graff and Michael Warner, eds., *The Origins of Literary Study in America: A Documentary Anthology* (New York: Routledge, 1989).
50. For a reading of Laurence Olivier's *Hamlet* that attends to the role of the pedagogical imperative, see Denise Albanese, "School for Scandal?: New Media *Hamlet*, Olivier, and Camp Connoisseurship," *Renaissance Drama* 34 (2005) Special Issue: "Media, Technology, and Performance," edited by Jeffrey Masten, Wendy Wall, and W. B. Worthen, 185–208 (Evanston, IL: Northwestern University Press, 2006).

4 The Shakespeare Film, the Market, and the Americanization of Culture

1. William Uricchio and Roberta Pearson, *Reframing Culture: The Case of the Vitagraph Quality Films* (Princeton, NJ: Princeton University Press, 1993).
2. After the production of just one film, *Love's Labour's Lost*, that did not meet with the same *success d'estime* of his earlier offerings, Branagh has offered no new theatrical releases in the United States, although one production—*As You Like It* (2006)—aired on the Home Box Office (HBO) subscription cable network in 2007. Available data suggest Intermedia Films played no part in the production, which was a joint project of HBO Films, BBC Films, and Branagh's own production company, The Shakespeare Film Company.
3. Quoted in Lawrence Levine, *Highbrow/Lowbrow: The Emergence of Cultural Hierarchy in America* (Cambridge, MA: Harvard University Press, 1988), 53.
4. Terence Hawkes, *Meaning by Shakespeare* (New York: Routledge, 2002), 153. It should be noted that Hawkes's account does not quite make the point for which I use his title. Rather, he argues against textual essentialism (with meaning as the "product" sold by its supreme author) in favor of understanding specific instantiations dialectically.
5. Carol Innerst, "The Bard Draws a Pass to Pop Culture on Campus: Many Colleges Are Skipping Shakespeare," *Washington Times,* December 17, 2007. Innerst is reporting on a survey of "70 leading colleges and universities" conducted by the National Alumni Forum in light of the Georgetown controversy. For information about and documentation of events at Georgetown, I am grateful to Kim Hall and Henry Schwartz.
6. For suggestive analyses of Kurosawa's versions of Shakespeare, see John Collick, *Shakespeare, Cinema and Society* (Manchester: Manchester University Press, 1989), 150–187.

7. Michael Denning, *Culture in the Age of Three Worlds* (London: Verso, 2004), 97–120.
8. Michael Bristol, *Shakespeare's America, America's Shakespeare* (New York: Routledge, 1990), 19.
9. See, for example, Linda Boose and Richard Burt, eds., *Shakespeare the Movie: Popularizing the Plays on Film, TV, and Video* (London: Routledge, 1997).
10. *Hamlet*, directed by Kenneth Branagh (1996; Warner Brothers International DVD, 2007) and *William Shakespeare's Romeo + Juliet*, directed by Baz Luhrmann (1996; Fox DVD, 1997). In light of Peter Donaldson's wonderfully persuasive reading of the plus sign in Luhrmann's title, I have corrected my own representation of it; see Donaldson, "'In fair Verona' : Media, Spectacle, and Performance in *William Shakespeare's Romeo + Juliet,*" in *Shakespeare After Mass Media*, ed. Richard Burt (New York: Palgrave Macmillan, 2002), 59–82.
11. See Toby Miller, Nitin Govil, and John McMurria, *Global Hollywood 2* (London: BFI Publishing, 2005).
12. James Loehlin, "'Top of the World, Ma': *Richard III* and Cinematic Convention," in Boose and Burt, *Shakespeare the Movie,* 67–79; the quoted passage appears on 67.
13. See, for instance, J. C. Bulman and H. R. Coursen, eds., *Shakespeare on Television: An Anthology of Essays and Reviews* (Hanover, NH: University Press of New England, 1988); Anthony Davies and Stanley Wells, eds., *Shakespeare and the Moving Image: The Plays on Film and Television* (Cambridge: Cambridge University Press, 1994).
14. Graham Holderness, "Boxing the Bard," in Bulman and Coursen, *Shakespeare on Television*, 14–18.
15. Theodor Adorno, "The Fetish Character in Music and the Regression in Listening," in *The Culture Industry: Selected Essays in Mass Culture* (New York: Routledge, 1991), 29–60.
16. Kenneth Branagh, *Hamlet by William Shakespeare: Screenplay, Introduction, and Film Diary* (New York: Norton, 1996).
17. In suggesting there is something easy and knowable about the mise-en-scène, I do not mean to imply that the setting cannot be read more complexly: surely the icy glitter of the palace's public chambers have consequences for our understanding of Hamlet's unease in them. But the temporal code within which they might signify is nevertheless rife with associations for certain kinds of spectators.
18. Consider Branagh's remarks concerning his casting choices for Hamlet during a public discussion at the Smithsonian Institution in Washington, D.C., in December 1996:

    In the end...I don't think you can second guess the audience or think that somehow to provide those people in those parts is to guarantee you a certain kind of audience, because I've been aware over the years, in fact for a lot of people, the knee-jerk reaction is lack of acceptance and a suspicion. And in fact I think it can do you more harm than good...There would be a price to pay for some people. I'm sure it won't work for everyone, but for me it was a great treat to see all those different approaches come together. I believe the man belongs to everyone, you know, across the world, and across cultures, across sexes, and so implicitly I wanted to suggest that with the accent-blind, nationality-blind, color-blind casting. (Transcription made by Diane Williams)

See also Ramona Wray and Mark Thornton Burnett, "From the Horse's Mouth: Branagh on the Bard," in *Shakespeare, Film, Fin de Siècle*, ed. Mark Thorton Burnett and Ramona Wray (New York: St. Martin's, 2000), 165–178.

19. The most recent data from the Internet Movie Data Base indicate that *Hamlet* has not recouped its production costs: budgeted at $18 million, the movie's total U.S. gross was given as $4.4 million. The Internet Movie Data Base (www.imdb.com), the source for my figures, must be used with caution, for there is reason to suspect its accuracy. In consulting Shakespeare movies listed on the site over a period of several months, I found the data were infrequently updated and unevenly collected: the international data are comprehensive in some cases, scattered in others, and nonexistent in still others. Nevertheless, imdb.com is roughly useful, if only as a preliminary basis for an argument about profitability (accessed January 15, 2010).
20. imdb.com (accessed May 23, 2010).
21. The quotation comes from the transcription cited in note 18.
22. The claim is Richard Burt's: see "The Love That Dare Not Speak Shakespeare's Name: New Shakesqueer Cinema," in Boose and Burt, *Shakespeare the Movie*, 240–268. It may be true that DiCaprio has wide erotic appeal (and not just to men), and that Leguizamo's other cinematic roles might leave a regendering trace across his performance as the parodically macho Tybalt (who is shown as the favorite of Juliet's mother). Nevertheless, Burt's indiscriminacy effaces the extent to which the script demands that only Mercutio of the three be read as sexually ambiguous. The distinction is important to maintain, given the film's insistent conjoining of race and other forms of exoticism.
23. I have hazarded the approximate "Anglo-Saxon or Celtic" as a description of Benvolio because of Dash Mihok's red hair and fair skin—as well as the costume he wears to the Capulet ball, an odd combination of Viking helmet and Scottish kilt (all the costumes are resonant of mythic characterizations; thus Dave Paris's astronaut garb, Romeo's knight in shining armor, and Juliet's angel).
24. Michael Denning, *The Cultural Front: The Laboring of American Culture in the Twentieth Century* (London: Verso, 1997), 401.
25. Peter Donaldson's discussion of Australian drag performances as part of the context for Mercutio's star turn is apposite here; see Donaldson, "Fair Verona."
26. Celeste Olalquiaga, *Megalopolis: Contemporary Cultural Sensibilities* (Minneapolis: University of Minnesota Press, 1992), 41–42.
27. My students would argue with me that the love scenes between Romeo and Juliet are the exceptions to my rule: as one put it, "What would the film even mean if they weren't sincere?" Still, I think this response speaks more to the investment in pure romance my students bring to the film than to the film's representation of

that romance. For me the scenes function merely as telling points of semiotic difference, not unlike the pale skin tones given to the lovers.
28. Don Hedrick, "War is Mud: Branagh's Dirty Harry V and the Types of Political Ambiguity," in Boose and Burt, *Shakespeare the Movie*, 45–66.
29. The commercially successful soundtrack also functions to deemphasize the importance of the script.
30. See Paul Smith, *Millennial Dreams* (London: Verso, 1997).
31. Bristol, *Shakespeare's America*, 10.
32. Roland Barthes, *Mythologies* (1957), trans. Annette Lavers (New York: Hill and Wang, 1973), 12.

5 Social Dreaming and Making Shakespeare Matter

1. Engaging with this domain is Richard Burt's aim in *Unspeakable ShaXXXspeares: Queer Theory and American Kiddie Culture* (New York: St. Martin's Press, 1998).
2. Constance Penley, *NASA/Trek: Popular Science and Sex in America* (London: Verso, 1997).
3. "Act V": episode 218, *This American Life*; first broadcast August 9, 2002; go to www.thisamericanlife.org for audio. All transcriptions are my own.
4. Jack Zipes, "Traces of Hope: The Non-Synchronicity of Ernst Bloch," in *Not Yet: Reconsidering Ernst Bloch*, ed. Jamie Owen Daniel and Tom Moylan (London: Verso, 1997), 1–12. The phrase "learned hope" is a translation of a concept, *docta spes*, associated with Bloch. I have generally benefited from the many insights concerning Bloch to be found in this collection.
5. Amy Scott-Douglass, *Shakespeare Inside: The Bard behind Bars (Shakespeare Now!)* (London: Continuum, 2007); Jean Trounstine, *Shakespeare behind Bars: The Power of Drama in a Women's Prison* (New York: St. Martin's Press, 2001); Neils Herold, "Movers and Losers: Shakespeare in *Charge* and *Shakespeare behind Bars*," in *Native Shakespeares: Indigenous Appropriations on a Global Stage*, ed. Craig Dionne and Parmita Kapadia (Aldershot, UK: Ashgate, 2008), 153–179. See also the documentary *Shakespeare behind Bars*, directed by Hank Rogerson (Philomath Films, 2005).
6. Michael Warner has stressed the importance of coming into a relation with strangers as part of what it means to be a public; equally important, of course, is the abstractness of the position on offer. See *Publics and Counterpublics* (New York: Zone, 2000).
7. Courtney Lehmann, *Shakespeare Remains: Theater to Film, Early Modern to Postmodern* (Ithaca, NY: Cornell University Press, 2002).
8. For a general sense of his position, see Alan Sinfield, *Faultlines: Cultural Materialism and the Politics of Dissident Reading* (Berkeley and Los Angeles: University of California Press, 1992).
9. Jurgen Habermas, *The Structural Transformation of the Public Sphere* (1962), trans. Thomas Burger (Cambridge, MA: MIT Press, 1989).

10. I have not done extensive empirical work on the matter of audience, but I find it notable that *This American Life* is particularly popular among students at my institution's MFA program. It is also worth noting that "Act V" is, according to the program Web site, a very popular episode and that Glass has several times generously lent his name and presence to help raise funds for Wilcox's prison theater program.
11. In *Unspeakable ShaXXXspeares,* Richard Burt offers a useful, audacious, and provocative account of the value academics tend to place in smartness that in some ways resonates with mine, albeit to different ends.
12. A colleague, Susan Tichy, has suggested that it's considered a breach of prison etiquette to ask prisoners about their crimes. That would make Hitt's insistence on knowing them all the more tactless, all the more clearly an abuse of the power to know that is already so clearly on his side.
13. Jonathan Dollimore, *Radical Tragedy: Religion, Ideology, and Power in the Drama of Shakespeare and His Contemporaries* (Chicago: University of Chicago Press, 1984), 191–195.
14. Niels Herold also invokes the idea of "losers" in connection with "Shakespeare behind Bars," although not in connection with economic transformation as such; see "Movers and Losers."
15. For a left critical analysis of the need to reimagine a public sphere, see John Frow, "Cultural Studies and the Neoliberal Imagination," *Yale Journal of Criticism* 12, no. 2 (1999): 424–430.
16. Richard Dyer, "Entertainment and Utopia" in *The Cultural Studies Reader,* ed. Simon During (New York: Routledge, 1993), 271–283; the quoted passage appears on p. 273.
17. In this it differs from Hank Rogerson's 2005 *Shakespeare behind Bars,* a film tracking the "Shakespeare behind Bars" Program over the course of a year at the Luther Luckett Correctional Center. It gives viewers a far more structured—and apparently far more promising—sense of the possible coalescence of performance and parole. But the promise is suddenly dashed when Sammie, a member of the troupe who has seemed to be a special point of investment in the film, is sentenced to six more years instead.
18. Hence an announcement I received for a production of *Stalag 17* at Northeast Correctional Center in Missouri, a men's prison, and for *The Caucasian Chalk Circle* at the Women's Eastern Reception, Diagnostic, and Correctional Center; both are in Missouri and are affiliated with Prison Performing Arts, the umbrella organization with which Wilcox works.
19. Herold, "Movers and Losers," 166.
20. Gayatri Spivak, "Can the Subaltern Speak?" in *Marxism and the Interpretation of Cultures,* ed. Cary Nelson and Lawrence Grossberg (Urbana: University of Illinois Press, 1988), 271–313.
21. Lata Mani, "Cultural Theory, Colonial Texts: Reading Eye-Witness Accounts of Widow Burning," *Cultural Studies,* ed. Lawrence Grossberg, Cary Nelson, and Paula Treichler (New York: Routledge, 1992), 392–394.

22. Stuart Hall uses the phrase "cultural dopes" in his useful analysis of debates around what counts as popular culture: "Notes on Deconstructing 'The Popular,'" in *People's History and Socialist Theory*, ed. Raphael Samuel (London: Routledge & Kegan Paul, 1981), 227–240.
23. It is worth noting that even Spivak later pulled back from the strength of her assertion; see Gayatri Spivak, "Subaltern Talk: Interview with the Editors" in *The Spivak Reader*, ed. Donna Landry and Gerald Maclean (New York: Routledge, 1996), 287–308.
24. Fredric Jameson, *Marxism and Form: Twentieth-Century Dialectical Theories of Literature* (Princeton, NJ: Princeton University Press, 1971), 145–146.
25. Ernst Bloch, *The Principle of Hope* (1959), 3 vols., trans. Neville Plaice, Stephen Plaice, and Paul Knight (Cambridge: MA: MIT Press, 1986), 3.
26. Tony Bennett, *Outside Literature* (London: Routledge, 2000), 286.
27. Hugh Grady, *Shakespeare's Universal Wolf: Studies in Early Modern Reification* (New York: Clarendon Press, 1986); Kiernan Ryan, "Marxism before Marx," in *Marxist Shakespeares*, ed. Jean Howard and Scott Shershow (New York: Routledge, 2000), 227–244, esp. 227–230.
28. See the arguments concerning the "structure of feeling" in *Marxism and Literature* (Oxford: Oxford University Press, 1977), 128–135.
29. Susan Buck-Morss, *Dreamworld and Catastrophe: The Passing of Mass Utopia in East and West* (Cambridge, MA: MIT, 2000).
30. For how education reproduces class, see Paul Willis, *Learning to Labor: How Working-Class Kids Get Working-Class Jobs* (New York: Columbia University Press, 1982).
31. Nancy Fraser has provided a useful summary of the critical discourse on Habermas as well as a diagnosis aiming to recuperate the concept: see "Rethinking the Public Sphere: A Contribution to the Critique of Actually-Existing Democracy," in *The Phantom Public Sphere,* ed. Bruce Robbins (Minneapolis: University of Minnesota Press, 1993), 1–32. For a critique of Habermas aiming to argue for a "proletarian public sphere," see Oskar Negt and Alexander Kluge, *Public Sphere and Experience: Towards an Analysis of the Bourgeois and Proletarian Public Spheres* (1979), trans. Peter Labanyi, Jamie Owen Daniel, and Assenka Oksikoff (Minneapolis: University of Minnesota Press, 1993). See also Dana Polan, "The Public's Fear: Or, Media as Monster in Habermas, Negt, and Kluge," in Robbins, *Phantom,* 33–41; Fredric Jameson, "On Negt and Kluge," in Robbins, *Phantom,* 42–74.
32. Warner, *Publics and Counterpublics.*
33. Frow, "Cultural Studies"; Michael Hardt, "The Withering of Civil Society," *Social Text* 45 (Winter 1995): 27–44.
34. Arjun Appadurai and Carole Breckenridge, "Why Public Culture?" *Public Culture* 1, no. 1 (1988): 5–9; see also Igor Kopytoff, "Public Culture: A Durkheimian Genealogy," *Public Culture* 1, no. 1 (1988): 11–16; and "Editors' Comments," *Public Culture* 1, no. 1 (1988): 1–4.

Works Cited

Adams, Joseph Quincy. "The Folger Shakespeare Memorial Dedicated April 23, 1932: Shakespeare and American Culture." *Spinning Wheel Magazine* 12 (nos. 9–10) 1932: 212–215; 229–231.

Adorno, Theodor. "The Fetish Character in Music and the Regression in Listening." In *The Culture Industry: Selected Essays in Mass Culture*, 29–60. New York: Routledge, 1991.

Albanese, Denise. "Black and White, and Dread All Over: The 'Photonegative' *Othello* and the Body of Desdemona." In *A Feminist Companion to Shakespeare*, edited by Dympna Callaghan, 226–247. Oxford: Blackwell, 2000.

———. "The Popular Mechanics of Rude Mechanicals: Shakespeare, the Present, and the Walls of Academe." *Shakespeare Studies* 32, edited by Susan Zimmerman, 295–321. Madison, NJ: Fairleigh Dickinson University Press, 2004.

———. "School for Scandal?: New Media *Hamlet*, Olivier, and Camp Connoisseurship." *Renaissance Drama* 34 (2005) special issue: "Media, Technology, and Performance," edited by Jeffrey Masten, Wendy Wall, and W. B. Worthen, 185–208. Evanston, IL: Northwestern University Press, 2006.

Althusser, Louis. "Ideology and Ideological State Apparatuses." In *Lenin and Philosophy and Other Essays*, translated by Ben Brewster, 127–186. New York: Monthly Review Press, 1971.

Anderson, Benedict. *Imagined Communities: Reflections on the Origin and Spread of Nationalism*. 2nd ed. London: Verso, 1991.

Andrews, John. "Shakespeare and the Lincoln Assassination." *The Shakespeare Newsletter* 42, no. 2 (1992): n. 213.

———. "Was the Bard Behind It?" *Atlantic Monthly*, October 1990, 27.

Appadurai, Arjun, and Carole Breckenridge. "Why Public Culture?" *Public Culture* 1, no. 1 (1988): 5–9.

Applebee, Arthur N. *Tradition and Reform in the Teaching of English: A History*. Urbana, IL: National Council of Teachers of English, 1974.

Archives of the Board of Education, Municipal Archives, New York.

Archives of the City University of New York.

Archives of Columbia University, New York.

Archives of Howard University, Washington, D.C.
Archives of the University of Virginia, Charlottesville, Virginia.
Aronowitz, Stanley. "Against Schooling: Education And Social Class." *Social Text* 22, no. 2 (2004): 13–35.
———. "The Last Good Job in America." In *Post-Work: The Wages of Cybernation*, edited by Stanley Aronowitz and Jonathan Cutler, 203–223. New York: Routledge, 1998.
Bacon, Delia. *The Philosophy of the Plays of Shakespeare Unfolded*. Boston: Ticknor and Fields, 1857.
Barthes, Roland. *Mythologies* (1957). Translated by Annette Lavers. New York: Hill and Wang, 1973.
Bennett, Tony. *Outside Literature*. London: Routledge, 2000.
Bennett, Tony, Lawrence Grossberg, and Meaghan Morris, eds. *New Keywords: A Revised Vocabulary of Culture and Society*. Oxford: Blackwell, 2005.
Berger, Harry, Jr. *Imaginary Audition: Shakespeare on Stage and Page*. Berkeley and Los Angeles: University of California Press, 1989.
Bloch, Ernst. *The Principle of Hope* (1959). Three volumes. Translated by Neville Plaice, Stephen Plaice, and Paul Knight. Cambridge: MA: MIT Press, 1986.
Bloom, Harold. *Shakespeare: The Invention of the Human*. New York: Riverhead Books, 1998.
Bolton, Richard, ed. *Culture Wars: Documents from the Recent Controversies in the Arts*. New York: New Press, 1992.
Boose, Linda, and Richard Burt, eds. *Shakespeare the Movie: Popularizing the Plays on Film, TV, and Video*. London: Routledge, 1997.
Bottomore, Tom. *Elites and Society*. 2nd ed. New York: Routledge, 1993
Bourdieu, Pierre. *Distinction: A Social Critique of the Judgment of Taste* (1979). Translated by Richard Nice. Cambridge, MA: Harvard University Press, 1984.
Bourdieu, Pierre, and Hans Haacke. *Free Exchange*. Palo Alto, CA: Stanford University Press, 1995.
Branagh, Kenneth, dir. *Hamlet* (1996). Warner Brothers International DVD, 2007.
———. *Hamlet by William Shakespeare: Screenplay, Introduction, and Film Diary*. New York: Norton, 1996.
Bristol, Michael. *Big-Time Shakespeare*. New York: Routledge, 1996.
———. *Shakespeare's America, America's Shakespeare*. New York: Routledge, 1990.
Brousseau, Elaine. "'Now, Literature, Philosophy, and Thought, Are Shakspearized': American Culture and Nineteenth Century Shakespearean Performance, 1835–1875." Ph. D. diss., University of Massachusetts, Amherst, 2003.
Brown, Stephen J. "The Uses of Shakespeare in America: A Study in Class Domination." In *Shakespeare, Pattern of Excelling Nature: Shakespeare Criticism in Honor of America's Bicentennial from the International Shakespeare Association Conference, Washington, DC, 1976*, edited by David M. Bevington and Jay L. Halio, 230–238. Newark, DE: University of Delaware Press, 1978.
Bulman, J. C., and H. R. Coursen, eds. *Shakespeare on Television: An Anthology of Essays and Reviews*. Hanover, NH: University Press of New England, 1988.

Bunker, Frank Forest. "The Functional Reorganization of the American Public School System." PhD diss., New York University, 1913. Washington, D.C.: Government Printing Office, 1916.

Burnett, Mark Thorton, and Ramona Wray, eds. *Shakespeare, Film, Fin de Siècle*. New York: St. Martin's Press, 2000.

Burt, Richard. "The Love That Dare Not Speak Shakespeare's Name: New Shakesqueer Cinema." In Boose and Burt, *Shakespeare the Movie*, 240–268.

———. *Unspeakable ShaXXXspeares: Queer Theory and American Kiddie Culture*. New York: St. Martin's Press, 1998.

Cartelli, Thomas. *Repositioning Shakespeare: National Formations, Postcolonial Appropriations*. New York: Routledge, 1999.

———. "Shakespeare and the Street: Pacino's *Looking for Richard*, Bedford's *Street King*, and the Common Understanding." In *Shakespeare, the Movie, II: Popularizing the Plays on Film, TV, Video, and DVD*, edited by Richard Burt and Lynda Boose, 186–199. London: Routledge, 2003.

Cartelli, Thomas, and Katherine Rowe. *New Wave Shakespeare on Screen*. Cambridge: Polity, 2007.

Collick, John. *Shakespeare, Cinema and Society*. Manchester: Manchester University Press, 1989.

Cowen, Tyler. *In Praise of Commercial Culture*. Cambridge, MA: Harvard University Press, 1998.

Daniel, Jamie Owen, and Tom Moylan, eds. *Not Yet: Reconsidering Ernst Bloch*. London: Verso, 1997,

Davies, Anthony, and Stanley Well, eds. *Shakespeare and the Moving Image: The Plays on Film and Television*. Cambridge: Cambridge University Press, 1994.

Denning, Michael. *The Cultural Front: The Laboring of American Culture in the Twentieth Century*. London: Verso, 1997.

———. *Culture in the Age of Three Worlds*. London: Verso, 2004.

Derrick, Thomas. *Understanding* Julius Caesar*: A Student Casebook to Issues, Sources, and Historical Documents* (Greenwood Press Literature in Context Series). Westport, CT: Greenwood Press, 1998.

Desmet, Christy, and Robert Sawyer, eds. *Shakespeare and Appropriation*. London: Routledge, 1999.

Desrosières, Alain. *The Politics of Large Numbers: A History of Statistical Reasoning*. Translated by Camille Naish. Cambridge, MA: Harvard University Press, 1998.

Dollimore, Jonathan. *Radical Tragedy: Religion, Ideology, and Power in the Drama of Shakespeare and His Contemporaries*. Chicago: University of Chicago Press, 1984.

Dollimore, Jonathan, and Alan Sinfield, eds. *Political Shakespeare: New Essays in Cultural Materialism*. 2nd ed. Ithaca, NY: Cornell University Press, 1995.

Donaldson, Peter. " 'In fair Verona': Media, Spectacle, and Performance in *William Shakespeare's Romeo + Juliet*." In *Shakespeare after Mass Media*, edited by Richard Burt, 59–82. New York: Palgrave Macmillan, 2002.

Donnelly, Ignatius. *The Great Cryptogram: Francis Bacon's Cipher in the So-Called Shakespeare Plays*. New York and London: R. S. Peale and Co., 1888.

Drakakis, John, ed. *Alternative Shakespeares*. London: Methuen, 1983.
Dyer, Richard. "Entertainment and Utopia." In *The Cultural Studies Reader*, edited by Simon During, 271–283. New York: Routledge, 1993.
"Editors' Comments." *Public Culture* 1, no. 1 (1988): 1–4.
Ehrenreich, Barbara, and John. "The Professional-Managerial Class." *Radical America* 11, Part 1 (March-April 1977): 7–31; 11, Part 2 (May-June 1977): 7–22.
Eliot, T. S. *Notes Towards the Definition of Culture* (1948). London: Faber and Faber, 1962.
Elson, Ruth Miller. *Guardians of Tradition: American Schoolbooks of the Nineteenth Century*. Lincoln: University of Nebraska Press, 1964.
English Course Description: English Language and Composition/English Literature and Composition May 2007, May 2008. College Board AP: www.collegeboard.com/student/testing/ap/sub_englit.html).
Epstein, Helen. *Joe Papp: An American Life*. New York: Da Capo, 1996.
Fiske, John. "Cultural Studies and the Culture of Everyday Life." In Grossberg, Nelson, and Treichler, *Cultural Studies*, 154–173.
Foucault, Michel. *Discipline and Punish: The Birth of the Prison*. Translated by Alan Sheridan. New York: Vintage Books, 1995.
———. "Governmentality." In *The Foucault Effect: Studies in Governmentality*, edited by Graham Burchell, Colin Gordon, and Peter Miller, 87–104. Chicago: University of Chicago Press, 1991.
Fraser, Nancy. "Rethinking the Public Sphere: A Contribution to the Critique of Actually-Existing Democracy." In *The Phantom Public Sphere*, edited by Bruce Robbins, 1–32. Minneapolis: University of Minnesota Press, 1993.
Frow, John. *Cultural Studies and Cultural Value*. Oxford: Clarendon, 1995.
———. "Cultural Studies and the Neoliberal Imagination." *Yale Journal of Criticism* 12, no. 2 (1999): 424–430.
Fultz, Michael. "African American Teachers in the South 1890–1940: Powerlessness and the Ironies of Expectation and Protest." *History of Education Quarterly* 35, no. 4 (1995): 401–422.
———. "Teacher Training and African American Education in the South 1900–1940." *Journal of Negro Education* 64, no. 2 (1995): 196–210.
Garber, Marjorie. "Shakespeare as Fetish." *Shakespeare Quarterly* 41, no. 2 (Summer 1990): 242–250.
Grady, Hugh. *Shakespeare's Universal Wolf: Studies in Early Modern Reification*. New York: Clarendon Press, 1996.
Graff, Gerald, and Michael Warner, eds. *The Origins of Literary Study in America: A Documentary Anthology*. New York: Routledge, 1989.
Greenberg, Clement. "Avant-Garde and Kitsch" (1939). In *Art and Culture: Critical Essays*, 3–21. Boston, MA: Beacon Press, 1961.
Greenblatt, Steven. *Will in the World: How Shakespeare Became Shakespeare*. New York: Norton, 2004.
Grossberg, Lawrence, Cary Nelson, and Paula Treichler, eds. *Cultural Studies*. London: Routledge, 1992.

Guillory, John. *Cultural Capital: The Problem of Literary Canon Formation*. Chicago: University of Chicago Press, 1993.

———. "Literary Critics as Intellectuals: Class Analysis and the Crisis in the Humanities." In *Rethinking Class: Literary Studies and Social Formations*, edited by Wai Chee Dimock and Michael Gilmore, 107–149. New York: Columbia University Press, 1994.

Habermas, Jurgen. *The Structural Transformation of the Public Sphere* (1962). Translated by Thomas Burger. Cambridge, MA: MIT Press, 1989.

Hall, Stuart. "Notes on Deconstructing 'The Popular.'" In *People's History and Socialist Theory*, edited by Raphael Samuel, 227–240. London: Routledge & Kegan Paul, 1981.

Hardt, Michael. "The Withering of Civil Society." *Social Text* 45 (Winter 1995): 27–44.

Harvey, David. *A Brief History of Neoliberalism*. Oxford: Oxford University Press, 2005.

———. *The Condition of Postmodernity*. Oxford: Blackwell, 1989.

Hawkes, Terence. *Meaning by Shakespeare*. London: Routledge, 1992.

Hedrick, Don. "War is Mud: Branagh's Dirty Harry V and the Types of Political Ambiguity." In Boose and Burt, *Shakespeare the Movie*, 45–66.

Herold, Neils. "Movers and Losers: Shakespeare in Charge and *Shakespeare behind Bars*." In *Native Shakespeares: Indigenous Appropriations on a Global Stage*, edited by Craig Dionne and Parmita Kapadia, 153–179. Aldershot, UK: Ashgate, 2008.

Hodgdon, Barbara. "The Critic, the Poor Player, Prince Hamlet, and the Lady in the Dark." In *Shakespeare Reread: The Texts in New Contexts*, edited by Russ McDonald, 259–294. Ithaca, NY: Cornell University Press, 1994.

———. "Replicating Richard: Body Doubles, Body Politics." *Theatre Journal* 50, no. 2 (1998): 207–205.

———. *The Shakespeare Trade: Performances and Appropriations*. Philadelphia: University of Pennsylvania Press, 1998.

Hofstadter, Richard. *Anti-Intellectualism in American Life*. New York: Knopf, 1963.

Hoggart, Richard. *The Uses of Literacy* (1957). With a new introduction by Andrew Goodwin. New Brunswick, NJ: Transaction Publishers, 1992.

Holderness, Graham. "Boxing the Bard." In Bulman and Coursen, *Shakespeare on Television*, 14–18.

———. "Preface: 'All this.'" In *The Shakespeare Myth*, edited by Graham Holderness, xi-xvi. Manchester: Manchester University Press, 1988.

Horkheimer, Max, and Theodor Adorno. "The Culture Industry: Enlightenment as Deception." In *The Dialectic of Enlightenment*, translated by John Cumming, 120–167. New York: Continuum Books, 1976.

Howard, Jean, and Marion O'Connor, eds. *Shakespeare Reproduced: The Text in History and Ideology*. New York: Methuen, 1987.

Huntington, Samuel. "Dead Souls: The Denationalization of the American Elite." *National Interest* (Spring 2004). http://www.freerepublic.com/focus/f-news/1111567/posts.

Ingraham, Laura. *Shut Up and Sing: How Elites from Hollywood, Politics, and the UN Are Subverting America*. Washington, D.C.: Regnery Publishing, 2003.

Innerst, Carol. "The Bard Draws a Pass to Pop Culture on Campus: Many Colleges Are Skipping Shakespeare." *Washington Times*, December 17, 1997.

International Movie Data Base: imdb.com.

Jameson, Fredric. *Marxism and Form: Twentieth-Century Dialectical Theories of Literature*. Princeton, NJ: Princeton University Press, 1971.

———. "Reification and Utopia in Mass Culture." *Social Text* 1 (Winter 1979): 130–148

Jordan, David Starr. *The Blood of the Nation: A Study of the Decay of Races through the Survival of the Unfit*. Boston, MA: American Unitarian Association, 1902.

———. *The Voice of the Scholar: With Other Addresses on the Problems in Higher Education*. San Francisco: Paul Elder and Company, 1903.

Joughin, John, ed. *Shakespeare and National Culture*. Manchester: Manchester University Press, 1997.

Kamps, Ivo, ed. *Shakespeare Left and Right*. New York: Routledge, 1991.

Kett, Joseph F. *The Pursuit of Knowledge under Difficulties: From Self-Improvement to Adult Education in America, 1750–1990*. Palo Alto, CA: Stanford University Press, 1994.

Kolin, Philip C., ed. *Shakespeare in the South: Essays on Performance*. Jackson: University of Mississippi Press, 1983.

Koons, Helene Wickham. *How Shakespeare Won the West: Players and Performers in American's Gold Rush 1849–1865*. Jefferson, NC: McFarland, 1989.

Kopytoff, Igor. "Public Culture: A Durkheimian Genealogy." *Public Culture* 1, no. 1 (1988): 11–16.

Lamont, Michèle. *Money, Morals, and Manners: The Culture of the French and the American Upper-Middle Class*. Chicago: University of Chicago Press, 1992.

Lanier, Douglas. "'Art Thou Base, Common, and Popular?': The Cultural Politics of Kenneth Branagh's *Hamlet*." In *Spectacular Shakespeare: Critical Theory and Popular Cinema*, edited by Courtney Lehmann and Lisa S. Starks, 149–171. Madison, NJ: Fairleigh Dickinson Press, 2002.

———. *Shakespeare and Modern Popular Culture*. Oxford: Oxford University Press, 2002.

Levine, Lawrence. *Highbrow/Lowbrow: The Emergence of Cultural Hierarchy in America*. Cambridge, MA: Harvard University Press, 1988.

Loehlin, James N. "'Top of the World, Ma': *Richard III* and Cinematic Convention." In Boose and Burt, *Shakespeare the Movie*, 67–79.

Looking for Richard dialogue: http://www.script-o-rama.com/movie_scripts/l/looking-for-richard-script-transcript.html.

Loomba, Ania, and Martin Orkin, eds. *Post-Colonial Shakespeare*. London: Routledge, 1998.

Luhrmann, Baz, dir. *William Shakespeare's Romeo + Juliet* (1996). Fox DVD, 1997.

Macdonald, Dwight. "Masscult and Midcult." In *Against the American Grain: Essays on the Effects of Mass Culture*, 3–75. New York: Random House, 1962.

Mani, Lata. "Cultural Theory, Colonial Texts: Reading Eye-Witness Accounts of Widow Burning." In Grossberg, Nelson, and Treichler, *Cultural Studies*, 392–394. New York: Routledge, 1992.

McGuffey, William Holmes. *New Sixth Eclectic Reader*. Cincinnati, OH: Wilson and Hinkle Co., 1867.

Meisel, James H. *The Myth of the Ruling Class: Gaetano Mosca and the "Elite."* Ann Arbor: University of Michigan Press, 1962.

Miller, Toby, Nitin Govil, and John McMurria. *Global Hollywood 2*. London: BFI Publishing, 2005.

Murphy, Andrew. *Shakespeare For the People: Working-Class Readers 1800–1900*. Cambridge: Cambridge University Press, 2008.

National Endowment for the Arts. "Shakespeare in American Communities." 2008. Available as a pdf from www.arts.gov.

Negt, Oskar, and Alexander Kluge, *Public Sphere and Experience: Towards an Analysis of the Bourgeois and Proletarian Public Spheres* (1979). Foreword by Miriam Hansen. Translated by Peter Labanyi, Jamie Owen Daniel, and Assenka Oksikoff. Minneapolis: University of Minnesota Press, 1993.

Nelson, Cary, and Stephen Watt. "America's Fast Food Discipline." In *Academic Keywords: A Devil's Dictionary for Higher Education*, 55–58. New York: Routledge, 1999.

New York City Superintendent of Schools Annual Report, 1899–1900. New York: Board of Education, 1899.

Newstok, Scott. "'Step aside, I'll show thee a president': George W. As Henry V?" http://www.poppolitics.com/archives/2003/05/George-W-as-Henry-Vh.

O'Dair, Sharon. *Class, Critics, and Shakespeare: Bottom Lines on the Culture Wars*. Ann Arbor: University of Michigan Press, 2000.

Ohmann, Richard. *English in America: A Radical View of the Profession*. New York: Oxford University Press, 1976.

———. *Politics of Letters*. Middletown, CT: Wesleyan University Press, 1987.

Olalquiaga, Celeste. *Megalopolis: Contemporary Cultural Sensibilities*. Minneapolis: University of Minnesota Press, 1992.

Pacino, Al, dir. *Looking for Richard*. Twentieth-Century Fox, 1996.

Penley, Constance. *NASA/Trek: Popular Science and Sex in America*. London: Verso, 1997.

Price, Thomas R. *The Construction and Types of Shakespeare's Verse as Seen in* Othello. New York: Press of the New York Shakespeare Society, 1888.

Public Theater Web site: http://www.publictheater.org/celebrating/past.php.

Rawlings, Peter, ed. *Americans on Shakespeare 1776–1914*. Aldershot, UK: Ashgate, 1999.

Readings, Bill. *The University in Ruins*. Cambridge, MA: Harvard University Press, 1996.

Roberts, Peter. *Shakespeare and the Moral Curriculum: Rethinking the Secondary-School Shakespeare Syllabus*. New York: Pripet Press, 1992.

Robbins, Bruce, ed. *The Phantom Public Sphere*. Minneapolis: University of Minnesota Press, 1993.

Rogerson, Hank, dir. *Shakespeare behind Bars*. Philomath Films, 2005.
Ross, Andrew. *No Respect: Intellectuals and Popular Culture*. New York: Routledge, 1989.
Sante, Luc. *Low Life: Lures and Snares of Old New York*. New York: Vintage, 1992.
Saxton, Alexander. *The Rise and Fall of the White Republic: Class Politics and Class Culture in Nineteenth-Century America* (1990). With a new foreword by David Roediger. London: Verso, 2003.
Scott-Douglass, Amy. *Shakespeare Inside: The Bard behind Bars (Shakespeare Now!)* London: Continuum, 2007.
"Shakespeare in American Communities" Web site: http://www.shakespeareinamericancommunities.org/overview/b_v.html See also http://www.arts.gov/national/shakespeare/index.html.
"Shakespeare in American Life" Web site: http://www.shakespeareinamericanlife.org
Shaw, Catherine M. "Edwin's Booth's *Richard II* and the Divided Nation." In *Textual and Theatrical Shakespeare: Questions of Evidence*, edited by Edward Pechter, 144–163. Iowa City: Iowa University Press, 1996.
Shiach, Morag. *Discourse on Popular Culture: Class, Gender, and History in Cultural Analysis, 1730 to the Present*. Palo Alto, CA: Stanford University Press, 1989.
Simon, Henry William. *The Reading of Shakespeare in American Schools and Colleges: An Historical Survey*. New York: Simon and Schuster, 1932.
Simon, John. *John Simon on Theater: Criticism 1974–2003*. New York: Applause Books, 2005.
Sinfield, Alan. *Faultlines: Cultural Materialism and the Politics of Dissident Reading*. Berkeley: University of California Press, 1992.
———. "Give an account of Shakespeare and Education, showing why you think they are effective and what you have appreciated about them. Support your comments with precise references." In *Political Shakespeares: New Essays in Cultural Materialism*, edited by Jonathan Dollimore and Alan Sinfield, 134–157. Manchester: Manchester University Press, 1985.
Smith, Paul. *Millennial Dreams*. London: Verso, 1997
Snyder, William Lamartine. *The Geography of Marriage: Or, Legal Perplexities of Wedlock in the United States*. New York: G. P. Putnam's Sons, 1889.
SparkNotes. *The Tempest, by William Shakespeare*. Contributors: Susannah Mandel, Adam Stewart, Brian Phillips, Patrick Flanagan, John Crowther, and Justin Kestler. New York: Spark Publishing, 2002
Spivak, Gayatri. "Can the Subaltern Speak?" In *Marxism and the Interpretation of Cultures*, edited by Cary Nelson and Lawrence Grossberg, 271–313. Urbana: University of Illinois Press, 1988.
———. "Subaltern Talk: Interview with the Editors." In *The Spivak Reader*, edited by Donna Landry and Gerald Maclean, 287–308. New York: Routledge, 1996.
Stallybrass, Peter, and Allon White. *The Politics and Poetics of Transgression*. London: Methuen, 1983.
Stoler, Ann Laura. *Race and the Education of Desire: Foucault's History of Sexuality and the Colonial Order of Things*. Durham, NC: Duke University Press, 1995.

Sturgess, Kim. *Shakespeare and the American Nation*. Cambridge: Cambridge University Press, 2004.

Sullivan, Dorothy. *William Holmes McGuffey: Schoolmaster of the Nation*. Rutherford, NJ: Fairleigh Dickinson University Press, 1994.

This American Life. "Act V." Episode 218 (broadcast date August 9, 2002). www.thisamericanlife.org.

Trachsel, Mary. *Institutionalizing Literacy: The Historical Role of College Entrance Examinations in English*. Carbondale, IL: Southern Illinois University Press, 1992.

Trounstine, Jean. *Shakespeare behind Bars: The Power of Drama in a Women's Prison*. New York: St. Martin's Press, 2001.

Uricchio, William, and Roberta E. Pearson. *Reframing Culture: The Case of the Vitagraph Films*. Princeton, NJ: Princeton University Press, 1993.

Vaughan, Virginia Mason. "*King John*." In *A Companion to Shakespeare's Works, Volume II: The Histories*, edited by Richard Dutton and Jean E. Howard, 379–394. Oxford: Blackwell, 2003.

Warner, Michael. *Publics and Counterpublics*. New York: Zone, 2000.

Warren, Ruth. "The Popularity and Influence of Shakespeare's English and Roman Historical Plays in America from the Beginnings to 1950." Unpublished M.A. thesis, College of the Pacific, 1955.

Watkins, William. *The White Architects of Black Education: Ideology and Power in America, 1865–1954*. Foreword by Robin D.G. Kelley. New York: Teachers College Press, 2001.

Weber, Max. "Classes, Status Group, and Parties" (1922). In *Weber: Selections in Translation*, edited by W. G. Runciman and translated by Eric Matthews, 43–56. Cambridge: Cambridge University Press, 1978.

Williams, Raymond. *Keywords*. New York: Oxford University Press, 1985.

———. *Marxism and Literature*. Oxford: Oxford University Press, 1977.

Willis, Paul. *Learning to Labor: How Working Class Kids Get Working-Class Jobs*. With a foreword by Stanley Aronowitz. New York: Columbia University Press, 1982.

Worthen, W. B. *Shakespeare and the Authority of Performance*. Cambridge: Cambridge University Press, 1997.

Zinoman, Jason. "First Thing We Do, Let's Seat All the Lawyers." *New York Times*, July 1, 2004. Arts and Leisure Section.

Index

Abu-Jamal, Mumia, 130
Academia
   and capitalism, 34–37
   as privileged, 4, 6, 18, 20, 31–35, 72, 92, 142
   in relation to the public, 3–4
   as site of labor, 26, 31, 36–37, 59, 114
"Act V," 120, 122–123, 126–138
   and civil society, 133–134, 137–138
   and identification, 127–129, 131–133, 134–136, 137–138
   and parole, 133–134, 135
   and social dreaming, 121, 123, 137–138
   and surveillance, 134, 137–138
   see also public radio; *This American Life*
Adams, John, 114
Adams, Joseph Quincy, 71
Adelman, Kenneth, 137
Adorno, Theodor, 17, 102
Advanced Placement (AP) in English Literature, 78
Alderman, Edwin, 85
All's Well That Ends Well, 42
Allen, Penelope, 46
Althusser, Louis, 31
American Masters (PBS), 124
American Revolution, 75
Anderson, Benedict, 73
Angelou, Maya, 33, 52
Anglophilia, 25, 34
Anti-intellectualism, 35
Anti-Stratfordianism, 88
Antony and Cleopatra, 75, 85
Appadurai, Arjun, 144
Apprentice, The, 24
Appropriation, 7, 19, 141
Arnold, Matthew, 21, 24, 53
Aronowitz, Stanley, 31, 36–37
As You Like It, 82, 83, 84, 85
As You Like It (dir. Branagh), 105–106
Association of Colleges and Preparatory Schools of the Southern States, 85

Bacon, Delia, 88
Bacon, Francis, 88
Barnard College, 80, 81
Barthes, Roland, 16, 19, 52, 115, 128
   Mythologies, 52, 115
BBC Films, 105
BBC/Time-Life Shakespeare (PBS), 62, 99, 124
Benjamin, Walter, 17, 139, 140
Bennett, Tony, 139
Bergman, Ingmar, 129
Blair, Tony, 34
Bloch, Ernst, 6, 121, 139–140
Booth, Edwin, 76
Booth, John Wilkes, 75–76
Booth, Junius Brutus, 76
Bottomore, Tom, 28
Bourdieu, Pierre, 24, 31

Index

Bradley, A. C., 59
Branagh, Kenneth, 8, 34, 56, 95–96, 99–100, 101–106, 113
Breckenridge, Carol, 144
Bristol, Michael, 114
Brook, Peter, 56
Brousseau, Elaine, 90
Brown, Stephen J., 32, 33, 36
Burt, Richard, 93
Burton, Richard, 96, 111
Bush, Laura, 14
Butler, Nicholas Murray, 80, 85
Byron, Lord, 27

Carlyle, Thomas, 27
Castle Rock Entertainment, 105
Cheney, Lynne, 33, 34, 52
Chianese, Dominic, 46
Churchill, George B., 75
City College (NY), 82, 83, 88
Civil War, 69, 75, 90
Cliffs Notes, 7, 49, 57–58, 59, 61
Cloisters, The, 43–44, 60
  see also Metropolitan Museum
College Entrance Examination Board (CEEB), 7, 32, 68, 70, 71, 72, 77, 78–81, 82, 83, 84, 85, 86, 89, 90, 92, 95, 98
Columbia University, 54, 55, 80, 81–82, 85, 90
Coriolanus, 75, 85
Corporation for Public Broadcasting, 124
Cort Theater (NY), 46, 49, 50
Crystal, Billy, 106
Cultural capital, 20, 24, 31–32, 99, 105, 114, 123, 126, 129
  see also Shakespeare and elite culture; Shakespeare and cultural hierarchy
Cultural materialism, 1–2, 3, 4, 17, 18–19, 25, 68, 116, 121, 123, 129, 132, 140
Cultural studies, 3, 16, 17, 18–19, 21–22, 33, 37, 98, 121, 137, 140–141
Culture wars, 15, 23, 36, 141
Cymbeline, 75

Danes, Claire, 107, 111
Delacorte Theater (NY), 42, 46, 65
  see also Papp, Joseph; Public Theater
Denning, Michael, 98, 108
DiCaprio, Leonardo, 107, 111, 115, 118
Dollimore, Jonathan, 2, 132
Domingo Placido, 23
Donnelly, Ignatius, 88
Drakakis, John, 2
Dyer, Richard, 133

Edward II (dir. Jarman), 98
Ehrenreich, Barbara and John, 31
Eliot, Charles William, 78, 85, 86
Eliot, T. S., 12, 28, 36, 45
Elites and elitism, 8, 12–13, 26–32, 132, 140–141
  and political discourse, 29–30
  see also cultural capital; Shakespeare and elite culture
Elite theory in sociology, 28–31
Elson, Ruth Miller, 75, 77, 86
Elyot, Thomas, 27
Eugenics, 8, 86–88
  see also Shakespeare and race knowledge
Evans, Walker, 19

Federal Communications Commission (FCC), 124
Finley, Karen, 12
Folger Shakespeare Library, 14, 71
For-profit universities, 35
Foucault, Michel, 28, 29, 31
Frankfurt School, 17
Fraser, Nancy, 143
French Revolution, 27
Frost, Robert, 138
Frow, John, 21, 143

Garber, Marjorie, 33, 34, 52
Gates, Bill, 24
General Agreement on Tariffs and Trades (GATT), 100
Georgetown University, 51, 53, 97, 99, 105, 128, 135

Gibbon, Edward, 27
Gielgud, John, 44–45, 47
Gioia, Dana, 13, 14, 15
Glass, Ira, 116, 125–126, 127–129, 132, 134, 138
   see also This American Life
Grady, Hugh, 139
Greenberg, Clement, 17
Greenblatt, Stephen, 3, 116
Guillory, John, 24, 29, 30, 31, 63

Haacke, Hans, 65
Habermas, Jurgen, 124, 143
Hadge, Michael, 54
Hamlet, 9, 46, 48, 54, 57, 59, 69, 74, 75, 82, 83, 85, 99, 117, 120, 122, 127, 128, 129–130, 131, 133, 134, 135, 138
Hamlet (dir. Branagh), 8, 34, 99–100, 101–106, 112, 124
   and bourgeois Anglophilia, 99, 104–106, 110, 124
Hamlet (dir. Olivier), 62, 101
Hardt, Michael, 143
Harvard University, 54, 55, 58, 78, 80, 85, 89
Harvey, David, 36, 59
Hawkes, Terence, 96, 100
Henry IV Part I, 74
Henry V, 46, 84, 85
Henry V (dir. Branagh), 101, 102, 105, 111
Henry V (dir Olivier), 101
Henry VIII, 74, 83, 89
Herold, Niels, 135, 137
Hitt, Jack, 129–131, 132, 133, 134, 135, 136, 137, 138, 143
Hobbes, Thomas, 27
Hodgdon, Barbara, 93
Holderness, Graham, 18, 19, 101
   Shakespeare Myth, The, 18
Home Box Office (HBO) Productions, 105–106
Hopkins, Antony, 98
House Un-American Activities Committee (HUAC), 64

Howard, Jean, 2
Howard University, 83–84, 86, 90
Huntington, Samuel, 11, 24, 25

Ideology critique, 1, 2, 137, 139
   see also cultural materialism; cultural studies; political criticism
Intellectuals, 30–31, 136
   see also academia
Intermedia Films, 96, 105–106
Internet Movie Data Base (imdb.com), 106

Jacobi, Derek, 44, 48
Jameson, Fredric, 21, 138, 139, 140
Jarman, Derek, 98
Jones, Bratt, 135–136, 137, 143
Jones, James Earl, 46–47, 52
Jordan, David Starr, 79, 86–88
Joughin, John, 2
Julius Caesar, 59, 69, 75–76, 80, 82, 83, 84, 85, 89
Juvenile Mentor, The (Pickett), 74

Kamps, Ivo, 2
Keynesian state, 30
Kimball, Frederic, 44, 46, 54, 56, 57, 61, 64
Kimball, Roger, 13
King John, 69, 74, 75, 89
King Lear, 75, 82, 83, 132
Kline, Kevin, 46–47, 48, 112

Lamont, Michèle, 24
Lanier, Douglas, 19–20
Leguizamo, John, 107, 109
Lehmann, Courtney, 123
Levine, Sherrie, 19
Levine, Lawrence, 4, 6, 12, 22, 23, 26, 62, 70, 71, 90
   Highbrow/Lowbrow, 22
Liberalism, 11, 29, 125, 131
Lincoln, Abraham, 75, 76
"Live from Death Row," 130
Live from Lincoln Center (PBS), 124

Loehlin, James, 101
Longfellow, Henry Wadsworth, 81
Looking for Richard (dir. Pacino), 6, 37, 39–57, 59–64, 67, 93, 97, 98, 99, 112, 113, 116, 128
   and "feeling," 49–53, 57
   and pedagogy, 7, 42, 53, 55, 60–62, 65, 67, 99, 113
   and performance, 6–7, 40, 41, 46–47, 53–55, 57, 60–63, 64
   and race, 47, 50–53
   and Shakespeare's place in the American imaginary, 38, 39–42, 44–45, 47, 48–49
   and study guides, 57–60, 61
Love's Labor's Lost, 81
Love's Labour's Lost (dir. Branagh), 105–106
Luhrmann, Baz, 8, 99, 106, 108, 111, 112, 114, 116, 128

Macaulay, William, 81
Macbeth, 69, 75, 80, 81, 82, 83, 84, 85, 86, 89, 91
Macdonald, Dwight, 17
Mani, Lata, 136–137
Mannheim, Karl, 28
Mapplethorpe, Robert, 13
Marcuse, Herbert, 139
Marx, Karl, 28, 109
Marxism, 29, 121, 139–140
Mass culture, 2, 16–18, 63, 70, 92, 95, 97, 98, 102, 114, 141
Mass education, 5, 69–72, 81, 93
   see also Shakespeare in education
Masterpiece Theater (PBS), 104, 124, 125
McCarthyism, 29, 64, 76
McGuffey's Readers, 7, 74, 80, 87, 89, 92
Merchant-Ivory Films, 104
Merchant of Venice, The, 46, 76–77, 80, 82, 83, 84, 85, 86–88, 89
Method acting, 40, 57, 113, 122, 130
Metropolitan Museum of Art (NY), 43
Mexico City, 106, 108–109, 110
Midsummer's Night's Dream, A, 14, 46, 69, 82, 85

Mihok, Dash, 107
Milton, John, 81, 138
Minstrelsy, 23, 90 Miscegenation, 69, 85, 90
Missouri Eastern Correctional Center, 120, 131
   see also "Act V," *This American Life*
Morrison, Toni, 138
Mosca, Gaetano, 28, 30
"Movers and Shakespeares," 137
Much Ado About Nothing (dir. Branagh), 101, 106

NAFTA (North American Free Trade Agreement), 108
National Endowment for the Arts (NEA), 6, 8, 12–16, 18, 23, 40, 64, 65, 119
National Public Radio (NPR), 125
National Review, 13
Natural Reader (Olney), 74
Neo-liberalism, 30, 35, 108–109, 114, 132–133, 143
New Criterion, The, 20
New York Board of Education, 73, 80, 82
New York City, 24, 40, 41, 42–44, 50, 79, 80, 81, 90
   Board of Education, 73, 80, 82
   see also Public Theater; Metropolitan Museum of Art
New York University, 80, 91

O'Connor, Marion, 2
O'Dair, Sharon, 21, 33, 36
Ohmann, Richard, 31, 32, 36
Olalquiaga, Celeste, 110
Olivier, Laurence, 23, 101
Opera, 22–24
Othello, 14, 46, 69, 74, 75, 81–82, 85, 89–90

Pacino, Al, 6–7, 37, 38, 39–51, 53–58, 59–65, 98, 113, 116, 128, 142
Papp, Joseph, 6, 40, 42, 46, 64–65
Pareto, Vilifredo, 28, 30

Pearson, Roberta, 62, 95, 97
Penley, Constance, 120
Perrineau, Harold, 107, 109
Plath, Sylvia, 138
Political criticism (of Shakespeare), 5, 6, 8, 16, 17–18, 20–21, 22, 76, 123, 127, 136
  see also cultural materialism
Popular culture, 1, 7, 17–18, 22, 136, 140–141, 142
  see also mass culture
Postcolonial criticism, 2, 136–137
Preston, Mark, 11
Price, Thomas, 82
Primers, 73–75, 92
Public Broadcasting Act, 124
Public Broadcasting System (PBS), 124
Public culture, 8, 9, 19, 65, 143–144
  see also Shakespeare and public culture
Public radio, 9, 39, 122–123, 124–125, 130, 138
  see also "Act V," *This American Life*
Publics, 3–4, 13, 38, 39, 41, 48, 62, 65, 67, 73, 81, 116, 124, 127, 138, 142, 143
Public sphere, 123–125, 143–144
Public Theater (NY), 6, 40, 46, 64–65
  see also Papp, Joseph

Ran (dir. Kurosawa), 98
Readings, Bill, 35
Reconstruction, 69
Redgrave, Vanessa, 45, 51
Richard II, 76, 83, 85
Richard III, 14, 40, 44, 46, 48, 49, 53, 54, 57, 59, 61, 62, 63, 74, 85
Romeo and Juliet, 14, 59, 69, 83, 85
Ryan, Kiernan, 139–140
Ryder, Winona, 54, 61

Sallie Mae, 14
Santorum, Rick, 11, 13
Sati, 136–137
Saxton, Alexander, 90
Scott, Sir Walter, 79, 81, 91

Sedaris, David, 125
Shakespeare
  and American accents, 7, 45–46, 49–50, 112–113
  American attitudes toward, 5, 8, 14–15, 22, 38, 39–41, 44, 45–46, 47, 48–50, 59, 67, 68–69, 100, 113–114, 132
  and Anglophilia, 7, 8, 25, 32, 34, 44, 46, 62, 69, 76, 89, 99, 104–105, 106, 110, 124
  as Anglo-Saxon culture, 1, 2, 32, 33, 34, 62, 69, 71, 77, 79, 82, 89, 91, 95, 98, 99, 114
  in Central Park, 42, 46, 65
  and college entrance examinations, 8, 24, 32, 68, 77–88
  and "compulsory lovability," 7, 50, 57, 63, 67, 142–143
  and citizenship, 7, 69, 73, 75–76, 84, 89, 132–133
  and civil society, 133–134, 137–138
  as cultural capital, 4, 18, 20, 32, 33, 63, 68, 77–78, 86, 92, 99, 105, 114, 116, 123, 128–129, 137, 141, 142
  and cultural hierarchy, 2–3, 7, 18–23, 37–38, 39–40, 62, 70, 92, 95–98, 99, 116, 119,140–141
  and domination or hegemony, 1, 2, 8, 15, 18–22, 25, 32, 33, 91, 99, 119, 128, 132, 136, 137, 140, 143
  and early cinema, 62, 71, 93, 97, 98
  in education, 5, 7–8, 15, 23, 25, 51, 55, 61, 63, 65, 67–93, 95, 98, 102, 113, 119, 120, 142
  and elite culture, 2, 4–5, 6, 12–16, 17, 20–25, 26, 30–33, 63, 64, 68–69, 70, 78, 84, 112, 114, 116–117, 120, 122, 123, 127–128, 140–142, 144
  and Hollywood, 95–100, 102, 106–107, 112–114, 115–116
  and identification, 9, 14, 127–129, 130, 132–133, 136

Shakespeare—*Continued*
 and immigration, 1, 2, 8, 62, 68, 69, 71–72, 79, 95, 98, 119
 and industrialization, 8, 17, 34, 68, 70, 72, 98
 and the market, 3, 8, 25–26, 39, 53, 58–59, 61–62, 63, 78, 92–93, 96, 99–100, 103–104, 105–107, 111, 113–114, 115–116, 119
 and myth, 16–17, 18, 136, 139
 in nineteenth-century primers, 73–75, 87
 and oratory, 47, 73–75, 80, 89, 90
 and pedagogical fantasy, 5, 8, 37–38, 42, 53, 60–62, 65, 67, 119, 142–143
 and postmodern irony, 58–59, 115, 123, 126–128, 132
 and prison education programs, 120–122
 see also "Act V," *This American Life*
 and public culture, 1, 4–5, 8–9, 17–18, 65, 68, 79, 95, 114, 116, 117, 119–120, 123, 138, 139–143
 and race, 50–53, 64–65, 68, 77, 83, 84, 90, 104, 107–108, 108
 and "race knowledge," 8, 34, 62, 68, 71, 72, 77, 84, 85, 86–88, 90–91, 98, 114
 and social class, 4, 5, 9, 20–21, 31–33, 51–52, 58, 62–63, 126, 128, 137, 141–143
 and social dreaming, 6, 8–9, 51, 53, 117, 119, 120–121, 138–141
 see also under individual plays and films
Shakespeare film, 8, 39, 64, 65, 95–98, 99–100, 104
Shakespeare-function, 5, 6, 16, 17, 41
"Shakespeare in American Communities" (NEA), 6, 8, 12, 14–16, 23, 25, 32, 41, 64, 126
Shakespeare in Love (dir. Madden), 95, 97
"Shakespeare in Washington," 14
Simon, Henry William, 74

Simon, John, 49
Sinfield, Alan, 2, 77, 123
Sirius Radio, 124
Snyder, William Lamartine, 90
Sorvino, Paul, 107
SparkNotes, 58–59, 62, 116
Spivak, Gayatri, 136–137
Stanford University, 79, 85–88
Star Trek, 120
Stratford-upon-Avon, 44, 48
Strictly Ballroom (dir. Luhrmann), 111

Taming of the Shrew, The, 96, 97
Tarver, Quindon, 107
Tempest, The, 42, 59, 75, 81, 82, 83, 85
Ten Things I Hate About You, 96, 97
This American Life, 116, 117, 122, 125–129, 134, 136, 137
 see also "Act V"
Throne of Blood (dir. Kurosawa), 98
Timon of Athens, 75, 85
Titus Andronicus, 75, 85
Titus Andronicus (dir. Taymor), 96, 97–98
Trachsel, Mary, 70, 89
Trump, Donald, 24, 25, 108
Twelfth Night, 84, 85

University of California, Berkeley, 86
University of Pennsylvania, 80
University of Virginia, 83, 84–85, 90
Uricchio, William, 62, 95, 97
Utopianism, *see* Shakespeare and social dreaming

Valenti, Jack, 14, 15
Vitagraph Quality Films, 62, 71, 93, 97
Volpone (Jonson), 27
Vowell, Sarah, 125

Waller, Danny, 135
Warner, Michael, 143
Warren, Ruth, 76
Weber, Max, 28, 31
Webster, Daniel, 81

Wilcox, Agnes, 134
William Shakespeare's Romeo + Juliet
(dir. Lurhmann), 8, 99–100,
106–115, 116
as economic indicator, 108–109,
113–114
and Hollywood aesthetics, 106–107,
112–114
and kitsch, 110–111, 115
and Latin American Catholicism,
109–111
and neocolonialism, 108–109, 114
and race, 107–108, 109

and Shakespearean language, 112–113
and youth culture, 106–107
Williams, Raymond, 6, 140
Keywords, 6
Williams, Robin, 106
Wilson, J. Dover, 59
World War II, 28, 34

XM Radio, 124

Yale University, 80

Zipes, Jack, 121